Migrants and Citizens

Migrants and Citizens

Demographic Change in the European State System

Rey Koslowski

Cornell University Press

ITHACA AND LONDON

First published 2000 by Cornell University Press

Printed in the United States of America

Library of Congress Cataloging-in-Publication Data

Koslowski, Rey.
    Migrants and citizens : demographic change in the European state system /
Rey Koslowski.
        p.   cm.
    Includes bibliographical references and index.
    ISBN 0-8014-3714-8 (cloth)
    1. Europe—Emigration and immigration.   2. Europe—Emigration and
immigration—Government policy.   I. Title.

JV7590 .K67 2000
325.4—dc21   00-022677

Cornell University Press strives to use environmentally responsible
suppliers and materials to the fullest extent possible in the publishing
of its books. Such materials include vegetable-based, low-VOC inks
and acid-free papers that are recycled, totally chlorine-free, or partly
composed of nonwood fibers. Books that bear the logo of the FSC
(Forest Stewardship Council) use paper taken from forests that have
been inspected and certified as meeting the highest standards for
environmental and social responsibility. For further information,
visit our website at www.cornellpress.cornell.edu.

Cloth printing   10   9   8   7   6   5   4   3   2   1

FSC Trademark © 1996 Forest Stewardship Council A.C.
SW-COC-098

For Susan Abbie McKenney

Contents

Acknowledgments

This book draws in part on papers I have given at conferences and workshops. The overall argument has not appeared in print before, but some sections of the book have been published elsewhere. Chapters 3 and 4 elaborate on some material from "Migration and the Demographic Context of European Political Institutions," in *Immigration into Western Societies: Problems and Policies,* edited by Emek Ucarer and Donald J. Puchala (London: Pinter Press, 1997). Parts of chapter 6 appeared in "Intra-EU Migration, Citizenship, and Political Union," *Journal of Common Market Studies* 32, no. 3 (September 1994): 369–402. Other sections of chapter 6 were published as "EU Citizenship: Implications for Identity and Legitimacy," in *The Contested Polity: Legitimacy and the European Union,* edited by Thomas Banchoff and Mitchell Smith (London: Routledge, 1999). Parts of chapters 6 and 8 are drawn from "EU Migration Regimes: Established and Emergent," in *Challenge to the Nation-State: Immigration in Western Europe and the United States,* edited by Christian Joppke (Oxford: Oxford University Press, 1998). Reprinted by permission of Oxford University Press.

Institutional support from several sources made this book possible. The University of Pennsylvania's School of Arts and Sciences supported the initial research and writing. I am grateful to the Center for German and European Studies at Georgetown University for a fellowship in 1996–97 that supported the research and writing of parts of chapters 4 and 6 and all of chapter 7, as well as revisions to the rest of the manuscript. I also thank Rutgers University–Newark for providing leave time and supplemental financial support as well as a sabbatical leave in the spring of 1999.

The book benefited greatly from the comments and advice that I received from many people at the universities where I have studied, researched, and taught as well as the broader community of migration scholars. First and foremost, I thank Friedrich Kratochwil for his guidance on my dissertation and his advice and unflagging support over the years. I also thank Daniel Deudney, Ellen Kennedy, and Jack Nagel for their help on the dissertation. Devin Hagerty and James Hentz helped me keep my eye on the prize, and their constructive criticism contributed to the coherence of my arguments. In addition, I thank Yosef Lapid, Walter McDougall, Amir Pasic, Nancy Schwartz, Beverly Springer, and Douglas Verney for their comments on chapters.

At Georgetown's Center for German and European Studies, I especially thank Sam Barnes and Greg Flynn for their support, Thomas Banchoff for his camaraderie, Lily Gardner Feldman for challenging discussions, and my fellow research associate and officemate, Ellen Anderson, for her great sense of humor. I also thank my colleagues at the political science department at Rutgers-Newark for their encouragement and advice, most notably Yale Ferguson, Richard Langhorne, Virginia Walsh, and Mel Dubnick.

A wonderful community of migration scholars reached out beyond institutional and/or disciplinary boundaries to help an aspiring graduate student and then junior professor. Special thanks go to Mark Miller who read my dissertation prospectus, cooked me a nice lunch, then sent me forth with a box full of his books and the names of other scholars who proved to be just as generous with their time. Jim Hollifield and Martin Heisler commented on several papers that are incorporated in the book and gave invaluable support through the years. Christian Joppke not only invited me to the European University Institute in beautiful Florence but also pushed me to address the issue of sovereignty head on, which gave the book one of its central themes. Rogers Brubaker provided useful criticism of material incorporated into chapters 4, 6, and 8. Many thanks to Rainer Bauböck, Roland Blank, Adrian Favell, Andrew Geddes, David Jacobson, and David Martin for comments on chapters 7 and 8. During my year at Georgetown, Charles Keely, Audrey Singer, and Rosemarie Rogers gladly served as sounding boards and shared their expertise.

Much of the third part of the book has been influenced by the exchanges that I have had with a group of younger scholars from the United States and Europe sponsored by the German American Academic Council and Social Science Research Council. I thank Rainer Münz and Ari Zolberg for bringing us together and for their continuing support. Discussions with members of my focus group, Andrea Smith, John Torpey, and Antje Wiener, as well as commentary by Yasemin Soysal, helped me refine my arguments on dual nationality. I also thank Gianni D'Amato, Virginie Guiraudon, Gallya Lahav, Nedim Ogelman, Bernhard Santel, and Sarah Wayland for continuing research collaboration that has contributed to arguments made in the book. Special thanks go to David Kyle for introducing me to the emerging issue of human smuggling.

At Cornell University Press, Roger Haydon provided substantive comments on early versions of the first chapters in addition to fine editorial guidance. I am grateful for the comments of two anonymous reviewers as well as the many other people whom I have failed to name but, nonetheless, contributed to improving the quality of this book.

Finally, I could not have completed this book without my wife, Susan McKenney. She kept me healthy and sane, read the entire manuscript, repeatedly, shared my excitement, consoled me after setbacks, and prodded me when I needed it. I am ever grateful for her patience and understanding over the past few years.

R. K.

Princeton, New Jersey

Migrants and Citizens

Introduction

*E*ast German communism disintegrates as thousands of young East Germans leave their country through Czechoslovakia and Hungary. West Europeans brace for mass migrations from eastern Europe as the Berlin Wall falls and the Iron Curtain lifts. Ethnic tensions flare as 25 million Russians find themselves outside Russia when the Soviet Union disintegrates. As millions flee Iraq, Bosnia, Haiti, Cuba, Rwanda, Albania, and Kosovo, safe havens and no-fly zones are declared, economic sanctions are tightened, invasions are staged, air strikes commence and international relief efforts are mounted. International migration has become central to international politics in the post–Cold War world.

According to United Nations estimates, the number of people living outside of their state of nationality has been growing—from approximately 85 million people in 1975, to about 105 million in 1985, to almost 120 million in 1990. The world's migrant population has also been gradually increasing relative to world population—from 2.08 percent in 1975, to 2.18 percent in 1985, to 2.28 percent in 1990 (U.N. 1995).[1] Although it is extremely difficult to predict the future of migration trends, the circumstances for increasing world migration are favorable. Jet airliners have reduced intercontinental travel to hours rather than weeks. Satellite television, telephones and the internet spread information of different life possibilities elsewhere and foster the development of migratory networks. The concentration of projected world population growth in the less developed parts of the world increases demographic pressure for migration from less

1

developed to more developed countries and migration among less developed countries (Hoffmann-Novotny 1997).

As physical and economic constraints on international migration recede, migration becomes more of a function of legal constraints imposed by states, and, therefore, an increasingly political matter. Still, 2.28 percent is a relatively small proportion of total world population and it can be argued that international migration therefore has a relatively small effect on international politics in general. The political significance of migration, however, is not simply a function of its magnitude.

The mere existence of international migration that states do not want calls into question the ability of states involved to control their borders—a fundamental attribute of sovereignty. Many observers of international relations routinely assume state sovereignty and territorial integrity. Yet it is not at all clear to what degree the world's states have the capability, and their policymakers the will, to stop their citizens from leaving or stop the citizens of other countries from entering (Cornelius, Martin, and Hollifield 1994; Sassen 1996).

The policy impact of migration is often out of proportion to the actual size of migratory flows because of public perceptions in the host country that migrants increase employment competition, challenge religious, cultural or ethnic homogeneity or pose threats to national security (Weiner 1995, x, 45–74). These perceptions, whether or not well founded, often influence domestic political contests and thereby influence policy making. When migration seems a threat, it can lead to changes in host state policies toward sending countries, changes that go beyond the immediate issue of immigration rules. Under such conditions, migration, even of small numbers of people relative to the total population of the host country, can have a significant impact on foreign policy (Tucker, Keely, and Wrigley 1990; Weiner 1993; Teitelbaum and Weiner 1995; Miller 1997; Shain 1999).

Relatively few emigrants can also have a disproportionate impact on sending countries. For example, only a small fraction of a country's citizens may work abroad, but their remittances may provide a country with most of its hard currency (Stanton Russell 1992). Similarly, emigrants and political refugees often participate in home country politics with an impact that is disproportionate to their numbers—because of their education and skills, the financial capital they accumulate, and the influence on host country foreign policies toward their home countries.

Moreover, the number of people who reside outside their state of nationality understates the political consequences of international migration. It does not include the descendants of migrants who may have the nationality of the state in which they reside. Citizens may still identify politically or sentimentally with their parents' and grandparents' home state and participate in home state politics. Conversely, they may identify with the host state, but their fellow citizens may identify them with their ancestors' home state and not fully accept these descendants of immigrants as fellow citizens. In sum, past migration is often the root of contemporary politics of race and ethnicity (Castles and Miller 1998, chap. 2).

The growing predisposition to understanding politics in terms of individual rights has also magnified the political significance of international migration. As a rights-based discourse increasingly informs political practice within states, individuals come to possess a growing panoply of civil, social, and political rights. This extension of rights domestically has been paralleled by the entrance of "human rights" into the discourse of international relations. In 1795, Immanuel Kant enunciated the rights of "hospitality" for aliens. "Hospitality means the right of a stranger not to be treated with hostility when he arrives on someone else's territory." Kant asserted further that

> the peoples of the earth have thus entered in varying degrees into a universal community, and it has developed to the point where a violation of rights in one part of the world is felt everywhere. The idea of a cosmopolitan right is therefore not fantastic and overstrained; it is a necessary complement to the unwritten code of political and international right, transforming it into a universal right of humanity. (Kant 1970, 105, 107–8)

Kant's concept of rights of hospitality has subsequently been codified in a succession of constitutional provisions and international treaties on human rights. Whereas students of international politics could once have treated even relatively large migrations in epiphenomenal terms, the recent proliferation of rights magnifies the political significance of even relatively small migrations by raising the issue of the rights possessed by foreign residents.

For all these reasons, the consequences of international migration for international politics are greater than one might expect. It is also important to remember that these consequences differ in both degree and kind. The uneven distribution of migrants among the world's states causes wide variations in the impact of migrants on relations between certain states. The consequences also differ depending on whether the migration is of permanent legal immigrants, political refugees and asylum seekers, legal guest workers or undocumented migrant workers as well as on the social composition, economy, form of government and dominant ideology of the states involved.

Generally speaking, large-scale movements of refugees have the most immediate and direct impact on international politics. Such movements are, as the outcomes of war, revolution, or ethnic conflict, inherently political (Zolberg, Suhrke, and Aguayo 1989; Keely 1996; Weiner 1996) and often involve host states in the conflict that led to the migration in the first place (Dowty and Loescher 1996; Posen 1996). Because the bulk of the world's refugees have moved from one developing country to another, the direct international consequences of migration are most evident in the less developed parts of the world. As with Malawi in the early 1990s, migration may mean hosting a million refugees in a country of ten million with little in the way of spare resources (UNHCR 1993, 100). As with Zaire in 1994, migration may mean 1.2 million Rwandan refugees pouring over borders in a matter of weeks, rapid spread of diseases fostered by concentrations of humanity in unsanitary conditions, and soldiers among the refugees effectively taking over refugee camps and preparing for military action in the state from which they fled (Adelman 1997).

Although the movements of refugees among less developed countries have had the most direct impact on international politics, the politics of international migration became particularly salient in Europe at the close of the Cold War. Western foreign policymakers and the media became transfixed with the prospect of a mass migration to western Europe.[2] In September of 1992, British Foreign Secretary Douglas Hurd said that he and his fellow European Union (EU) foreign ministers deemed that migration, "among all the other problems we face—is the most crucial." Like nineteenth-century America, "Europe is a magnet for people seeking greater opportunities, from the east and south. . . . We have already seen, most obviously in Germany but also elsewhere in the Community, the tensions and antipathies which can result from the inflow." But unlike nineteenth-century America "ours is not an empty continent" (qtd. in Savill 1992). Some European policymakers took a step further, arguing not only that migration was a new threat but also that the challenges it posed should be dealt with by European cooperation rather than by unilateral action. In the fall of 1995, Wolfgang Schauble, then parliamentary chairman and later leader of the German Christian Democratic Union (CDU), stated that no state could single-handedly protect its citizens from the new threats of mass migration, terrorism, ecological destruction, organized crime and political religious fundamentalism. "Therefore we cannot, and must not, be satisfied with the present degree of [European] integration. We must deepen integration, for we will solve neither today's nor tomorrow's problems with a Europe organized as a loose association based on inter-governmental, ad hoc agreements" (qtd. in Binyon 1995).

European foreign policymakers consider migration a threat to national security because, even though migration seemingly has little to do with the balance of power, it has everything to do with domestic politics. Policymakers often view immigration as a point of entry for the importation of political conflicts from abroad, a drain on social service budgets and a challenge to cultural identity,[3] issues with which opportunistic, populist politicians can manipulate public passions and erode support for the established political elite (Betz 1994). Although xenophobic populist parties have had only limited electoral success in European countries (and primarily in local and regional races), such populism indirectly influences policy making by way of mainstream conservative parties who, in protecting their right flanks, adopt some anti-immigration rhetoric and policies as their own (Thraenhardt 1997).

The impact of migration on the dynamics of international politics in Europe is more subtle than it is in less developed parts of the world. It depends more on the perception of threats than on real threats of attacks by armed refugee warriors. The political consequences of migration are often a function of liberal ideologies that extol human rights and raise difficult questions regarding the civil, social and even political rights of migrants. Migration control has become the objective of multilateral cooperation in order to preempt perceived threats and reduce the political dilemmas that are raised by migrants' rights. Hence, migration affects international politics in Europe by way of domestic political changes that prompt changes in foreign policies.

But why has migration become so politically salient in Europe so quickly? To understand the contemporary dynamics of the domestic-international political nexus, one must examine the historical legacy of European emigration as well as migration within Europe. The contemporary "migration crisis" in Europe is defined largely in terms of what appear to be unprecedented numbers of foreigners in European societies, but it was as recently as the 1970s that more people began migrating to the European continent than those leaving (Widgren 1990, 752). Contemporary east-west and south-north migration into Europe pales before earlier European out-migration. Also, centuries of intra-European migration before the mass emigration of Europeans to the New World gave individual west European societies multiethnic populations long before the arrival of Turkish and North African guest workers or of east European refugees.

The contemporary political consequences of migration differ from those of the nineteenth century because the nature of international migration has changed. Before World War I, most international migrants moved from Europe to settler societies with open immigration policies and inclusive citizenship laws. With little intention of returning, such migrants generally opted for assimilation into the host society and polity. Most of today's migrants are ostensibly temporary. They are asylum seekers and refugees from the seemingly interminable civil wars that continue to burn around the world. They are guest workers, illegal migrant workers, transient students, professionals and corporate employees who are part and parcel of the global economy (Salt 1989, 1992, 1993). Most of these temporary migrants may fully intend to return home, but many routinely stay in their host countries, have children there and become permanent settlers. The expectation that migration will be temporary, often held both by authorities in the host countries and the migrants themselves, has led to ambiguity in the political identity of migrants as well as underestimation, and even denial, among host country authorities of demographic realities and practical political problems.

Migration flows alone are not responsible for the crisis many Europeans perceive, and these flows are not necessarily indicative of migration's political significance. Rather, international migration to and within Europe has illuminated difficult problems that are latent in the modern political institutions of the nation-state itself. For example, restrictive citizenship laws that exclude migrants and their children from political participation have undermined the legitimacy of democracy in some west European states. Yet when naturalization rules are eased and large proportions of the permanent resident population reject naturalization, the result challenges the presumption of political assimilation. When states try to increase naturalization rates by permitting dual nationality, they challenge the principle of a singular nationality underlying the nation-state and blur the demographic boundaries of the states themselves as well as the international system they collectively constitute.

Migration has become politically salient so quickly because many of the political institutions of modern Europe are ill-suited to deal with immigration. Modern European political institutions of citizenship, democracy, and the welfare state developed within the organizational framework of the nation-state; they also developed in the demographic context of millions of Europeans leaving their countries. This demographic context shaped citizenship laws that bound the membership of European democratic states as well as the communities within which these states redistributed wealth. Now, as the flow of migration has reversed, these political institutions are, in a sense, dysfunctional. Yet changing them is very difficult. In the end, political crises develop, not necessarily because of the sheer numbers of migrants (which were much smaller than predicted at the outset of the 1990s) but because many institutions cannot accommodate even relatively small numbers without raising sensitive issues of national identity. Therefore, increasing state control of migration flows, whether unilaterally or through cooperation at the European level, is not in and of itself a "solution" to the political problems that migration poses.

The first part of this book places these arguments about migration and citizenship within a broader theoretical context. In chapter 1, I show how a focus on migration offers insights into the modern conceptualization of world politics as a system of interacting nation-states. I investigate the bearing of migration on assumptions of sovereignty, territoriality and political identity and explore the implications of demography for the development of political institutions in general. These arguments are supported in the three chapters of part 2.

In chapter 2, I explain why political developments in Europe are central to international relations and situate general arguments regarding territoriality and political identity into more specific debates over sovereignty in relation to European political union. I argue that sovereignty can be understood in terms of a state's ability to control its borders and determine its membership. It, however, can be fully understood only within the context of states' relations with one another—which means, in the case of EU member states, political integration. The sovereignty of EU member states is being transformed with changes in migration policy and citizenship figuring prominently in the development of a European polity. These arguments are supported in the three chapters of part 3.

The title of the second part of the book, "Demography Shaping Political Institutions," can be read in two ways. First, it can refer to those political institutions that shape demography. For example, scholars have pointed to the role of the state in migration (driving out refugees), mortality (war), and fertility (forced sterilization or child subsidies). Or the title can refer to how demographic change influences the development of political institutions. In this second part of the book, I only briefly discuss the ways the state has shaped population growth and migration and focus instead on the under-appreciated role of migration in the development of the nation-state and the political institutions associated with it.

Chapter 3 examines the role of migration in the development and expansion of the modern European system of states with particular attention paid to the epidemiological factor of migrant-born disease, the impact of migration on the balance of power, as well as the demographic context of polyethnic social formations. This historical overview supports a central argument: the modern nation-state is an atypical social and political form because it is based on the unprecedented population growth and emigration that began in the middle of the eighteenth century. Contemporary European politics can largely be understood as a mismatch of modern political institutions centered on the nation-state with a changing demographic context that now challenges these institutions.

Chapter 4 demonstrates how in European nation-states the political institutions of citizenship and democracy developed in the context of rapid population growth and mass emigration during the nineteenth century. These same political institutions are now being challenged by declining fertility rates and increasing immigration, which are returning European societies to their preexisting polyethnic condition. Particular emphasis is placed on the consequences of increasing immigration for the legitimacy of democratic rule in European states that base citizenship on ancestral lineage as well as on the dilemmas these states face in attempting to maintain the welfare systems upon which quintessentially European forms of social democracy rest.

Chapter 5 extends this argument by examining the consequences of migration, including how migration shaped the differing principles of citizenship for the political union of states. Previous unions in America and Germany are quite different from contemporary European integration, precisely due to the differing demographic contexts in which they developed. Hence, migration and member state citizenship present major theoretical and practical problems for constitutional designs of European political union that are based on analogies to the American and German federal experiences.

Each chapter in the second part of the book ends with a section that identifies a theoretical dilemma confronting modern political institutions in Europe today: increasingly multiethnic societies, citizenship laws that exclude resident aliens, and a conflict between democratic inclusiveness and political union. Part 3 examines contemporary changes in citizenship and migration policies that respond to these dilemmas. Responses in the form of EU citizenship, increasing dual nationality, and cooperation on border control also demonstrate a move in Europe toward a new form of political organization that transforms the conventions of territoriality upon which state sovereignty and the European state system rests.

Chapter 6 examines the development of a regime regulating migration within the EU and considers the role of migration in the process of European legal and political integration. I demonstrate the fundamental differences between the European polity that has been constituted by the Maastricht Treaty on European Union (TEU) and previous forms of political union with an analysis of European Union citizenship and its implications for voting, political identity, and constitutionalism.

Chapter 7 examines dual nationality in Europe and the political meanings of dual nationality for international relations in general. International norms against dual nationality initially developed in response to conflicts among states over the military obligations of their nationals and formed sa demographic boundary maintenance regime aimed at reducing cases of dual nationality. Now, state practices have changed to permit dual nationality, thus undermining Europe's demographic maintenance regime with interesting implications for the political identity of individuals and state sovereignty.

Chapter 8 examines the development of international cooperation on asylum policies and border control among EU member states and the development of an institutional framework for further cooperation and integration of migration policies. In contrast to the intra-EU migration regime, this cooperation has mainly focused on restricting the movement of non-EU nationals into the Union. The simultaneous emergence of an international regime governing migration to the EU, the influence of this regime on migration policy making in eastern and central Europe, and the decline of the regime that helps European states demographically delineate their boundaries vividly demonstrates a transformation of sovereignty in the emerging European polity.

Part 1

Theoretical Issues

Migration and the
Conceptualization of World Politics

*P*ractical policy questions regarding international migration strike a deep chord in contemporary European politics that reverberates beyond the policy realm because they raise difficult theoretical questions about political identity, belonging to a polity, and membership in a state: Who are we? How do we draw the line between "us" and "them"? Can "they" become "us"? If so, how long does it take; what does it take? At first glance, these questions may seem relevant only to domestic politics and appear to have precious little to do with international politics. This is the case, however, only if these questions have already been answered so well that the answers can be taken for granted. If one can assume that a state's population identifies with the state, only then can one speak of a nation-state as an international actor. Taking for granted the answer "Soviet," or "Yugoslav," to the first question—Who are we?—has proved a very poignant reminder of the hazards involved in making such assumptions.

As foreigners increasingly make up greater proportions of a state's population, long established answers about political identity have greater difficulty withstanding even casual scrutiny. Answers like "Germany is not an immigration country" [1] ring hollow in the face of the new demographic reality that 13 percent of all children born in Germany are not born German citizens and 6.5 percent of the children born in Germany as German citizens have one foreign parent. [2] In combination with the brave new world of the single European market, European monetary union, and NATO expansion, this new demographic reality makes the very idea of a German nation-state at long last emerging from decades of division seem oddly quaint. Due to Germany's historical legacy and the fact that Germany hosts Europe's largest population of resident aliens, questioning German national identity has become something of an industry for pundits as well as scholars. With racist and xenophobic social movements and political parties thriving in the United Kingdom, France, Italy, and Austria (see Betz 1994), "the Germans" are by far not the only Europeans facing a loss of certainty about national identity triggered by international migration on the one hand and European integration on the other.

This combination of increasing migration and European integration not only challenges national identity, it challenges the notion of sovereignty—the central organizing principle of traditional approaches to comprehending world politics as a system of interacting nation-states. Political integration makes it difficult to simply "locate" sovereignty with respect to jurisdiction over any given issue, be it trade, defense, law enforcement, currency, or foreign policy. Increasing international migration yields growing discrepancies between a nation's demographics and its state's borders that undermine the validity of the nation-state as a unit of analysis itself. Although wrestling with these conceptual problems of identity, territoriality, and sovereignty may be difficult, the exercise will not only help us better understand the contemporary politics of migration and citizenship, it will also demonstrate the importance of migration and citizenship to understanding world politics in general.

Migration, the State, and International Relations Theory

With respect to the conceptualization of world politics, international relations theories can be divided into two opposing groups in a debate over the state as a unit of analysis: state-centric theories, primarily realism and neorealism, and non-state centric theories, which developed as alternatives to realism and focus on transnational interaction and non-state actors.

State-centric theories conceptualize world politics in terms of an international system of territorially delineated states. Due to the existence of government within states, domestic politics is characterized by order and hierarchy; due to the absence of world government, politics among states is characterized by anarchy. Traditional realists posit that international politics is primarily about war and peace, and neorealists argue that international politics is structured by the distribution of the military capabilities of states. In contrast to traditional realism, however, neorealist analysis is conducted almost exclusively in the "third image," or on the level of the international system, rather than on the "second image," or at the level of politics within the state.[3]

Unfortunately third-image, state-centric, capability-driven analysis does not adequately deal with international migration because international migration can lead to changes (or the potential for changes) in domestic politics that reverberate on the international level in the form of foreign policy changes that are not necessarily the result of changes in military capabilities. For example, domestic political stability may attract international migration, which increases population and economic growth.[4] This growth, in turn, increases military power in the international arena. At the same time, however, even small migrations often prompt political movements directed at immigrants (especially in periods of economic recession). Exclusion of minorities can then polarize domestic politics and become a major factor of political destabilization, up to and including national self-determination and irredentism. International stability can hinge on both the integration of permanent resident aliens into polities and on international cooperation among states to stem future migration. In this way, international migration may influence relations among states whether or not that migration has changed the balance of power.

Given that international migration may lead to domestic political changes that in turn have international consequences, the political problems raised by migration often do not fit the domestic hierarchy/international anarchy dichotomy. These political problems, however, raise theoretical questions regarding the domestic hierarchy/international anarchy dichotomy itself and the conceptualization of world politics in terms of territoriality upon which that dichotomy rests.

In opposition to state-centric theories, a host of theories taking a transnationalist approach have been advanced.[5] This group of theories includes functionalism (Mitrany 1946), neofunctionalism (Haas 1958), social communications theory (Deutsch et al. 1957), interdependence theory (Keohane and Nye 1977), world society theory (Burton 1972), and epistemic community theory (Haas 1992a). Theorists taking a transnationalist approach try to understand world politics in its totality. They point out that states are not the only actors in world politics. Non-state actors—such as multinational corporations; international trade unions; international scientific, technical, and functional organizations; and global religious organizations and foundations—also play crucial roles in world politics.

Moreover, transnationalist theorists argue that state-to-state relations only represent part of world politics, and that many politically significant actions bypass states themselves. Robert Keohane and Joseph Nye identified four global interactions: communication, or the movement of information, including beliefs and ideas; transportation, or the movement of physical objects, including merchandise and arms; finance, or the movement of money and instruments of credit; and travel, or the movement of persons (Keohane and Nye 1972, xii). Theorists taking a transnationalist approach contend that such interactions demonstrate the state's "permeability," and some theorists even argued that as the volume of transnational interactions increased, states would increasingly become "obsolete." Moreover, many transnationalist theorists attempted to shift the focus of analysis away from military capabilities, national interests, and war to economic interdependence, common interests, and international cooperation.

Most arguments challenging state-centric theories dealt with economic interdependence arising from increasing international trade and monetary flows (Keohane and Nye 1977). International migration is another such cross-border flow that demonstrates the permeability of the state (Mitchell 1989), but analysis of the international movement of people languished. This is unfortunate because the international movement of humans is potentially much more significant than the international movement of goods or money. Unlike goods and money, migrants have a will of their own[6] and can themselves become significant economic and political actors. Migrants challenge assumptions of territoriality not just when they cross borders but also when they send home hard currency, participate in home country politics, influence the foreign policy-making of host and home states, and develop alternative diasporic identities. As international relations scholars largely abandoned theories of transnationalism and the study of migration in the 1980s, anthropologists and sociologists turned their attention to migrant social and political networks that spanned state borders, and some have made "transnationalism" a major "new" analytical focus in their fields (Glick Schiller, Basch, and Blanc-Szanton 1992; Portes 1995; Kearney 1995; Appadurai 1996; Cohen 1997).

As theories of economic integration and interdependence challenged the primacy of the realist concern with military capabilities, analyses of economic interdependence developed into a neoliberal institutionalist theoretical framework. Neoliberal institutionalism focuses on the international regimes facilitating cooperation among states (Krasner 1983) and the international institutions, which perpetuated cooperation even as the hegemonic power that initially established these institutions went into decline (Keohane 1984). Neoliberal institutionalism is a type of synthesis of the state-centric conceptualization of world politics and the transnationalist agenda of focusing on international cooperation. It begins analysis with an unproblematic understanding of states as constituent units of the system, and as unitary actors, yet focuses on the existence of "cooperation under anarchy."[7] By viewing the nature and interests of states as exogenous to domestic politics and the international environment, world politics can be understood in terms of the interaction of rational "international actors" in which microeconomic models and game theoretical approaches are applied (Keohane 1988).

The question of international cooperation has become the focus of the few studies of migration and international political economy undertaken by migration specialists, with regime theory becoming the primary theoretical framework (Mitchell 1989; Hollifield 1992a, 1992b; Zolberg 1992; Koslowski 1998). While liberal regime theories may be useful in examining the question of international cooperation in the area of migration, approaching the issue of migration in international politics primarily as a matter of international cooperation threatens to understate the importance of migration by relegating it to just one of many diverse regime issues— such as textiles, telecommunications, and fur seals (Aggarwal 1983; Cowhey 1990; Mirovitskaya, Clark, and Purver 1993). Since human migration across international borders differs from the movement of products or other factors of production because humans possess the capacity to become significant political and economic actors, the consequences of migration for world politics go beyond questions of its regulation or lack of regulation by states, whether unilaterally, bilaterally, or multilaterally. Beginning with unitary-actor assumptions and importing microeconomic tools to analyze international cooperation regarding migration may be a useful exercise (Kessler 1997), but it is much more important to examine the role of migration in the development of microeconomic linkages across state boundaries, the impact of migration on the macroeconomics of host and home countries, and the relationship of these microeconomic linkages and macroeconomic consequences to the nature of political interactions among states. If one views migration as a transnational phenomenon rather than an issue of cooperation and then problematizes the unitary-actor assumption, it becomes evident that migration is a factor that impinges on the nature of the state as an international actor.

Although regime theory for the most part remained state-centric, the development of regime theory also prompted calls for reframing the study of world politics in terms of international governance (Kratochwil and Ruggie 1986) and rethinking the assumptions of territoriality in the process of theoretical conceptualization (Kratochwil 1986; Ruggie 1993). This book contributes to the latter effort by focusing on the bearing international migration has on theoretical assumptions of territoriality. Not only has migration historically played a critical role in the development of political institutions, which theorists take for granted, but contemporary migration also raises practical problems for territorially organized institutions and theoretical problems for assumptions of territoriality.

Migration, Territoriality, and Identity

Migration is hardly a new phenomenon in world history given that humans have lived much longer in nomadic hunter-gatherer societies than in sedentary agricultural and industrial societies. International migration is relatively new, but only because part of total human migration became designated as "international" with the development of an international system. As boundaries delineating the system's constituent units developed, human migration was divided into two categories: international (or more accurately, interstate) migration and internal (intrastate) migration.

The phenomenon of international migration as a subject of inquiry does not fit well into the conceptual frameworks of international relations theory, political theory, and comparative politics because most scholars in these fields have been primarily concerned with politics either within or among states. Weber's understanding of the state as "a human community that [successfully] claims the monopoly of the legitimate use of physical force within a given territory" (Weber 1946, 78) has become the conceptual anchor around which theoretical frameworks in all these disciplines are often organized. The fact that international migration does not fit well into these theoretical frameworks is indicative not of a mere problem in incorporating an understanding of a marginal phenomenon, but of a problem in the conceptualization of world politics in general. Migration presents practical political problems that have not been well understood because political and international relations theories have generally assumed the continuity of people and place, nation and state, *demos* and democracy.

In political theory and comparative political analysis the conceptual categories of state, democracy, representation, and so on, have generally developed with an implicit understanding that the polity[8] is geographically defined and with the implicit assumption that the people of any given polity remain within that polity. Similarly, the articulation of an independent theory of international relations, based on the differentiation of world politics into territorial nation-states, assumes a continuity of the nation with the state (Lapid 1994). Although in many cases this was a convenient fiction to begin with, international migration furthers the discontinuity of people and place and thereby exposes the problems of the initial assumptions, as well as the problems with theories based on those assumptions.

Using a thought experiment helps clarify the conceptual problem that migration raises in regard to territoriality and political identity. Imagine that every five years 5 percent of the world's population moves from one state to another. Within a generation it would make little sense to speak of the United States, China, India, Germany, or other countries as totalities called "states" designating a central bureaucratic apparatus, territory, and people—as is generally the case among international relations scholars. If each state were understood to be "a human community that [successfully] claims the monopoly of the legitimate use of physical force within a given territory": Which human community? Who would legitimate the use of force? How?

Formal political structures may remain under such conditions of mass migration, but the changing demographic composition of the polity would profoundly alter the political dynamics within the polity, as well as the relationship of the polity to its formal structures. In this hypothetical situation, it would be difficult to think of a polity in strictly geographically-delineated terms and then empirically analyze its internal politics and foreign policies, because any conclusions based on the characteristics of that polity could well become obsolete as quickly as the demographic composition of the polity changed.[9] The global rate of international migration has not approached the level described in this hypothetical example, but it has in certain parts of the world. For example, during the early nineteenth century, the demographic composition of Texas changed rapidly as European and American immigrants increased in proportion to "native" Mexicans. As demographics changed, so did the identity of the polity as a whole.

The hypothetical example draws attention to the territorial orientation of political and international relations theory. The project of theorizing begins with well-defined territorial boundaries as a given. Modern conceptions of politics operative in contemporary theory, however, developed in the historical context of the rise of the nation-state. Just as the development of the state involved the territorial differentiation of polities and control over inhabitants, our modern understanding of politics has developed a similar theoretical delineation along territorial lines.

If a political theorist is concerned with making theoretical statements about the universal and eternal elements of politics, humanity as a whole is the unit of analysis. The actual composition of the polities into which humanity may be divided should not make a difference. In practice, political theory has rarely been organized around all of humanity as the unit of analysis. Even though theorists often argue in general terms about democracy, authority, justice, representation, freedom, and so on, such arguments have usually been made in reference to the state and even implicitly in reference to the state within which the author lives. All too often, universal attributes are projections of perceived similarities among members of the polity within which the author lives, of perceptions of the author's own self, or of hypothetical constructs of "human nature" based on deductions from such perceptions.

If a theorist is concerned with world politics as a whole, then political practice in its totality should be the object of study. In contrast, world politics is usually thought of in terms of the interaction of territorially defined units—states. There is a good reason for conceptualizing world politics in terms of the relations among states, namely the historical development of the organization of political practice centered on and around the state. It is important to understand, however, that this is also a historically contingent activity and that it is not the only way one might conceptualize world politics (Kratochwil 1986).

In contrast to arguments about the permeability of the state, our hypothetical situation would raise a more fundamental issue: What is the state as an international actor? If the state is more than a formal legal structure, an umbrella for a host of public and private institutions, a central bureaucracy, a military apparatus, a domestic law enforcement establishment, a system of public indoctrination and education, but is also a "people" that, together, comprise a territorially delineated totality and give it agency, mass migration would call into question a fundamental component of that totality. In terms of the relationship of international migration to political and international relations theory, it is not simply that political and international relations theories have difficulties dealing with the marginal issue of migration. Rather, the fact that migration presents a dilemma, in that it does not fit into the theoretical framework, illuminates a more general problem with assumptions of territoriality in theory.

A constructivist approach to the problems raised by migration is useful because constructivist analysis is not wedded to legal or political structures as "units of analysis" per se.[10] Rather, constructivism focuses on human practice, the contingency of practice, and the mutual relationship between agents and structures (Onuf 1989; Wendt 1987; Dessler 1989; Wendt 1992; Koslowski and Kratochwil 1994). The international system is understood as an interacting collection of human-made institutions including, but not limited to, states.[11] Institutions are settled or routinized practices constituted and regulated by norms (Kratochwil 1989), and states are institutions whose existence is dependent upon the reproduction of particular sets of practices. Not simply a legal entity or a formal organization, the state is an ensemble of normatively constituted practices by which a group of individuals forms a special type of political association. This political association is perpetuated by reproduction of the constituent individuals into successive generations of members of the association [12] as well as by reproduction of the normatively constituted practices of individual members.

If one understands both the international system and the state in terms of the reproduction of a given set of normatively constituted practices, international and domestic politics are not hermetically sealed within their own spheres. Political practice is divided into these two realms only by the historical fact of the state as the institutional setup that organizes politics. Therefore, changes in domestic politics can transform the international system and changes in international politics can transform domestic structures. Moreover, politics need not be understood as only taking place either inside or outside of the state.

This constructivist approach to understanding world politics illuminates the contingent nature as well as the constitutive role of territoriality. Territory is not just physical land or space. For a given space to be territory, a set of political practices must be reproduced (Sack 1986). That is, territory is contingent on the continual reproduction of territorially-oriented practice. For instance, John Ruggie explained how accommodation of the religious worship by diplomats from countries with other religions led to the institution of extraterritoriality. Ironically, extraterritoriality was necessary for the functioning of an international system of territorially defined states (Ruggie 1993, 164–67). With this poignant example, Ruggie demonstrates how territoriality is a social construct, which depends on the development of mutual understandings and the reproduction of particular practices.

The conceptualization of world politics in terms of territoriality is historically contingent on territorial social and political organization. Humans lived in mobile hunter-gatherer bands for hundreds of thousands of years until they began to domesticate plants and animals in approximately 8000 B.C. Some humans continued in their nomadic existence by supplementing hunting and gathering with pastoralism; others established sedentary societies based on agriculture, which became the basis for what has come to be called civilization. Whereas nomadic peoples maintained non-territorial forms of social organization, agriculturally based civilizations developed territorial forms of social organization "built upon the recognition of mutual rights subject to common law within a given territory" (Kratochwil 1986, 29). The modern territorially delineated conceptualization of world politics is based on the transition from nomadic to sedentary existence of approximately ten thousand years ago and the subsequent global expansion of agricultural and industrial civilizations at the expense of hunter-gatherer and pastoral societies, which was completed over the last five hundred years. Not only was the end of the continuous migration of nomads necessary for territorial political institutions to take root, it was the emigration out of agricultural and industrial centers that spread the conventions of territoriality around the world.

Throughout history, migration has influenced the political dynamics within and between premodern civilizations. Before the advent of printing, postal systems, and telecommunications technology, human migration was the primary means of technology transfer, cultural borrowing, and the translocation of political models. Before the development of the germ theory of disease, public health systems, and modern medicine, the transportation of microorganisms by migrating humans led to recurrent population-decimating epidemics.

Given the importance of technology transfer, cultural borrowing, and the translocation of political models to the development and interaction of polities, migration should occupy a prominent position in international relations theory. Unfortunately, looking back from our advanced technological societies, it is easy to miss the millennia of transfers and borrowings fostered by migration. Although general technological, political, and economic advancements were driven by these transfers and borrowings, the consequences of migration for international politics have largely been forgotten due, ironically, to the technology transfer migration originally fostered.

Looking back from a world in the midst of a population explosion, it is difficult to imagine that until the twentieth century, survival and even expansion of populations involved war, not only with other humans, but with microorganisms that were often far more deadly. Contact between populations that had developed immunities to a deadly disease with those that had not often led to disastrous epidemics that devastated civilizations in a way that we now have difficulty comprehending. The centrality of the transmission of disease to the interaction of societies is underscored by the fact that until the end of the nineteenth century, more soldiers died from disease and infection than died in battle. Hence wars were often decided as much by advantages in immunities to diseases and proper sanitation as by guns, ammunition, and morale.

Despite the historical role of migration in the development of territorially organized political institutions, most conceptions of human social and political organization take sedentary civilization as the norm and most examinations of migration begin with the assumption that humans are by nature sedentary and, thus, that it is migration that needs explanation

(Hoffmann-Novotny 1997). Given that human existence has for the most part been nomadic and that the transition to sedentary life was in large measure a matter of the application of the new technology of agriculture, territorial social organization is not inherently natural but rather a social and historical artifact.

Territoriality is a social practice that, however well institutionalized, need not be immutable in the demographic context arising from changing technologies and economic processes. Postindustrial service-based economies, trade expansion across borders, transnational firms, and accelerating global capital mobility may all be factors for increasing, rather than decreasing, international migration as a whole. However, sedentary society can be presupposed for the immediate future. Nevertheless, technological change has rapidly increased the potential for international migration, and future changes in technology as well as in economic organization could mean that the current high proportion of humans maintaining sedentary existence within territorial social organizations may not continue in the future to the degree to which it occurs now.

Indeed, even agricultural production no longer inherently renders the sedentary societies typical of ten thousand years of peasant farming. The United States possesses one of the world's most productive agricultural sectors. Its exports feed millions of people around the world. Yet due to technological advances, the number of people directly involved in food production has dropped to a small fraction of the American population. Moreover, the technological and commercial transformation of American food production has been a major factor in increasing international mobility. Migrant workers, both legal and illegal, perform a large portion of the nonmechanized agricultural labor.

If sedentary society need not be considered eternal, neither should territorial social organization. And if territoriality is only one of several ways in which politics has been organized in the past and may also be organized in the future, the territorial orientation of the modern conceptualization of world politics is clearly just as historically contingent.

Much as the emergence of the state involved the territorial differentiation of polities and control over inhabitants, our modern understanding of politics has developed a similar theoretical delineation along territorial lines. Territoriality is not only a social construct. Territoriality also patterns our thinking about politics, and this thinking is reified in the reproduction of practices that makes possible territory as an institution. Reification of territorially oriented thought through the reproduction of territory as an institution is fundamental to our conceptualization of politics, and a fact that may or may not be escaped. Self-consciousness of the nature of territoriality does not necessarily lead to its transcendence in practice. Hence, world politics continues to be organized territorially regardless of the anomalies presented by certain political problems, such as those posed by migration. The question then becomes one of the proliferation of such problems and the propensity of territoriality to be reproduced and to retain its position in our understanding of politics. In this regard, examining the role of migration in the development of modern territorially organized political institutions is useful in gaining insight into contemporary conceptualizations of world politics.

The Demographic Context of Political Institutions

The demographic context of political institutions refers, most basically, to the obvious fact that without people there are no political practices and without political practices there are no political institutions. Because the demographic factors of mortality, fertility, and migration determine the number of people in as well as the composition (age, gender, ethnicity, etc.) of the members of the polity, demographic factors shape the development of political institutions.

As we have discussed, the development of territorially organized political institutions depended on the end of migration on the part of entire societies. Had societies continued to migrate, whatever territorially delineated political institutions that did emerge would have had to either transform with the movement of the societies to which they belonged or simply be left behind with the smoldering campfires around which these institutions might have been initiated. Indeed, territorially delineated social and political institutions in civilizations did not uniformly and simultaneously occur across the face of the Earth. As I will demonstrate in chapter 3, Eurasian civilizations and their territorial political institutions gradually differentiated themselves from their environments while nomadic barbarians maintained non-territorial forms of social and political organization. Since this zone of nomadic peoples separated the civilizations that emerged, it became a buffer zone and medium through which civilizations indirectly interacted. In this sense, the demographic context of nomadic peoples surrounding civilization centers informed the development of territorially delineated political institutions as well as the relations between them.

Even though humanity did eventually settle down and territorially organized agricultural civilizations established the norms upon which politics as understood today is based, these civilizations still maintained relatively high rates of migration in and out of urban concentrations. Such migration continued to inform the development of political institutions by changing the ethnic composition of the polity. Since the beginning of civilization, a cycle of peasant in-migration to replace urban populations depleted by disease, coupled with the out-migration of urban elites to the peripheries, produced polyethnic societies that have been common to all Eurasian civilizations, including ancient Greece and Rome as well as their European successors (McNeill 1986). Polyethnic societies are characterized by a hierarchical political order and a division of labor along ethnic lines, in which different ethnic groups belong to different social classes and fill different occupational niches within those classes. The interaction of polyethnic empires with their environments differs fundamentally from that of modern nation-states. Whereas the boundaries of nation-states are fairly well delineated both geographically and demographically, the boundaries of premodern polyethnic empires were not that distinct.

In contrast to conceptualizations of world politics that take demographic and social history into account, traditional international relations theory is built on the nineteenth-century historiography that told the story of the rise of the nation-state, the struggle for power within nation-states, and the diplomacy and war between them (Herz 1959, 39–110). Contemporary international relations theorists even take a further step and conflate the modern state, city-state, and empire under the rubric of "self-regarding unit" (Waltz 1979, chap. 5). Neorealists argue that such self-regarding units, usually identified as states, have been producing an international anarchy through their interaction going back to the ancient Greek city-states (Art and Waltz 1971, 4; Waltz 1979, 174, 186; Gilpin 1981, 7, 85–96). Some theorists have questioned whether states in this sense actually existed and produced an international anarchy during the Medieval period (Ruggie 1983). This question has become a point of debate regarding the viability of neorealism as a general theory of international politics (Fischer 1992; Hall and Kratochwil 1993; Fischer 1993), with one prominent neorealist contending not only that "states and other political entities behaved according to realist dictates" in the seven centuries since 1300 but also that realism explains world politics for the past twelve hundred years (Mearsheimer 1994, 44–46).

Such neorealist vision of a past system of interacting nation-states is problematic given that European societies followed the polyethnic norm until sustained rapid population growth during the eighteenth and nineteenth centuries fostered the rise of large ethnically homogenous societies. Only then did European nation-states develop as the "containers" of political institutions, and only after that could one meaningfully speak of their interaction with one another (see chapter 3).

Moreover, the development of these modern European political institutions occurred in the context of mass migration from Europe to the rest of the world. By the nineteenth century, the expansion of agricultural civilizations extinguished most of the world's non-territorially organized hunter-gatherer and pastoral societies. Nevertheless, during the nineteenth century, the expansion of the predominant European civilization together with its industrialization led to an unprecedented migration that caused significant proportions of European societies to become nomadic. During the great migration of 1820–1924, 50 million people moved to the New World. By the end of this migratory period, people of European origin who lived outside of Europe constituted one-eleventh of the world's population (Thomas 1961, 9).

While modern European political institutions developed in the context of massive emigration, American, Canadian, Australian, New Zealand, and Latin American polities developed in the context of immigration. Migration from Europe to the New World facilitated early state formation through the expulsion of religious minorities and emigration of dissenters. In the context of immigration, New World polities developed with inclusive forms of citizenship and assimilative forms of democracy. This course of political development complemented the emergence of European nation-states that developed more ethnically exclusive national citizenship, which in turn bounded the democratic evolution of those nation-states. That is, the development of New World polities had a certain symbiotic relationship with the development of Old World polities. Polities in both New and Old Worlds developed along lines of territorially organized states; however, as elaborated in chapter 4, demography influenced the political institutions of the states that developed with respect to the types of democracies that emerged.

The demographic context of modern European political institutions has significant theoretical implications. Given the demographic circumstances of the eighteenth through the early twentieth centuries, commonly held conceptions of politics that presuppose the continuity of people and place may have been adequate for understanding the European state system at the time. Recent changes in the demography of European societies, however, have precipitated practical and theoretical problems outside of this traditional conceptual framework in the part of the world where the framework initially developed.

For example, constitutive norms like "everyone should
state," which became embodied in a corpus of nationality la
oped during the nineteenth century, made possible the diff
world politics into a system of nation-states. By differentiating the international
system demographically, nationality laws became both constitutive
of the international system as well as influential in the interaction of states.
European states that experienced extensive emigration tended to adopt nationality laws based on the principle of ancestral lineage (*jus sanguinis*) so
as to maintain ties with emigrants and facilitate the return of their children;
settler societies of the New World tended to adopt nationality laws based
on the principle of birthplace (*jus soli*) in order to facilitate the political
incorporation of immigrant children. Since members of the international
system accepted both jus sanguinis and jus soli as legitimate principles for
ascribing nationality, cases of dual nationality were unavoidable. Hence,
individual states' differing citizenship principles led to conflicts of law
among states regarding taxation, marriage, divorce, inheritance, voting,
and military obligation. During the nineteenth century such conflicts of
law led to serious disputes among states and even to war. These disputes
prompted the negotiation of bilateral treaties and multilateral conventions
against dual nationality, embodying the norm that "everyone should belong to a state and one state only," which further helped differentiate one
nation-state from another.

By the end of World War I, the nation-state became firmly established as
the institutional unit around which world politics was organized. At the
same time, ironically, native population growth in European countries began to decline and, by the 1970s, the centuries-old trend of net migration
leaving Europe reversed direction, returning the demographic makeup of
European societies to the earlier polyethnic norm. Since the political institutions associated with the ideal of the nation-state remained in place, this
change in European demography wrought by migration has led to practical problems for representative democracy in the very place where the state
and the international system originated.

The citizenship based on ancestral lineage that developed in the context
of emigration excludes growing numbers of permanent resident aliens and
their children when such citizenship continues on in the context of immigration. As the number of resident aliens grows in proportion to population, the gap between the citizenry and inhabitants grows as well. In many
European democracies, nationality laws based on ancestral lineage that at
one time might have promoted democratic inclusiveness became the basis

for excluding resident aliens from political participation. In this way, the changing demographics of twentieth-century European societies illuminate an inherent problem in democratic theory and raise practical challenges for state legitimacy based on democratic principles.

These theoretical problems and practical challenges are particularly evident when democratic states enter into a political union, as in the contemporary EU. The focus on migration, as elaborated in chapter 5, illuminates a conflictual relationship among democracy, citizenship based on ancestral lineage, and federal political union that has always been latent in theory. Migration, however, produces enough practical problems and concrete examples to make apparent an incompatibility among the three. This theoretical conflict challenges the notion, commonly assumed by proponents of European political union as well as integration theorists, that democracy and federation are always compatible. The conflict also demonstrates how a focus on migration can be used as a prism to better understand the operation of territorial assumptions in international and political theory.

The rapidly increasing political salience of international migration is not just a matter of the growing numbers of migrants. It is also driven by the way in which international migration challenges modern political institutions such as the nation-state and, in turn, raises serious questions regarding how we think about world politics. The disjunctures between nation and state, the polity and its members, and the demos and democratic state draw attention to the shortcomings of common theoretical frameworks by raising nagging doubts about basic assumptions on the convergence of political identity and territory. Although the state remains the institution around which political practice is currently organized, it is important that we accept the temporality of territoriality as the organizing principle of politics.

The refocusing on migration is not just a theoretical operation aimed only at exposing territorial assumptions in the conceptualization of migration. Rather, a greater awareness of demographic and social history leads to a reconsideration of the impact of migration on the development of modern political institutions themselves. Given that contemporary theory rests upon reflections on modern political institutions, the root of misconceptualization lies in taking for granted the status of modern political institutions. Political institutions, however, are no more or no less than the practices of people that have been repeated through the generations. More people, fewer people, different people—all these demographic factors influence whether or not a given set of political practices is reproduced, whether old political institutions continue on or new ones emerge. As fewer people are born as nationals of the existing nation-states of Europe, there are fewer people to practice the politics of the nation-state. In their stead, different people from elsewhere come. While these peoples' political practices may reproduce many political institutions, the nation-state is usually not one of them.

CHAPTER TWO

European Integration
and State Sovereignty

*I*f not the nation-state, then what? In Europe, there are supranational political institutions in Brussels and hypernational ones in Belgrade. Europe as a whole is not "beyond the nation-state" (Haas 1968), as the debacle in Bosnia and the lack of a common EU foreign policy in response made painfully clear. Nevertheless, persistent European integration has made it difficult to honestly think of France, Germany, the United Kingdom, Italy, and the rest of the EU's members in terms of nation-states as traditionally understood. The enigmatic EU defies easy description, let alone simple explanation, and thus has been reconceptualized in terms of a secular medieval past or a postmodern future. Whatever one may decide to call it, the EU is an archetypal example of political practice being institutionalized in a way that transforms the content and meaning of state sovereignty.

The integration of member state migration policies and citizenship laws is an important component of this transformation of sovereignty. The deepest changes involve the migration of EU member state nationals within the EU and the codification of their rights into an unprecedented form of membership—EU citizenship. Recent agreements on increasing cooperation, however, signal the integration of member state migration policies governing migration to the EU itself. The development of free movement within the EU has pressured member states to develop common policies on visas, asylum, and illegal migration. The member state cooperation spilling over from the issue of labor mobility to that of policing has diametrically opposed goals. Whereas the objective of the intra-EU migration regime has been free movement across borders, member state cooperation on migration from without has focused on restriction.

In an attempt to facilitate the incorporation of immigrants who have already established permanent residency, many European states are changing their naturalization practices to permit dual nationality. In so doing, some of the very same EU member states that have been building a regime for asylum policies and border control are undermining international cooperation on nationality laws aimed at reducing cases of dual nationality and multiple military obligations. Recent advocacy to allow dual nationality in European states opens old debates already resolved (at least partially) through the acceptance of a set of international legal norms against dual nationality that had developed over the preceding century. Because these changes are rooted in the interaction of domestic and international politics, state-centric approaches to understanding world politics are limited in their ability to explain such paradoxical developments.

The European State System and the Question of Political Union

If the subject is the conceptualization of world politics, then why focus on Europe? The human practices that formed the collection of institutions known as the international system first developed in Europe and then, during the nineteenth and twentieth centuries, embraced the entire globe (Bozeman 1960; Bull and Watson 1984). By definition, states are the primary actors of the classical European state system and, through the extension of European conventions to the entire globe, states have become the component units of the international system that structures contemporary world politics. Even after non-Europeans threw off their imperialist yokes, leaders of the polities that emerged from decolonization adopted European conventions of state sovereignty, sought recognition of their participation in the international system through membership in the United Nations, and became some of the most vociferous defenders of the conventions of sovereignty and the state system (Claude 1966; Jackson 1990). Regardless of the way it happened, or whether or not it should have happened, world politics is organized by the institutions that developed from within the European system of states.

Insight into the rise of Europe in relation to the rest of the world is not the only crucially important aspect for understanding the development of the international system. The organization of politics at the source of the contemporary international system has been crucial to the further conceptualization of world politics. European unification, or lack thereof, has been a theme around which central debates over the nature of international politics revolved from at least the time of Abbe Saint-Pierre and Jean-Jacques Rousseau (Rousseau 1991, 53–100). Traditional realist international relations theory was in large measure conceptualized in negative terms using the ideals of European unification, and later world government, as foils. Realists have maintained the premise that European unification is next to impossible (Waltz 1959, 183–84), depicted the close economic cooperation of EU member states as a function of bipolarity (Waltz 1979, 70–71, 91), and argued that this cooperation is destined to collapse with the end of the Cold War (Mearsheimer 1990).

The founding of the European Community (EC) with the Treaty of Rome in 1958 challenged the working assumptions of realist theory and inspired scholars to develop new approaches to understanding international politics that came to be known as integration theory, the most prominent being neofunctionalism. Neofunctionalist theory closely followed the strategic move of Jean Monnet, who gave up on the dream of a European federation and pragmatically shifted toward the economic integration of national industries under supranational authorities. Neofunctionalists believed that integration of one sector of the economy would "spill over" to other sectors and that this process of economic integration would eventually lead to the political integration of European states into some sort of federation.[1] While it has become clear that European integration has not followed the neofunctionalist trajectory, neither has integration "rolled back" to the status quo ante of the classical system of sovereign states, as realists had previously predicted (Hoffmann 1966).

Persistent European integration, marked by the Single European Act and the Treaty on European Union, makes it difficult to describe the current international system and the units comprising it, let alone explain its operation or predict its future. The EU challenges many of the assumptions of international relations theorists, but this is not necessarily due to optimistic projections of European unification into some sort of state. Rather, the EU can most usefully be viewed as an alternative to the state system that Hedley Bull termed "the new medievalism" (Bull 1977, 254) or, more prospectively, that John Ruggie termed "the first truly postmodern international political form" (Ruggie 1993, 140). That is, the current condition of European politics does not fit into traditional classificatory schemes. From this perspective, the EU is not viewed simply in teleological terms as a stage in the evolution toward a larger territorial state, whether unitary or federal in organization. The EU is instead seen as a new form of political organization that is itself a point of reference for theory. The analytical objective, then, is not so much a matter of explaining the integration process and answering the question of whether or not some sort of United States of Europe will emerge—it may never happen. What is more useful is trying to understand the EU for what it is now, rather than for what it might become. Hence, it is useful to identify state practices that are indicative of political transformation, and it is in this regard that changing European practices regarding migration, citizenship, and their bearing on state sovereignty become particularly significant.

Jean Bodin initially conceived of sovereignty as the power to make law.[2] Following Bodin, realist international relations theorists conceptualized world politics in terms of states that have supreme "law-making and law-enforcing authority" (Morgenthau 1974, 315) in a given territory. That is, realists assume states have both juridical and empirically effective sovereignty. European integration challenges state sovereignty, in both juridical and empirical senses, when the European Commission represents member states in trade policy negotiations with other sovereign states, when the EU's Council of Ministers issues single market directives based on qualified majority voting, and when the European Court of Justice issues rulings that have direct effect and take supremacy over conflicting member state laws.

While supranational European institutions usurp policy-making prerogatives that have been the classic markers of sovereignty, international migration and changing conventions of citizenship pose a double challenge to state sovereignty. First, penetration of state borders by unwanted migrants violates the premise of territorial sovereignty. Second, the presence of permanent migrants and their children who remain outside of the polity are anomalous to the concept of popular sovereignty over a given territory. State efforts to ameliorate such democratic anomalies, whether by increasing naturalization via permitting dual nationality or by extending local voting rights through EU citizenship, blur the boundaries of state membership. This raises the issue of exactly whom the state is sovereign over.

State Sovereignty over Territorial Borders

From a realist perspective, sovereignty with respect to international migration means that states control their borders and can decide whether or not to permit entry and exit; that even after admitting migrants the state can reverse its decision through expulsion, should it be deemed in the national interest; and that states choose which migrants will or will not receive nationality (Hendrickson 1992).

The realist assertion that states are ultimately sovereign and have the capability to control their borders, while true, is not all that enlightening. States obviously have the capabilities to control unwanted migration across their borders (as the Soviet Union and east European states once so effectively demonstrated). But do they? One cannot impute practice from capabilities.

In response to the realist position, James Hollifield has argued that advanced industrial democracies—such as Germany, France, and the United States—have been reluctant to exercise state sovereignty and take extensive measures to halt migration or begin expulsions due to the espousal of liberal economic ideologies and adherence to their own principles of human rights as well as international human rights treaties to which they are a party (Hollifield 1992a). Taking a skeptical stance on this position, Gary Freeman (1994) argues that state capabilities of liberal democracies may in fact vary with respect to different types of migration and vary from state to state, and there is evidence that during the early 1990s state capabilities in some liberal democratic states may be growing. Christian Joppke (1998) argues that, at least in the area of asylum policy, state capability in the United States, Germany, and Great Britain to control migration is not diminishing.

The issue of migration and state sovereignty, however, needs to be approached not only on a case-by-case basis for individual states but also within the context of the international system and for European states within the context of European integration. From the outset, sovereignty denoted both the state's supreme law-making and law-enforcing authority in a given territory as well as the recognition of such authority by the other states of the international system as expressed in the legal doctrine of sovereign equality. "Sovereignty is not a concept that is sensibly applied to a single state or to numerous states in isolation from one another. It is inherently a relational concept" (Caporaso 1993, 78). Sovereignty is a social construct of states interacting in a system, and at the heart of this social construct is the seeming contradiction of bounded supreme authority (Kratochwil 1995, 23–25).

The common understanding of sovereignty as state autonomy to behave as it will is not just conceptually but also empirically inaccurate. As Abram and Antonia Handler Chayes point out, in practice, most states comply with most international treaties, most of the time. They note that treaty compliance is largely not a function of supranational legal enforcement mechanisms or military or economic sanctions, but more often than not it is a function of the state's desire to remain a member of "reasonably good standing in the regimes that make up the substance of international life"

(Chayes and Handler Chayes 1995, 27). Hence, when it comes to migration, sovereignty has two dimensions: expressions of sovereignty through independent actions (such as increasing border checks, tightening asylum laws, carrying out deportations) and sovereignty vis-à-vis other states in cooperative efforts within specific areas, of which migration is only one of many.

Being a member of the international community in good standing with respect to migration is not exceptionally difficult, because international cooperation on migration has been limited. As opposed to trade, arms control, and even the environment, there is little in the way of an international migration regime on the global level. Paraphrasing Stephen Krasner's definition (Krasner 1983, 2), migration regimes are implicit or explicit principles, rules, norms, and decision-making procedures around which actors' expectations converge in the issue of migration. Although there is an international refugee regime, an international labor migration regime has yet to develop. The international refugee regime is based on the norms of the 1951 Geneva Convention and institutionalized in the office of the United Nations High Commissioner for Refugees (UNHCR). International cooperation has focused on: managing refugee flows to minimize conflicts between states; supporting countries of first asylum with the means to accommodate large refugee flows; facilitating resettlement of refugees from countries of first asylum to other states; assisting in voluntary repatriation to home countries once threats to personal security subside; and taking preventative action with respect to human rights abuses (Loescher 1993). Except in the case of some Third World states whose empirical sovereignty is already questionable at best (Jackson 1990), this cooperation has not significantly impinged on state sovereignty because the international refugee regime only provides a modest framework for facilitating state management of refugee issues—it is not primarily concerned with the rights of refugees themselves. Since the end of the Cold War, previous state commitments to the international refugee regime have weakened as advanced industrial states have become less willing to resettle increasing numbers of refugees from countries of first asylum or, alternatively, to provide sufficient financial contributions to support refugees in the host states where they remain (UNHCR 1993, 31–50; Loescher 1994).

If border control is an attribute of state sovereignty and international regimes reflect power relationships governed by national interests and are marginal in their consequences (Grieco 1988), then, from a realist perspective, the development of international migration regimes is not expected to happen at all. In contrast to the global situation, however, an international migration regime has developed in Europe. Over the decades, EU member states have adopted an extensive set of principles, rules, norms, and decision-making procedures dedicated to providing labor mobility within the EU. The regime governing intra-EU migration was first articulated in the Treaty of Rome, reaffirmed in the 1986 Single European Act (SEA), and formally codified in the EU citizenship provisions of the Treaty on European Union (TEU). Hollifield notes that unlike the relations among states in general, "sovereignty with respect to the populations of member states has been ceded to the Community" (Hollifield 1992b, 580) because most citizens of EU member states have freedom of movement among member states and rights to employment in fellow member states. With respect to populations of member states, for EU member states to transfer sovereignty to a supranational body defies realist logic. Cooperation in response to east-west migrations made possible by the end of the Cold War is especially surprising when, according to the neorealist vision, the end of bipolarity was to eliminate the external pressure for European cooperation.

In contrast to the robust intra-EU migration regime, a regime governing migration into the EU from non-member states is under construction with the 1990 signing of the Dublin Convention on jurisdiction for asylum applications and the Schengen Convention on border controls, as well as with ongoing negotiations under Title VI of the Maastricht Treaty, the "Third Pillar" of the EU dedicated to Cooperation in Justice and Home Affairs (JHA), and the June 1997 Amsterdam Treaty. This regime is still relatively incomplete, and its influence on state behavior is not necessarily immediate and direct.[3]

EU governance of migration within the Union is closely linked to cooperation on migration to the EU. Achieving a single European market comprising an "area without internal frontiers in which the free movement of goods, persons, services and capital is ensured" has pressured member states to develop common policies on visas, border controls, asylum application, and illegal migration. Member state cooperation on intra-EU labor migration may have led to cooperation on dealing with migration to the EU; however, member states have diametrically opposed goals in the different areas. The objective of the intra-EU migration regime has been free movement across borders; member state cooperation on migration from without has focused on restriction. Given this focus on restricting migration, it appears that EU member states have been willing to give up their sovereignty with respect to the movement of their own nationals within the Union, but have been reluctant to do so for the migration of non-EU member state nationals to the EU. As we will see in chapter 8, the issue of sovereignty with respect to European cooperation on migration is much more complicated.

Territoriality, State Sovereignty, and Citizenship

As mentioned above, international migration has grown in political significance due in no small part to the growing predisposition toward understanding politics through the prism of individual rights—both those enumerated in the constitutions and rulings of the courts of individual states as well as human rights articulated in international conventions. The expansion of migrants' civil and social rights in the states in which they reside has led some scholars to speak of the "devaluation of citizenship," given that the possession of a state's nationality is no longer necessary to enjoy many of the rights of citizenship (Schuck 1989). Pointing to the extension of social rights to Europe's guest workers, their new forms of social membership, and international human rights regimes that reinforce these new forms of membership, Yasemin Soysal argues that "the recent guestworker experience reflects a time when national membership is losing ground to a more universal model of membership, anchored in deterritorialized notions of persons' rights" (Soysal 1994, 3). Emphasizing the role of the Universal Declaration of Human Rights and the European Convention for the Protection of Human Rights, David Jacobson argues that the devaluation of citizenship has enabled migrants' appeals to international human rights codes and their enforcement by judicial bodies to transform nationality "from a principle that reinforces state sovereignty . . . to a concept of nationality as a human right; the state is becoming accountable to all its residents on the basis of human rights law" (Jacobson 1996, 10).

There is a transformation of citizenship and state sovereignty taking place. This transformation of citizenship, however, is primarily driven by internal constitutional changes and domestic politics and less so by the proliferation of individual rights generated by international human rights regimes and secured by supranational institutions. More is involved than a zero sum devaluation of national citizenship in favor of a universal personhood of international human rights. The transformation of citizenship is also, and perhaps more importantly, an outcome of the consequences (often inadvertent) of declining international cooperation to maintain demographic boundaries through restrictions on dual nationality as well as of state actions to remedy internal democratic deficits through compromise measures—such as the extension of partial political rights and the establishment of EU citizenship.

International norms against statelessness and dual nationality helped establish an international system of nation-states by delineating its parts in
terms of population. Just as states conclude border treaties—which delineate their jurisdiction geographically, along with multilateral boundary
conventions that provide international rules for this practice—states delineate their jurisdictions demographically. States have entered into multilateral conventions on statelessness and dual nationality in order to legitimate their competencies over defined jurisdictions and to minimize
conflicts. These multilateral efforts reduced the number of cases of statelessness and dual nationality and instituted a regime for the resolution of
conflicts over the remaining cases.

As long as the number of cases that persist stays relatively small, conflicts of nationality law can be marginalized in relations among states because the consequences of statelessness and dual nationality are ultimately
borne by individuals whose interests, if in conflict with those of the states
concerned, can easily be disregarded. Increased international migration
places pressure on the state system's demographic boundary maintenance
regime by increasing the number of people who find themselves caught between two states and, as a result, suffer adverse consequences. In response
to increasing migration and growing numbers of resident aliens who are
excluded from the polity, several European states (e.g., Switzerland, the
Netherlands, and Germany) have tried to increase their naturalization rates
by relaxing their policies on renunciation of previous citizenship for resident aliens who naturalize. As I will explain in more detail in chapter 7,
such policy changes have undermined the international regime dedicated to
reducing cases of dual nationality, which has in turn led to a blurring of the
demographic boundaries that delineate one state from another.

In the face of increasing migration, some European states have also extended certain rights of citizenship for resident aliens to maintain their legitimacy. Due to the possession of rights under EC law enjoyed by nationals of EU member states, intra-EU migration has prompted legal cases over
the rights of nationals of one EU member state residing in another that
pit the objective of free movement and the principle of non-discrimination
against member state sovereignty. At the same time, as European states enter into a political union while their citizens take advantage of new free-
doms in regard to movement of labor, problems of maintaining democratic
legitimacy arise because of member state citizenship laws that exclude from
political participation resident aliens who migrated from fellow EU member states. As I will explain in more detail in chapter 6, EU citizenship was
meant to address this democratic deficit; however, this form of multiple

membership is constitutive of an increasingly complex, multilayered, and multifocal European polity and is indicative of the transformation of sovereignty within the EU.

The lifting of internal border controls, multilateral cooperation on external border controls, and changing norms and practices of state attribution of citizenship represent significant departures from classical state sovereignty and thereby challenge traditional assumptions of the nation-state as the organizational structure of politics in Europe. EU member states have been building an institutional framework for cooperation on asylum policies and border control, which has mainly restricted the movement of non-EU nationals into the Union. In contrast, some of the very same states are violating existing international norms against dual nationality in attempts to incorporate more foreigners into their polities. These norms initially developed in response to conflicts between states over the military obligations of their nationals and formed a demographic boundary maintenance regime aimed at reducing cases of dual nationality. The rise and decline of these regimes provide examples of the pervasive interaction of domestic and international politics in contemporary Europe as well as highlight the changing patterns of authority and political identity in the emerging European polity.

Part 2

Demography Shaping
Political Institutions

Part 2

Demography Shaping
Political Institutions

CHAPTER THREE

Nation-States

C ontemporary world politics is organized around the institutions that developed in modern Europe. Nation-states and the international system they collectively constitute provide the structure of modern world politics, while the evolutionary and revolutionary processes of democratization have provided much of the dynamics. The practice of democracy existed in ancient European city-states as well as in premodern tribal societies such as the Iroquois (Mansbridge 1983, 10–13; Mohawk 1992; Crawford 1994). Citizenship as political membership and participation existed in Athens, and citizenship as the possession of a set of rights developed in Rome (Riesenberg 1992). It was only after the American and French Revolutions of the late eighteenth century, however, that the political institutions of democracy and citizenship provided organizing principles of large-scale polities functioning within the "container" of the modern European nation-state.

The nation-state is very much an ideal type that accurately depicts social reality only in regard to demographic conditions prevalent in Europe during a relatively brief period of time. Before the eighteenth century, the structure of European society had followed the norm of all Eurasian civilizations—polyethnicity. These civilizations maintained polyethnic social structures due to an age-old pattern of epidemics that decimated urban population centers of individual civilizations as well as migration from their rural hinterlands and even from beyond their frontiers. Only with sustained rapid population growth, which began after 1750, did nations that embraced states develop. Since the end of World War I, European social structure has been returning to the "civilized" norm of polyethnicity.

Modern political theories utilize concepts that emerged in the course of reflection on the development of democracy and citizenship within nation-states. Contemporary international relations theory concerns itself with the international system consisting of the interaction of these states. By using migration as a theoretical prism, I demonstrate theoretical conflicts among the conceptual categories associated with these modern political institutions. Because modern theories that use these conceptual categories often assume the continuity of people and place—for example, beginning with nomenclature, the idea of "international" relations assumes states whose populations can be differentiated along national lines—they are deficient in making sense of important contemporary political practices. Specifically, the assumption of the continuity of people and place may have been operable given demographic circumstances in modern Europe, but the changing demography of Europe has led to practical problems that are outside of the conceptual apparatus this assumption yields.

Migration and the Development of the International System

The conception of the state as a self-regarding unit that functions as a unitary actor in the international system presupposes a certain political and legal relationship between individuals and the state they inhabit—specifically, that they belong to it in some way, be it as subjects, nationals, or citizens. During the Middle Ages, individuals were subject to a wide variety of overlapping secular and religious authorities. Hence, monarchs had no uniform jurisdiction and lacked sovereignty in the modern sense. The common presumption that nation and state coincide and together form actors at the level of the international system holds for a fairly limited period in history. If one claims that an international system has existed in premodern times, then empires were the "units" of the system. The territories of premodern empires, however, were often bounded by rather indistinct frontiers—rather than by clearly delineated boundaries—and their societies were polyethnic in composition. Such indistinct frontiers and polyethnic social composition led to practices that did not conform to neorealist descriptions of the interaction of self-regarding units, because it was not at all clear at the time how the units were delineated and who the "self" was.

Richard Little[1] addresses the problem with neorealism's projection of contemporary understandings of the nation-state into the past under the rubric of self-regarding units and Waltz's contention that in the interaction of self-regarding units, "the logic of anarchy obtains whether the system is composed of tribes, nations, oligopolistic firms or street gangs" (Waltz 1990, 37). In contrast to the neorealist assumption of an anarchy "made up of identical interacting units operating within a closed system" (Little 1993, 99), Little documents the existence of anarchies with functional differentiation among units in his examination of the Greek city-states, the Diadochi empires, and the Roman empire. In an attempt to provide a better understanding of the continuity and transformation of international systems, Little appeals to world historians, William H. McNeill in particular, to explain the development and interaction of empires.

In *The Rise of the West,* as well as its abridged form *A World History,* McNeill shows how four civilizations in the Middle East, Greece, India, and China emerged around 500 B.C. Although the Middle East contained the world's predominant civilizations before 500 B.C., during the next two millennia—to A.D. 1500—these four civilizations developed a rough equilibrium among themselves. Barbarians of the steppes adopted various practices from them all and, in the process, maintained their own autonomy. McNeill describes the relationship among civilizations in the following terms:

> Throughout the ensuing centuries, growth and modification within each of these civilizations never ceased. The area of the earth occupied by each civilization tended to expand. This, of course, increased the bulk and variety within each civilized heartland and reduced the insulating barbarian zones between them. Contact from one end of Eurasia to the other tended, despite some setbacks, to increase in frequency as the centuries passed. This permitted leaders of one culture to borrow and adapt items from other civilizations which happened to interest them. Such cross-cultural borrowing was, indeed, one of the principal stimuli to innovation within each separate civilization. Yet such borrowings were always voluntary, spontaneous, never forced. (McNeill 1967, 121–24)

Even though these civilizations maintained their autonomy, they did not directly interact with one another as in a balance of power system (Little 1993, 95–96). Rather, the civilizations had many indirect exchanges of information, technology, philosophy, religion, and culture that increased production and military capabilities. These exchanges were often mediated by nomadic peoples inhabiting the central Asian steppe that separated them. Hence, the civilizations maintained an equilibrium, but it was not a balance of power. This is the case because, for the most part, the civilizations did not directly interact with one another; they did not form shifting alliances;

and, although they developed military technologies borrowed from other civilizations via encounters with nomadic barbarians common to them all, the civilizations did not engage in countering perceived threats from other civilizations through the "internal balancing" of arms racing.

Moreover, the units of this system were functionally differentiated in that the nomadic barbarians filled a particular role in the system formed by the five units. The steppe nomads functioned as a buffer between the other four units that enabled them to develop in the way they did. Also, the nomadic barbarians maintained non-territorial forms of social and political organization, while the civilizations developed territorially delineated social and political organizations. In a sense, the non-territorially organized barbarian polities filled an environmental niche, which complemented the development of four more territorially organized polities.

The borrowing of ideas constitutes cultural diffusion, but it was human beings who crossed the frontiers of civilizations and carried the ideas that were borrowed.[2] Knowledge was indirectly transmitted from one territorially organized agricultural civilization to the other through the migrating inhabitants of the pastoral societies that separated them, particularly by the military elites of these pastoral societies who penetrated deeply into civilizations on recurrent invasions. Ideas were also transmitted directly by traders and missionaries who moved across the steppe from one civilization to another.

In addition to cultural exchanges, McNeill argued that migrating humans (and the animals that came with them) transported microparasites that had a tremendous impact on the development of civilizations and their interaction (McNeill 1977). This biological exchange across civilizations has important theoretical implications for international relations theory, and particularly for the realist paradigm. Traditional realists and neorealists contend that war or the threat of war is the eternal condition of international relations. Conquest and defense against, or deterrence of, conquest are the objectives of the preparations for war, the threat of war, and war itself. Historically, conquest and migration have been two dimensions of the same process: overtly, as when colonists follow an advancing army to hold areas taken, or more subtly, as when migrants replace native populations through differential rates of mortality and fertility. Simply considering military conquest as a form of international migration in order to make my argument is a bit disingenuous. Apart from actual military engagements, however, due to the exchange of microparasites, contact between disease-experienced populations and previously isolated populations has played a crucial role in the development of empires, ancient and modern, as well as in their interaction with one another and their relative success.

McNeill has conceptualized microparasitism and the macropara$
of warriors who use advances in military technology to feed off the peasant
majority as twin processes at work in history.[3] Much as populations that
have developed immunities to a particular disease expand at the expense of
populations that have no such immunities, warriors who develop a new
military technology break open the defenses of societies that lack a counter-
vailing technology. The processes of military incursion and epidemic then
operate in tandem as the warriors penetrate societies and the diseases they
carry devastate the invaded population. Of course, the outcome of such
contact can be reversed if warriors armed with superior technologies but
lacking immunities invade a population that has built up immunities to a
certain disease. In such cases the incursion of the warriors may not lead to
an expansion of control, despite technological superiority, and if the warriors infect their home populations, large self-inflicted population losses
may occur.

As the great human migration to the unpopulated areas that could sustain hunter-gatherer societies came to an end about 8000 B.C., an era
marked by the development of agriculture, civilization, and the conquest
and enslavement of other peoples began. Within an already occupied world,
migration could take four different forms: one population destroys and
replaces another population; one population enslaves the other; one population conquers the other, but the conquerors develop a symbiotic relationship with the conquered; or outsiders infiltrate a population, but do not dis-
place the ruling group. Radical destruction was typical of nomadic pastoral
societies, which had a minimal division of labor and were delineated by kinship lines. The other three forms of migration were typical of agricultural
societies with greater division of labor and based on hierarchical polyethnic social order (McNeill 1987, 18), which became known as civilizations.

A cyclical pattern of migratory flows of peasants and elites both in and
out of urban concentrations of humanity was fundamental to the development, maintenance, and expansion of the Eurasian civilizations in the
Middle East, India, China, and Mediterranean Europe (McNeill 1978, 5).
The concentration of humanity into urban living spaces increased the
spread of diseases that killed off high proportions of urban populations.
Successive waves of epidemics made it impossible for cities to routinely reproduce themselves. Without sustained immigration from the surrounding
countryside, the urban population would have died off; without cities, civilization would not exist. About a thousand years after the formation of
the first cities, armies that concentrated populations in a similar manner
formed. With respect to population, armies functioned in certain respects
very much like "mobile cities" because the movement of armies concen-

trated populations in their wake and the demography of the armies themselves shared the dynamic of epidemic die-off and recruitment of rural re-
placements (McNeill 1978, 7).[4]

At a certain point, cities became large enough to provide enough human
hosts to support a population of microorganisms that reproduced through
direct human-to-human contact (e.g., smallpox, measles, mumps, etc.). Inhabitants of cities and armies that survived these diseases built up immunities that often lasted for the rest of their lives, rendering only children susceptible to infection. In this way, these infections became what we now call
"childhood diseases." During times when urban die-off was relatively low
and the urban population swelled or local famines deprived urban populations of sufficient food supplies, urban dwellers moved to the frontiers of
the civilization. Native populations that had no previous contact with urban disease pools and lacked immunities became infected and died in large
numbers, emptying areas for even more migration from the city. This dynamic led to ever greater periodic migrations from the city that, in turn,
subsequently prompted increased immigration of peasants in order to sustain the urban population.

A smaller, but no less important, migration of elites in and out of the
cities occurred. Searching for scarce resources, traders and soldiers, often
with missionaries in tow, ventured beyond the frontiers of the civilization.
If the local peasantry could not fulfill manpower needs, labor became one
of those scarce resources. Hence, cities sent armies to conquer peoples from
beyond the frontiers of the civilization and bring back captives to enslave.
In the opposite direction, nomadic barbarians invaded and pillaged cities
but had little use for slaves in their pastoral economies.

The cyclical pattern of migration between the urban centers and peripheries of Eurasian civilizations rendered their societies polyethnic in nature
(Armstrong 1982, 122–26; McNeill 1986). The ethnic group that originally composed the bulk of the urban population generally dominated linguistically. Waves of epidemics occasionally decimated cities to such a degree that the language of new rural migrants eventually dominated, as when
Semitic Akkadian overtook Sumerian in Mesopotamia. Slavery and occupational caste systems contributed greatly to polyethnic social formation.
Slaves usually worked in construction gangs, but they also assumed important roles as household servants and soldiers. Some cities became so dependent on slavery for replenishing their populations that the slaves eventually
took over political control (McNeill 1977, 163–64; Doyle 1986, 107). Although not enslaved, ethnic groups from outside the city were recruited to
particular occupations that the dominant urban groups considered unde-

sirable. As with certain forms of slavery, the importation of free laborers led to the functional division of labor along ethnic lines that organized occupational niches for migrants.

The international system of nation-states that we have come to take for granted was far from a forgone conclusion of historical inevitability. Rather, the international system is the projection of European political practices and conventions onto the rest of the world—at first through imposition and then through perpetuation, partly due to the conscious reconstitution of European-style state through the decolonization process and partly due to sheer force of habit in the face of few remaining alternatives. Of course, alternative forms of political organization may have been possible, but the distinctly European form triumphed in a protracted half-millennium struggle with the other civilizations of the world.

The equilibrium that developed among the four Eurasian civilizations centered in China, India, the Middle East, and Greece between 500 B.C. and A.D. 1500 was rocked by four shocks (McNeill 1967, 124). The first two, expansion of Greek civilization to the Middle East and expansion of Indian civilization to China and Japan, eventually left relatively little lasting influence. The third shock—expansion of the Middle Eastern civilization with the rise of Islam and its spread to North Africa and Spain and then India, Eastern Europe, and central Asia—left a more permanent mark, particularly on the development of Indian civilization. However, it was the fourth and final shock that overturned the balance among the civilizations. This process began when west Europeans first conquered the Americas and explored the world's coastlines. Then, in the period between 1700 to 1850, what came to be known as Western civilization established an economic and military superiority over the rest of the world that enabled its political expansion through projection of the European state system to the entire globe. Migration played a crucial role in this expansion, particularly with the transportation of disease. The great out-migration of Europeans also redistributed power from European nation-states at the core to the settler societies in the periphery and changed the political dynamics of the continent left behind.

Conquest, trade, crusading, and slaving across the disease pools of the Mediterranean, Middle Eastern, Indian, and Chinese civilizations led to a gradual sharing of diseases and the development of common sets of immunities. Epidemic diseases that led to catastrophic die-offs gradually became endemic diseases that took a proportion of each generation's children but immunized surviving populations. This cross-immunization, however, did not stop the spread of diseases from previously isolated regions, nor was this cross-immunization of familiar diseases global in scope. For example, Mongol invaders most likely picked up the bubonic plague during raids of Yunnan and Burma (1252–53) and transported it to western Europe (McNeill 1977, 132–76). The plague was immeasurably more devastating than the military defeats and pillage by the invaders, as upwards of one-third of western Europe's population succumbed to it.

An even more dramatic die-off occurred as Europeans came into contact with populations previously unexposed to endemic Eurasian diseases (most importantly, smallpox). Essentially, relatively few Spaniards were able to conquer the Aztec and Inca civilizations because European migration to the New World crossed disease pool boundaries, with immense demographic consequences (Crosby 1972, 47–58; McNeill 1977, 1–5, 176–208; Braudel 1981, 36–38; Diamond 1997, 210–13).[5] In like fashion, diseases carried by Europeans wiped out much of the native populations in Siberia, Australia, southern Africa, and New Zealand. The introduction of European diseases worked in tandem with the introduction of European plants and domesticated animals that managed to drive out native species. The migration of Europeans and their plants, animals, and pathogens fundamentally transformed the ecosystems of three of the Earth's continents in a way that led to the biological domination of European plant and animal species as well as Europeans themselves in the world's temperate regions (Crosby 1986, 294–308). The thesis that disease experience enables "civilized" peoples to easily conquer more primitive peoples (which has come to be known as McNeill's law) is supported by the counterfactual evidence that contemporaneous European forays to disease-experienced civilizations such as China, Japan, and the Ottoman Empire were more easily rebuffed (Crosby 1986, 132–44).

The crucial role of migration in the European conquest of the Americas, Australia, Oceania, and southern Africa has important implications for international relations theory. The expansion of European civilization through conquest, or (depending on one's point of view) the devastation of native civilizations and the ecosystems that supported them by European barbarians, was not simply the result of superior military forces or differential technological and economic development that could then be utilized militarily (Kennedy 1987; Gilpin 1981). Rather, mere human contact (or the transportation of intermediary animal hosts) fostered infections among disease-inexperienced populations. When populations that had become immune to childhood diseases opposed those who had not developed similar immunities, the disease-inexperienced populations usually lost. In other words, European armies, missionaries, traders, and colonists unconsciously deployed biological weapons in addition to the conventional armaments of their soldiers during the conquest of native American, Siberian, Australian, and New Zealand peoples.

The conquest of the Americas in the sixteenth century by monarchies of seafaring west European countries empowered west Europeans, as compared to potential central and east European rivals including the two largest European countries of the fifteenth century: Moscovy and the Polish-Lithuanian Commonwealth. Technological advances of the Industrial Revolution facilitated the nineteenth-century European dominance of Asia and Africa, but the resources amassed, transportation technologies developed, and economic and political institutions established in western Europe during the earlier conquest of the Americas were later used in further empire building. Although historians have demonstrated the consequences of migrant-borne diseases for the rise and decline of civilizations, international relations scholars have not considered these consequences in traditional accounts of the development of the international system and changes in the balance of power among its constituent units. If the European dominance over the rest of the world established after 1500 was as much the result of unconscious biological warfare as of conventional military capabilities, the traditional view of world military history and the realist theoretical postulates derived from this history could be called into question.

After about 1750, the demography of Eurasian civilizations began to change as the population growth rate increased rapidly, while the decimation of isolated native peoples continued (Braudel 1981, 33). Europe's population grew rapidly after 1750 due to the homogenization of Eurasian disease pools; the introduction of new foods (like potatoes and corn) from the Americas; the institutionalization of public health and sanitation systems; and, in the nineteenth century, the development of the germ theory of disease and the advancement of medical science in treating disease (Jones 1987, 140–43). European population growth fueled a great out-migration from Europe that underpinned the extension of the European state system to the globe and also led to a redistribution of power within the emerging international system at the close of the nineteenth century.

The idea of the balance of power is the sine qua non of many international relations theorists. Few stop to consider that past migration was critical to the distribution of power within the contemporary international system. The westward migration of Americans and new immigrants from Europe across North America in the nineteenth century, the southern migration of Russians in the sixteenth and seventeenth centuries, and the eastward migration of Russians across Asia in the eighteenth and nineteenth centuries provided the demographic basis for the emergence of the United States and the Soviet Union as superpowers in the twentieth century.

The potential for this development was perhaps first recognized by Tocqueville. In his conclusion to the first volume of *Democracy in America,* Tocqueville speculated that due to emigration from Europe to the United States as well as rapid population growth and eastward migration of Russians, the United States and Russia would each "one day . . . hold in its hands the destinies of half of the world" (Tocqueville 1969, 413). Similarly, Morgenthau recognized the importance of migration to the United States as he argued that immigration fueled the development of American power and the international redistribution of power vis-à-vis western Europe (Morgenthau 1978, 131). These insights have been lost on subsequent theorists who took the demographic basis of power for granted and instead focused more exclusively on military capabilities, including the technology and economics of those capabilities.

The rapidity and scope of migration that enabled the United States and Russia to develop as superpowers were not simply a function of the superior technology and military capabilities of the conquering populations. Indigenous populations of North America, the western steppe lands of Eurasia, and the forests of Siberia had been decimated by waves of epidemics before European populations began to grow after 1750. These epidemics left ostensibly "empty" lands open for the later settlement of millions of migrants.

Smallpox and other childhood diseases carried by Spanish and French explorers, traders, and missionaries in the sixteenth and seventeenth centuries killed off native populations of the western, midwestern, and southern regions of North America, before the arrival of eighteenth-century English colonists and subsequent American pioneers (Crosby 1986, 209–15). Native Americans in the North American interior who had not come in contact with diseases brought in by European explorers or other native Americans infected with European diseases were highly susceptible to the diseases carried by westward moving American settlers during the nineteenth century.

Disease and migration played a similar role in the expansion of Moscovy to the southwest and the east. The bubonic plague is best known for killing off a third of western Europe's population; however, the plague took its greatest toll, proportionally speaking, on the nomadic peoples of the steppes. By 1500, the southwestern steppe lands drained by the Don and lower Volga were relatively empty, devoid of significant agricultural communities or large-scale nomadic grazing, even though the land was ideal for both (McNeill 1977, 171). After Ivan the Terrible took Kazan and Astrakhan from the Tartars (1552–56), Moscovy gained control of the entire Volga and Russian pioneers began to settle the black earth region. Similarly, Polish-Lithuanian pioneers moved southeast during the sixteenth century. Poland and Moscovy utilized outlaw bands of frontiersmen called "Cossacks" to secure the western steppe. The frontier regions controlled by Cossacks, whether Russian, Polish, or Lithuanian, were called "Ukraines" or "Okraines" (Armstrong 1982, 78). In 1647–48, the Ukrainian and Dnieper Cossacks rebelled against their Polish overlords. Hamstrung by internal political strife, the Polish-Lithuanian Commonwealth was unable to strike a compromise accommodation. When the Cossacks turned to Moscovy for protection (1654), war broke out between Poland and Russia. The combination of Poland's internal conflicts and Russia's growing military power led Poland to negotiate the Treaty of Andrusovo (1667) in which Poland conceded Kiev, Smolensk, and eastern Ukraine to Moscovy. Not only did the productivity of these lands provide an economic basis for Moscovy's expansion into a European empire, the region became a bridgehead for the subsequent partition of Poland (Davies 1982, 345).

Moscovy's growing power in opposition to Poland, Sweden, and Prussia was supported by Moscovy's eastward expansion. Paul Kennedy argues that Russia's "status as a 'gunpowder empire' enabled it to defeat the horsed tribes of the east, and thus to acquire additional resources of manpower, raw materials, and arable land, which in turn would enhance its place among the Great Powers" (Kennedy 1987, 95). The rapid advance of Russian pioneers, who were beyond the Urals by the 1580s and reached the Pacific by 1640, was not simply a function of gunpowder. The horsemen of the eastern steppes had already been decimated by the plague (McNeill 1977, 171–73) and, much like Native Americans, isolated Siberian peoples had not developed immunities to the childhood diseases of Eurasian civilization, suffering deadly epidemics upon contact with Russian pioneers (Crosby 1986, 38–39).

While European population growth and out-migration were laying the foundation for a redistribution of power from the European core to the settler societies on the periphery, population growth and migration also had tremendous consequences for the political dynamics of Europe itself.

Polyethnicity and the European State System

The cyclical pattern of migration between the urban centers and peripheries of Eurasian civilizations also produced polyethnic European societies well into the modern era. In juxtaposition to European demographic history, political history in the tradition of nineteenth-century historiography tells the story of the development of nation-states (Hayes 1931; Iggers 1968). France and England were the prototypes, albeit quite different in nature. Spain, Portugal, and Sweden have also served as examples of this quintessentially modern political form. Germany and Italy only tenuously conformed to the model, and only in the latter half of the nineteenth century.

The problem with the notion of the nation-state is that it did not always conform to the reality of European societies. The populations of what were to become the nation-states of Europe were not very ethnically homogenous until the dramatic growth of European populations in the eighteenth century. The idea of the nation-state is a nineteenth-century adaptation of the ideal of the early Athenian and Roman polities that is projected back into European history. This was an ideal, given that both ancient Athens and Rome began as relatively ethnically homogenous city-states but became polyethnic civilization through migration (Koslowski 1994, 45–69). This chapter traces the trajectory of European societies from polyethnicity to national unity and back to polyethnicity and examines the bearing of this transformation on relations between European states, particularly with the transition from polyethnicity to national unity.

France is generally considered the archetypal nation-state, but the population of what is now France was formed through successive waves of invasion and intermixing (Braudel 1990, 21–167). The French people began as a mixture of Romanized Gauls and Germanic barbarians (Braudel 1990b, 98). Eventually, the Franks established a kingdom in Gaul led by the house of Merving. Their king, Clovis, converted to Christianity in 496 and moved the capital to Paris. During the two centuries of Merovingian rule, the Gallo-Roman and Frankish peoples gradually merged; towns were reestablished, but the overall population still decreased and manpower shortages persisted. In the context of this population decline, Celts from Wales colonized what is now Brittany during the sixth and seventh centuries and reestablished the Celtic language and culture (Braudel 1990b, 110–14). Polyethnic amalgamation continued during the Carolingian dynasty as Charlemagne briefly brought Gaul and most of the Germanic lands under unified rule. Subsequent invasions by Vikings, Avars, Magyars, and Saracens increased the diversity of the ethnic mix. Most notably, descendants of Viking invaders established the Duchy of Normandy, which produced subsequent rulers of England and much of France. The division of the Carolingian Empire among the three surviving grandsons of Charlemagne by the Treaty of Verdun in 843 and the ascendance of Hugh Capet to the throne of the Kingdom of France in 987 began a process of delineating an independent identity of France separate from Germany. Shortly thereafter, however, the Norman conquest of Britain in 1066 led to a mixture of the peoples and cultures of Britain and France that only the Hundred Years War (1337–1453) between the English and French monarchies would eventually once again separate (Holmes 1992, 89–108, 150–61, 294–302).

The idea of an English nation-state is similarly problematic in terms of demographic history. The British islands were inhabited by a Neolithic people who were then invaded by two different stocks of Celtic-speaking people from the Continent—the Gaels, who remain in Ireland and northern Scotland, and the Cymri and Brythons (Britons), whose language survives in present-day Welsh. Subsequent waves of invasions and migrations—beginning in 55 B.C. with the Romans; then the Jutes, Angles, and Saxons from northwest Germany in the middle of the fifth century; the Danes at the end of the eighth century; and Normans from France in 1066—rendered a very polyethnic society in England (Holmes 1992, 63–64). Indeed after the Norman invasion, French remained the language of the ruling elite for a century and a half. Only after the loss of Normandy in 1204 did a common language emerge from the languages of the conquered Anglo-Saxons, the Norman conquerors, and the Latin clergy. After the English colonization of Ireland began in 1171 and the Welsh resistance was quelled at the end of the thirteenth century, emigration of settlers from the Anglo-Saxon metropole to the Celtic periphery and migration of Irish laborers to English towns became a long-lived pattern that furthered the polyethnic amalgamation of English society.

The population of what was to become Spain formed through the mixture of Gallo-Romans with invading Vandals, Sueves, Alans, and Visigoths. Comprising approximately a fifth of the population, the Visigoths established a kingdom stretching from the Bay of Biscay to the Rhone and from Gibralter to the Loire during the fifth century. The Visigoths were quickly Romanized, and King Reccared converted to Roman Catholicism in 587. Berbers and Arabs overran the Visigoth kingdom in 711. Christians and Jews were tolerated in what became a hierarchical polyethnic society ruled by Moslems until 1212, when the Moslem ruling elite was defeated and expelled.

Polyethnic civilizations also developed around the cities of northern and central Europe. Migrating traders founded cities around ecclesiastical sees, which were often old Roman centers of communication and transportation. "The city arose when merchants who had traveled about in strong bands bound together by oath (Gothic *Hansa,* 'cohort'; Slavic *Gospodi,* 'people of the pact') found that there was enough commerce in communication nodes to justify settling down" (Armstrong 1982, 107). The population of these towns was sustained by rural migrants encouraged by the maxim *Stadtluft macht frei* (city air makes one free), which originated in the eleventh century. The maxim became a legal principle that freed serfs who had resided in cities for at least one year and effectively provided refuge from the sporadic violence of the medieval European countryside. Migrants, however, were recruited from far beyond the immediate countryside. For example, "between 1158 and 1259, 31 percent of Luebeck's settlers had come from Rhineland-Westphalia, 17 percent from other distant regions, and 29 percent from Lower Saxony, some hundred miles distant, leaving only 22 percent from neighboring Holstein, Lauenburg and Mecklenburg. Newer Hansa League towns around the Baltic recruited heavily from Luebeck" (Armstrong 1982, 109). The expansion of urban populations in northern Europe drew upon migrants from further south as well. For example, "as early as 1084 northern European princes had licensed Jews as money lenders, since they were among the few agents available from the advanced lands of the Mediterranean who were willing to participate in the eleventh-century development of the north" (Jones 1987, 120). Since Jews were excluded from land ownership and guild membership (Simmel 1950, 402–8) and given Christian prohibitions against usury, Jews filled the occupational niche of moneylenders, eventually to the monarchs of Europe (Arendt 1951, 11–28).

Successive waves of migration led to the development a polyethnic society in the Polish-Lithuanian Union, which in 1494 was the second largest country in Europe after Russia. After the Mongols retreated from Poland in the middle of the thirteenth century, the Polish nobility invited German settlers to areas depopulated by Mongol invasions. It has been estimated that in the fourteenth century Germans constituted 20–25 percent of Poland's overall population and over 50 percent of Poland's urban population (Armstrong 1982, 116). The ethnic diversity of the Polish-Lithuanian Union further increased during the fifteenth century as Jews from the Holy Roman Empire and Spain, as well as Armenians, migrated to Poland (Armstrong 1982, 118). During the sixteenth century, the Union was reconstituted into a commonwealth; religious freedom was institutionalized; and Polish, Latin, Ruthenian, German, Armenian, and Hebrew were recognized as official languages. Political incorporation and religious toleration turned Poland into a refuge that attracted people from outside Poland's borders throughout the century.

As in Poland, Hungarian kings encouraged the immigration of German settlers. Geza, ruler of the Magyars from 972–97, initially invited German missionaries. His son, St. Stephen, married a Bavarian princess and is said to have told his heir that "guest and foreign peoples . . . are very useful, they bring varied values and customs, weapons and knowledge with them, all of which ornament the Royal Court and make it splendid, while frightening the haughty foreigners. For weak and defenseless is a country which has but a single language and uniform customs" (qtd. in Armstrong 1982, 114). As early as 1150, Saxons from the Moselle were invited to settle southern Transylvanian regions. After the Mongol invasions German migration accelerated. During the thirteenth and fourteenth centuries, Germans came to dominate urban populations of the Hungarian kingdom.

Demographic changes facilitated the formation of nation-states in several ways. First, as religious minorities were expelled from the kingdoms of early modern western Europe, the remaining populations reproduced and raised their children in the dominant religion, thus increasing religious homogeneity (provided that new religious minorities did not immigrate). Furthermore, decreasing mortality and increasing fertility among European populations that began in the eighteenth century magnified the impact of the expulsion of religious minorities and the reproduction of the remaining populations. Not only did the religiously homogenous indigenous population grow faster, but this population growth reduced the need for immigration to replace urban populations. In this way, as I will explain later in more detail, increasing population growth enabled European societies to break from the polyethnic norm.

Aristide Zolberg (1985) has pointed out that the process of west European state formation included the expulsion of minorities, primarily on religious grounds, that cumulatively produced about one million refugees in the period spanning the late fifteenth and late seventeenth centuries. Isabella and Ferdinand expelled the Jews from Spain (approximately two hundred thousand) in 1492 and the Moors from Castile in 1502. In 1609, Philip III expelled the Moriscos, descendants of Moors who converted to Christianity. The Hapsburgs also expelled approximately over one hundred thousand Protestants from their territories in the Low Countries; Puritans and Quakers were driven from Britain; and over two hundred thousand Huguenots left France at the time of the revocation of the Edict of Nantes in 1685. While expulsion of religious minorities increased the religious homogeneity of some west European kingdoms, it increased the ethnic heterogeneity of many central and eastern European kingdoms. For example, the expulsion of Spain's Jews increased the polyethnicity of Poland.

The European state system's delineation of state boundaries not only made it possible for individuals to escape political and religious persecution, it also facilitated the development of capitalism. European economic growth and, in turn, the collapse of mercantilist restrictions on mobility fostered international labor migration. Mercantilists of the sixteenth and seventeenth centuries considered population as a source of economic wealth and military power, given that growing populations provided low cost labor to produce exportable goods and staffed the armies that monarchs used to expand their territorial holdings. Hence, states that followed mercantilist prescriptions attempted to bar emigration of skilled workers while welcoming immigration of skilled foreigners (Isaac 1947, 13–19). For example, at the time of the Revocation of the Edict of Nantes in 1685, the Huguenot clergy was expelled from France but, in keeping with mercantilist thinking, lay people were prohibited from leaving. Nevertheless, between 1681 and 1720 one-quarter of the French Protestant population fled, and among those approximately two hundred thousand refugees were the most wealthy and skilled members of the Huguenot community (Zolberg, Suhrke, and Aguayo 1989, 5–6). Huguenot refugees increased the ethnic diversity of Sweden, the German states, and Ulster, where they helped develop the metal, paper, and linen industries (Scoville 1951, 347–60).

The fragmented European state system provided a political structure in which migration could thus become significant economically. The religious wars of the Reformation and the jockeying for power within the European state system led to a situation in which one state would become the refuge for the skilled and rich who were persecuted or overly-taxed in the other (Jones 1987, 115–26). In addition to the migration of skilled Protestants from France, Italian engineers were hired by Ivan III to rebuild Moscow in the 1470s. Miners from southern Germany developed the tin and copper industry of Cornwall. The Murano glassmakers of Venice worked all across Europe (Jones 1987, 116). Italian merchants migrated throughout Germany in the sixteenth century (Braudel 1972a, 214–16). Jewish moneylenders persecuted in one of the German or Italian states moved to others and brought their capital, language skills, and commercial networks with them (Braudel 1972b, 805–17). As skilled laborers and entrepreneurs migrated throughout Europe, often despite individual states' efforts to stop them, technologies spread and entrepreneurs across Europe were able to accumulate capital. As economic, technological, and artistic elites migrated within Europe, the diffusion of knowledge and capital furthered the development of capitalism in the individual members of the European state system and led to the economic advancement of Europe as a whole.

As the Dutch developed an overseas commercial empire during the seventeenth century, Amsterdam grew rapidly with an influx of immigrants from the surrounding countryside as well as from Flanders, the German states, and Scandinavia. "Although it is impossible to know how many people came to the republic or to Amsterdam, gross immigration numbered in the hundreds of thousands. . . . By the late 1680s, over a quarter of the burghers of Amsterdam were Germans" (Moch 1992, 54). Large-scale seasonal labor migration to the Dutch countryside also developed. By 1650, the Dutch developed an international market for cheese, which prompted the development of a commercialized dairy industry and required seasonal labor for making hay. Westphalians came to bring in the crop. Eventually German peasants also became peat diggers, brickmakers, construction workers, and flax workers. "By 1730, at least 15,000, if not 25,000, migrant workers traveled annually in a broad 'North Sea system' to the province of Holland" (Moch 1992, 42).

Expulsion of Jews and Moors may have increased the religious and ethnic homogeneity of Spain's population; however, the demographic effect of expulsions on Spain's population was compounded by severe plague epidemics, celibacy, late marriage, and emigration, all of which throughout the sixteenth century left labor shortages filled by French peasants (Pounds 1990, 261–62, 265; Braudel 1972, 417–18). During the seventeenth and eighteenth centuries, a circulatory migration pattern developed between Spanish cities and the highland region of France. Young men would go to work in Spain for several years, and many stayed. As late as 1797, a French report noted that there were eighty thousand French nationals in Spain, many of whom were married to Spanish women (Moch 1992, 85).

Although the religious homogeneity of populations fostered national unity, the delineation of a people along religious lines differs from nationalism. Indeed, the French Revolutionaries proclaimed religious freedom in order to gain the support of inhabitants of France, regardless of religion, and these revolutionaries forged a new national identity in the process. Similarly, German nationalism was an attempt to overcome the fragmentation of German-speaking peoples into Catholic and Protestant states that had been instituted by the Treaty of Westphalia. It would be a mistake to confuse the early modern west European states with nineteenth-century European nation-states, because political delineation along religious lines differs from delineation along national lines. Nevertheless, it is important to recognize that nationalism is older than the nation-state.

National identities began to form around urban dialects as early as the sixteenth century (Pounds 1990, 215–16). Originating from the Latin *natio*, which the Romans used to characterize Jews, Greeks, and German tribes (Hinsley 1973, 20), the word "nation" was first used in reference to a part of the migrating members of the cosmopolitan European elite—denoting groupings of students within medieval universities (Greenfeld 1992, 4). It was not until the Reformation and the translation of the Bible into the vernacular, however, that the nation became a delineation around which political identification began to coalesce. Nevertheless, this "nationalism" was not a mass phenomenon but rather was evident among only a small proportion of the European population—the elites. Nationalism developed particularly among commercial elites, most notably those of England (Greenfeld 1992, 29–87). Throughout the sixteenth, seventeenth, and eighteenth centuries, nationalism competed with cosmopolitanism in the orientation of the lifestyles, cultural preferences, and political identification of European elites.

The aristocratic elites who dominated polyethnic societies did not necessarily identify with their subjects, making highly suspect the routine practice by historians and political scientists of projecting the nation-state back onto the early modern period. Hannah Arendt notes that in 1727 the Comte de Boulainvilliers, a defender of the French nobility,

> interpreted the history of France as the history of two different nations of which the one, of Germanic origin, had conquered the older inhabitants, the "Gaules," had imposed its laws upon them, had taken their lands, and had settled down as the ruling class, the "peerage" whose supreme right rested upon the "right of conquest" and "the necessity of obedience always due to the strongest. . . . Boulainvilliers denied any predestined connection with the soil; he conceded that the Gaules" had been in France longer, that the "Francs" were strangers and barbarians. He based his doctrine solely on the eternal right of conquest and found no difficulty in asserting that "Friesland . . . has been the true cradle of the French nation." (Arendt 1951, 162)

While members of the eighteenth-century French nobility identified with their German ancestors, eighteenth-century Prussian nobility often identified more with their French contemporaries than with their German subjects. Frederick the Great and his family spoke French; "the despised German language was rarely heard in the house" (Gooch 1947). Indeed, it was precisely the transnational identification of aristocracies that became a focus of opposition among the commercial classes.

Moreover, Boulainvilliers's argument is itself very problematic in that the French and other European aristocracies were hardly "nations" in and of themselves. European aristocracies were polyethnic, not only in the sense of cultural cosmopolitanism but biologically speaking as well. Due to the longstanding practice of dynastic intermarriage as a means of forming alliances, expanding and consolidating territory, and providing hostages to secure peace treaties, most rulers of modern European states shared common ancestors and many married "foreigners." The political unification of France depended on marriage and inheritance rather than on "geographical inevitability" (Pounds 1990, 117), and the Hapsburgs became politically successful in large measure through territorial agglomeration by marriage (Fichtner 1976, 243–65).

Migration and intermarriage was a basis for intercultural exchange and the development of a shared cosmopolitan culture among European elites. In addition to royal houses, the other families that composed the various aristocracies practiced intermarriage and migrated across state lines in order to advance their careers. State apparati were staffed by polyethnic cadres. For example, "under the *ancien régime* any one nation's diplomatic advisors were mixed in nationality" (Jones 1987, 112).

The armies fielded by the monarchies were often composed of foreign mercenaries, with "virtually an international officer corps staffing all the national armies" (Jones 1987, 115; see also Mockler 1970). At the beginning of the sixteenth century, the French army's infantry was larger than its cavalry, and the infantry was mostly foreigners (Rice 1970, 98–99). It has been estimated that at any given time during the seventeenth century, between fifty thousand and sixty thousand Swiss mercenaries were abroad and over nine hundred thousand Swiss died in the military service of foreign countries (Pounds 1990, 264). Throughout the sixteenth to eighteenth centuries, tens of thousands of Irish soldiers served in continental European armies, particularly in those of Flanders, Spain, and France. In 1798, approximately half of the privates in the Prussian army were foreigners; of the seven to eight thousand officers in 1806, one thousand were foreigners (Vagts 1959, 66, 85).

Generally speaking, prior to the eighteenth century, populations of what were to become European nation-states were far from ethnically homogenous. Not only did peasant populations primarily identify with local or regional political entities rather than with more all-inclusive linguistically delineated nations, migration between localities, regions, and nations— particularly from peripheral regions of one "nation" to the growing cities of another—perpetuated the norm of polyethnic societies.

Population Growth and the Nation-State

Although the original idea of modern nationalism developed in sixteenth-century England, as Liah Greenfeld points out, "Particularistic nationalism, reflecting the dissociation of the meaning of the 'nation' as a 'people' extolled as the bearer of sovereignty, the central object of collective loyalty, and the basis of political solidarity, from that of an 'elite,' and its fusion with the geo-political and/or ethnic characteristics of particular populations, did not emerge until the eighteenth century" (Greenfeld 1992, 14). The development of particularistic nationalism in the eighteenth century was facilitated by a rapid and sustained increase in the rate of population growth in Europe, which began about 1750 and led to a demographic shift from polyethnicity to ethnically homogenous populations.[6] This demographic shift made possible political identification along national lines involving majorities of urban populations during the French Revolution. Nevertheless, it was not until the end of the nineteenth century that increasing communication, commerce, and travel between urban and rural populations fostered a standard national language that propagated, through education and the mass press, throughout the entire population of the prototypical nation-state of France (Weber 1976). Only in the nineteenth century did the nation-state emerge as a locus of political identification of its inhabitants, and only then could it be considered a unified actor in the international system as is now commonly depicted.

In accordance with the mercantilist view that growing populations increased wealth, states facilitated population growth during the seventeenth and eighteenth centuries through the introduction of new crops (such as the potato), new agricultural techniques, and advances in "disaster management" (Jones 1987, 134–43). State regulations, quarantines, and border controls (*cordon sanitaire*) aimed at limiting the spread of epidemics and epizootics had also become well established in the eighteenth century and contributed to the fact that western Europe's last major outbreak of the bubonic plague occurred in Marseilles in 1720. While the states' population protection policies helped increase populations, population growth enabled the development of the ethnically homogenous societies we have come to call "nations." Ironically, polyethnic aristocracies facilitated the development of more ethnically homogenous nation-states within which representative democracy would develop and replace the ancien régime.

As rural populations in Europe began to grow rapidly about 1750, the necessity of immigration from beyond urban hinterlands to maintain urban populations diminished. Rather, great cities could find enough migrants from their immediate environs to sustain their populations and their economies. Immigrants from closer to the city were more ethnically and culturally akin to the dominant group of the urban population than those from further away and found learning the urban language and assimilating to urban ways easier. For example, replenishing urban populations with local recruits enabled the great cities of London and Paris to increase their ethnic and cultural homogeneity. As these migrants adopted London and Parisian dialects, and as emigration from the city to the periphery spread the use of these urban dialects, the standardization of language and the development of national cultures around those urban dialects intensified (McNeill 1986, 44).

The relationship between population growth, cultural homogenization around a capital city, and nation-state formation is further demonstrated by cases in which nation-state formation was retarded. In contrast to England and France, the territories of German-speaking central Europe did not have one great urban concentration, but rather several large cities.[7] Cultural and linguistic homogenization also occurred, but it did so around several urban dialects and cultural centers. When combined with territorial fragmentation resulting from the Treaty of Westphalia, the fragmented cultural homogenization process in Germany is an important reason for the late development of a unified nation-state among German-speaking peoples.

As assimilation and identification with the dominant urban ethnic group became a goal shared by rural migrants and urban elites alike, the ideal of equal status of all members of the nation developed as well. This nationalist ideal supplanted the norm of political control by the dominant ethnic group and acceptance of economic exploitation of newcomers from the rural hinterlands. In the French Revolution, disaffected sections of the middle class mobilized the masses of rural migrants by appealing to national identification against the prevailing hierarchical system based on status determined by birth and a functional division of society (McNeill 1987, 35).

With the advent of large-scale democracy, the delineation of the "people" or the "nation" as both rulers and ruled became crucial. The demographic composition of a polity did not present theoretical problems to the state until popular sovereignty became, at least nominally, the primary legitimizing principle of the state and states had to adopt democratic political institutions to demonstrate their adherence to that legitimizing principle.

In the era of absolute monarchies, the boundaries of the state were geographic and the inhabitants within that geographic realm were subjects of a sovereign ruler in accordance with the principle of *domicilium facit subitum* (domicile makes one a subject) that became established in legal doctrine during the sixteenth and seventeenth centuries (Grawert 1973, 79). Political legitimacy was based on dynastic lineage, and political rights were based on status within the social hierarchy. Politically, the composition of a population within a king's realm did not make much difference since the inhabitants were only subject to his commands. The subject status of inhabitants changed along with the territories that were exchanged by sovereigns as the outcome of marriage, succession, and war.

While the inhabitants of a king's realm were his subjects, they were not "citizens" of the kingdom. The only "citizens" at the time were members of towns and city-states. Citizenship, unlike subject status, was not necessarily a condition one was born into. Rather, it was a matter of active participation and belonging in a community, and the status of being a citizen was a function of the community's recognition of one's belonging. Much as in ancient Athens, citizenship was not a function of mere residence in the town or city-state. Given that citizens participated in deciding the fate of the community, citizenship was very exclusive and incorporation of outsiders into the citizen body was possible, but difficult. As in Athens, early modern towns were often ruled by citizen elites whose composition was governed by a de facto, if not de jure, principle of ancestral lineage. As Peter Riesenberg has termed it, this "first" citizenship began in the ancient city-states, reemerged in medieval Europe, and even survived in localized spheres carved out of the rule of absolutist monarchs. It was quite different from the "second" citizenship that emerged with the American and French Revolutions and denoted membership in large-scale territorial states (Riesenberg 1992, xv–xxiv).

The relationship between states and their inhabitants changed with the development of popular sovereignty during the American and French Revolutions because even as the state retained its geographic demarcation, it became constituted by the newly sovereign people—the citizens of the state. Subjects became also citizens, who, as a whole, became sovereign. In this way, citizenship and subject status became conflated as citizens made laws to which they were subject. As citizens constituted a new polity and became the authors of the state's laws, the question of who is a citizen and who is not also defined what a state is and is not.[8]

In a constitutional sense, the question of defining the demos became fundamental to defining the state. For example, during the American Revolution, the inhabitants of Britain's North American colonies chose either to remain British subjects or to adhere to a new polity and become citizens of the newly independent American states (Plender 1988a, 16). Areas mostly composed of adherents to the new polities became the United States, while thousands of Tories who chose not to become citizens of the American states emigrated north to remain British subjects in Canada.

The invention of the federal state at the Constitutional Convention of

1787 rested on the concept of citizenship in both the states and the federal republic formed by the states in their totality. Initially, United States citizenship was attained through citizenship in one of the member states. The American federation became more than the American confederation and other traditional confederations that preceded it, precisely because the citizens of its constituent states became citizens of the federation. The federation's citizens elected the Lower House of the federal legislature[9] and, in turn, the federal government's laws had direct effect upon the citizens (Tocqueville 1969, 155–58; Wheare 1964, 2). As a federation, the United States did not follow the pattern of the European nation-state; nevertheless, it came to be treated in like fashion in terms of its membership as a single unit in the international system through the formulation of the federal state. Hence, the United States became understood as a nation-state even without having a nation in the European sense of the word.

Two years later, the question of defining the demos also became fundamental to defining the state with the outbreak of the French Revolution. The revolution "institutionalized political rights as citizenship rights, transposing them from the plane of the city-state to that of the nation-state, and transforming them from a privilege to a general right" (Brubaker 1990, 106).[10] If by its own declared principles, the legitimacy of a state depends on democracy, the answer to the question of who is to possess political rights precedes any process of legitimization. Hence, the delineation of the members of the French state as opposed to all others became constitutive of the French state.

The delineation of state membership also became critical to modern methods of warfare. In addition to the political rights of voting and holding office, citizenship also entailed obligations such as military service. Since the French Revolution and the *levee en masse,* popular sovereignty has not only been constitutive of the nation-state but has also influenced the conduct of war between states. While Napoleon demonstrated the effectiveness of armies drawn from the entire citizenry, or "the nation," the other states of Europe adopted the practice of conscription whether they were democratic or not. In order to defend their realms against Napoleon's armies, autocratic rulers embraced the concept of national citizenship as they adopted mass conscription. This practice, in turn, prompted the development of rules of nationality in the relations among members of the European state system during the nineteenth century. These rules were eventually codified in a systematic manner during the beginning of the twentieth century, in large measure intended to minimize multiple nationality and conflicts over the military obligations of naturalized citizens.

Given that ethnically homogenous societies presuppose sustained population growth and corresponding political identification, the common practice among international relations scholars of assuming the nation-state as a unit of analysis is somewhat problematic for periods of native population stagnation or decline and/or lack of widespread political identification along national lines. Further, the common practice of conceptualizing international politics in terms of the interaction of nation-states before 1750 is very problematic. Although it is appropriate to analyze the interaction of states, these states encompassed polyethnic hierarchical societies with authority delineated along dynastic lines. Hence, the nature of the interaction of these states differed fundamentally from the interaction of the nation-states that emerged during the nineteenth century. For example, before the development of national citizenship, sovereigns routinely transferred territories and the subjects that went with them with minimal domestic political repercussions. Once notions of citizenship fostered the development of national identities among the masses during the nineteenth century, it became "increasingly impossible to resort to territorial concession as a means of maintaining the balance of power. As soon as the inhabitants cared whether or not they were French, German, or Austrian, their sovereigns could no longer manage the balance by simply transferring territory" (Koslowski and Kratochwil 1994, 224; see also Kratochwil 1982).

Moreover, the archetypal European nation-state and the institutions of representative democracy associated with it presupposed certain demographic conditions. Hence, the superimposition of the nation-state template on areas that did not share a similar demographic development has led not only to a whole host of misconceptualizations, but also to seemingly intractable problems with practical politics. For example, the west European ideal of representative democracy within states delineated along national lines flew in the face of eastern Europe's demography. Even though eastern Europe experienced the same sort of population growth that occurred in France and Great Britain, the identification of urban and rural populations was much more uneven. This partly resulted from the fact that German-speaking populations dominated many towns. Many Slavic-, Hungarian-, and Romanian-speaking migrants from the countryside surrounding the towns became Germanicized, but in other towns that were not dominated by Germans, non-Germanic languages became prevalent. Hence, the process of cultural homogenization did not take place in a geographically contiguous manner and national identities emerged in a patchwork formation (Cobban 1970).

While these emerging identities were accommodated in an ad hoc manner within the hierarchical structure of the Hapsburg Empire, movements to establish representative democracy along west European lines ran headlong into the demographic reality of the patchwork of ethnic identities. This incompatibility between democracy and demography made it impossible to maintain a large-scale polyethnic polity, and World War I consigned the Hapsburg Empire to history (Stourzh 1991). The distribution of ethnic groups was so scattered that even the Treaty of Versailles and its formation of nation-states around major concentrations of large ethnic groups led to a similar series of ethnic conflicts and secessionist and irredentist movements. While the recent tragedy of the former Yugoslavia reminds us of this problem with the nation-state as a conception of political order, demographic change in western Europe once again calls the ideal of the nation-state into question in the very place where it arose.

Population Decline, Migration, and Contemporary European Politics

As the Ottoman and Hapsburg empires collapsed and a League of Nations emerged in the wake of World War I, the nation-state had assumed its place as the central organizing principle of European politics. Also about this time, the demography of west European societies, somewhat ironically, began to return to the old civilized norm of polyethnicity. This transformation is primarily based on slackening population growth and increasing migration. Incorporation of colonial populations into European polities and the reawakening of subnational identities have contributed as well.

Two world wars, widespread use of birth control, and changing social norms have led to aging and even declining native populations in many of Europe's advanced industrial countries. The fertility rates of all EU member states dropped to below the replacement rate of 2.1 children born per woman, and the EU average has sunk to a postwar low of 1.43 (see table 1). Increasing migration from peripheral areas of Europe surrounding its industrialized northwestern core, as well as migration from outside of Europe, became necessary to compensate for indigenous population decline and provide sufficient manpower to sustain economic growth (Kindleberger 1967; Hollifield 1992a, 50–73). By the 1970s the centuries-old trend of net migration leaving western Europe reversed direction.

In the immediate postwar period, west European reconstruction and industrial expansion required a large, steady supply of low-skilled workers. Beginning in the 1950s, west European governments recruited workers from Italy, Greece, Spain, and Portugal for dangerous, dirty, and menial

Table 1   Fertility Rates in EU Member States, 1970–84, 1990–94, and 1995

	1970–74	1975–79	1980–84	1990–94	1995
Belgium	1.94	1.71	1.59	1.61	1.54
Germany	1.62	1.44	1.36	1.32	1.24
Denmark	1.96	1.70	1.42	1.73	1.80
Spain	2.89	2.63	1.83	1.28	1.18
France	2.31	1.86	1.87	1.72	1.70
Greece	2.32	2.32	1.97	1.37	1.40
Ireland	3.80	3.46	2.87	2.00	1.87
Italy	2.27	1.92	1.55	1.29	1.17
Luxembourg	1.96	1.54	1.48	1.65	1.68
Netherlands	1.97	1.58	1.51	1.59	1.53
Portugal	2.76	2.42	1.99	1.53	1.41
UK	2.04	1.72	1.80	1.78	1.71
Austria	—	—	—	1.47	1.39
Finland	—	—	—	1.82	1.81
Sweden	—	—	—	2.04	1.74
EU average	—	—	—	1.50	1.43

Source: 1970–84: Central Bureau of Statistics of the Netherlands, reported in Ardittis 1994, 25; 1990–94 and 1995: Eurostat 1996d.

jobs left unfilled by their own citizens (Castles and Kosak 1973). Displaced persons and refugees from eastern Europe provided the growing German economy a steady supply of labor until the Berlin Wall was built in 1961. Germany, as well as other industrialized European countries, then turned to recruiting guest workers from Turkey, Yugoslavia, and North Africa during the 1960s and early 1970s. Recruitment halted during the recession of 1973–74.

Although employers and host country politicians assumed that guest workers would return to their countries of origin, many workers made host countries their new homes and sent for their families to join them. During the 1980s, it became clear that temporary guest workers were becoming permanent resident aliens (Castles, Booth, and Wallace 1984). The 1980s were also marked by increases in family reunification and births to guest worker families as well as by an influx of refugees from eastern Europe and the Third World in the second half of the decade.

By January 1, 1993, there were almost eighteen million legal resident aliens in the EU (Eurostat 1996b). Due to low fertility rates, the contribution to total population growth by migration between 1980 and 1990 was greater than or equal to the contribution from births in Austria, West Germany, Italy, Luxembourg, Sweden, and Switzerland (OECD 1992, 15). Migration was responsible for all the population increase in Austria and

Germany, as births roughly matched deaths in Austria while deaths exceeded births in Germany. Moreover, by 1993, children born to resident aliens came to constitute a significant proportion of all births in many west European countries: 8.5 percent in Belgium, 11.7 percent in England and Wales, 10.8 percent in France, 14.0 percent in Germany, 37.8 percent in Luxembourg, 6.8 percent in the Netherlands, 13.0 percent in Sweden, and 24.2 percent in Switzerland.[11] Except for a large proportion of those born in England and Wales, most of these children were not born into citizenship due to the prevalence of jus sanguinis ascription of nationality prevalent in continental Europe (see chapter 4).

Europe's imperial heritage has also contributed to the demographic reversion to polyethnicity. Indeed, the common understanding of nineteenth- and early twentieth-century Great Britain and France as democratic nation-states is somewhat ill conceived. Although France and Great Britain can be said to have been ruled democratically by 1930,[12] if one includes all of the territories they controlled outside of Europe in one's definition of the British and French polities, it is clear that only a fraction of the total population was included in the demos. In this sense, French and British democracy was restricted to members of a citizen elite that ruled themselves as well as the disfranchised populations of the territories they controlled.

For example, the French revolution made subjects of the crown into citizens of the nation, but the inhabitants of French colonial possessions remained subjects. According to the French Civil Code, children whose fathers were French citizens became citizens regardless of where they were born (Brubaker 1990, 195–97, 201–2). Those born in French colonies to non-French citizens, however, were not born into French citizenship. This situation even held for certain parts of France itself. France invaded Algeria in 1830, and in 1848 Algeria was incorporated into France as three departments. Over a million French settlers migrated to Algeria, and it was these settlers and their descendants who were represented in Parliament, given that French citizenship was not extended to Algerian Muslims until after 1947 (Miller 1979, 21).

Having avoided a revolution like the one in France, the British monarchy's subjects remained subjects. This included the inhabitants of the British Empire, since the Imperial Act of 1914 stipulated that all inhabitants of the dominions and colonies were British subjects (Heater 1990, 103). A succession of reforms beginning in 1832 extended the vote to an ever greater proportion of British subjects until suffrage became "universal" in 1918 (Marshall 1964, 86). "Universal," however, referred to the king's subjects in the United Kingdom itself, not all of the king's subjects in the Empire. The ill-defined status of subject and the lack of clear-cut rules of citizenship persisted until Canada forced the issue of British citizenship when it created its own citizenship in 1946 and India achieved independence in 1947. The British Nationality Act of 1948 allowed the Dominions, the United Kingdom, and southern Rhodesia to create citizenship within an overarching British nationality (Dummett and Nicol 1990, 135).

If one includes the population of European empires in the European society and polity, one can argue that the societies of European states with possessions abroad remained polyethnic in the nineteenth century and that several ostensibly democratic European polities essentially remained hierarchical until postwar decolonization. Even if one just views Europe and its nation-states in the more traditional circumscribed way, the European colonial legacy still increased the polyethnicity of Europe through migration. As France and Britain wrestled with the contradictions of democracy, citizenship, and empire, a pattern of migration from the imperial peripheries to the British and French metropoles developed after World War II. Even though, strictly speaking, the West Indians in Great Britain and the Algerians in France were not foreigners according to nationality laws, they and their children contributed to the postwar reversion of European society to the norm of polyethnicity.

Increasing migration within and to European societies has been the primary reason for increasing polyethnicity, but changes in ethnic identification have similar demographic and political consequences. Generally speaking, changes in a population are governed by births, deaths, and net migration. Changes in identification, however, can lead to demographic changes by a change in categorization. For instance, the Native American population of the United States grew by more than 70 percent from 1970 to 1980, not because Native American fertility rates dramatically increased or mortality rates dropped. Rather, "more people chose to identify themselves as Indians to the census" (Alonso 1987, 95). A similar process has been taking place in Europe, whereby many Spaniards are identifying themselves as Catalans and Basques, Germans as Bavarians, French as Corsicans, Italians as Lombards, Britons as Scots, and so on.

Politically, this reorientation of identity has been manifested in movements for greater regional autonomy within nation-states. On the EU level these movements for greater autonomy have been expressed in the idea of a "Europe of regions" that infers a transfer of policy-making responsibility from the nation-state to both the EU "above" and the regions "below." Increasing identification of individuals with political entities that preceded the nation-states in which they are located increases the polyethnicity of

European society in two ways. First, it simply increases the number of politically salient ethnic identities. Second, it produces new minorities in a manner analogous to migration because the regional political entities are not uniformly composed of people who identify with them.

Contrary to traditional state-centric conceptualization of world politics, the nation-state has only been an appropriate unit of analysis for a limited and relatively brief period of history. This becomes clear when one examines social and demographic history and the pivotal role of migration in it. Migration is crucial to understanding the dynamics of the development and interaction of civilizations. The dynamics of the biological interaction of humans and the pathogens that preyed upon them led to a cyclical pattern of migration within and among civilizations. Moreover, migration became the basis for much of the technological and cultural borrowing that maintained a rough equilibrium among the four Eurasian civilizations. This cyclical pattern of migration also produced polyethnic societies, which interacted with their environments in ways that are quite different from those of the ethnically homogenous political units that are often assumed in international relations theory. Moreover, the introduction of diseases by peoples who were disease-experienced into populations without immunities led to epidemics that became important factors in determining the outcomes of political and military conflicts. The combination of declining growth in native European populations, migration from Europe's periphery to its industrial core, migration to Europe from former colonies, and the development of regional identities is returning the demographic makeup of European societies to the polyethnic norm.

CHAPTER FOUR

Citizenship

Declining native population growth, the postwar migration of guest workers, and the recent influx of asylum seekers have changed European demography by increasing the proportion of resident aliens within west European populations. Nevertheless, most immigrants and a large proportion of their children have been excluded from citizenship because the nationality laws that developed in many European countries are based on ancestral lineage. Commenting on postwar European migration, McNeill notes:

> Consequently, polyethnic lamination—the clustering of different groups in particular occupations in a more or less formal hierarchy of dignity and wealth—is again asserting itself. . . . This change constitutes a reversion to the civilized pattern of the deeper past, when the world's great empires were ruled by small groups—their members often recruited from a multiplicity of ethnic backgrounds—presiding over hierarchies of specialized occupations, each of which tended to be dominated by a particular ethnic group. Such social arrangements do not accord well with liberal theory, which recognizes no significant differences among citizens. When such differences in fact exist, theory gets into difficulty. (McNeill 1987, 35)

In this chapter, I show how theory gets into difficulty when demographics change. European political institutions and liberal theories that recognize no significant differences among citizens developed in the demographic context of growing populations and emigration of between the late eighteenth and early twentieth centuries. In Europe's contemporary demographic context of shrinking populations and increasing immigration, these political institutions confront practical problems of inclusion. These practical problems, in turn, illuminate theoretical anomalies inherent in modern theories developed in the previous demographic context.

The formative nature of migration in the development of modern political institutions is most clearly evident in the institutions of citizenship and representative democracy. Modern nationality and citizenship laws emerged in Europe contemporaneously with an unprecedented period of population growth and emigration. This demographic context of migration was crucial to the development of the principles of jus sanguinis and jus soli. The development of democracy in continental Europe during the nineteenth and early twentieth centuries coincided with a great emigration that prompted many of these democratizing states to bound their newly formed citizenries using the rule of jus sanguinis.

This historical development raises the theoretical question of whether democracy and citizenship based on ancestral lineage are compatible. Liberal democratic European states that based citizenship on jus sanguinis may have maintained democratic inclusiveness when their populations were rapidly growing and many of their citizens moved abroad. In the context of declining populations growth rates and increasing immigration, however, jus sanguinis decreases democratic inclusiveness and thereby undermines the legitimacy of the democracies that abide by this principle.

Migration and the Principles of Citizenship

Originating in the political practice of ancient Greece, citizenship meant membership in the city-state. According to Aristotle, "He who has power to take part in the deliberative or judicial administration of any state is said by us to be a citizen of that state; and, speaking generally, a state is a body of citizens sufficing for the purposes of life. But in practice a citizen is defined to be one of whom both the parents are citizens; others insist on going further back; say to two or three or more ancestors" (Aristotle 1941, 1177–78). When in 451 B.C. pay for the jurors of the popular court made it possible for the poorest citizens to serve, the bulk of Athenian citizens became participants in Athens' democracy. At the same time Athenian citizenship was restricted to children of Athenian citizens,[1] thereby excluding resident aliens, known as *metics,* from the democratic polity that was being constituted.

In contrast to Athens' increase in political participation and restrictive bounding of citizenship, in Rome the political content of citizenship was diluted as citizenship in the republican city-state was extended to the inhabitants of territories under Roman rule, first by the extension of citizenship to all Italians in 89 B.C. and then by the edict of Caracalla (A.D. 212), which extended citizenship to all free inhabitants of the empire (Sherwin-White 1939, chap. 5). George Sabine notes, "The modern notion of a citizen as a man to whom certain rights are legally guaranteed would have been better understood by the Roman than by the Greek, for the Latin term *jus* does partly imply this possession of private right" (Sabine 1961, 5).

During the American and French revolutions the ancient ideal of citizenship in the city-states of democratic Athens and republican Rome was projected to large-scale polities. Moreover, the French innovation of national citizenship also meant the development of laws differentiating membership of one nation from that of another. National citizenship had an external as well as an internal dimension. That is, national citizenship became constitutive not only of the nation-state but also of the international system that, in their totality, nation-states formed. During the nineteenth century, the inhabitants of the states participating in that system received a "nationality" or formal state membership (*Staatsangehörigkeit*) when states identified those people who belonged to it and those who did not (Grawert 1973; Hammar 1990a, 41–49).

In terms of international law, nationality encompasses subjects as well as citizens. At the end of the eighteenth century the terms "subject," "national," and "citizen" were used indiscriminately (Plender 1988a, 8). As popular sovereignty eventually became a norm of state legitimization (at least nominally) a distinction between subject and citizen became clear. In contrast, as polities became more inclusive through the spread of universal suffrage, nationality and citizenship increasingly overlapped. The interrelationship of the terms is expressed in Oppenheim's definition: "Nationality of an individual is his quality of being subject of a certain State and therefore its citizen" (Oppenheim 1955, 642–43). Weis notes, "Conceptually and linguistically, the terms 'nationality' and 'citizenship' emphasize two different aspects of the same notion: State membership. 'Nationality' stresses the international, 'citizenship' the national, municipal, aspect" (Weis 1979, 5–6).

Nationality refers to the status of being subject to a state's laws, taxes, and military conscription while enjoying the right of protection by the state even when abroad. Citizenship refers to a bundle of civil, political, and social rights possessed by individuals (Marshall 1964). States have developed a set of shared norms delineating who is subject to which state's laws, and many of these norms have been codified in international law. The particular bundle of rights that, together, make up what is understood as citizenship may vary from state to state; within each state, the degree to which nationals possess these different rights may also vary from person to person.

Moreover, as Weis notes, "Every citizen is a national, but not every national is necessarily a citizen of the State concerned" (Weis 1979, 5–6). Ships, aircraft, and corporations (i.e., legal persons), as well as individuals, possess nationality, but only individual human beings can be citizens. A citizen of American Samoa is a United States national, but not a citizen of the United States (Neuman 1998, 253). A felon may lose his or her citizenship rights but still retain his or her nationality. Citizenship can also mean more than nationality in that it often denotes active political participation (Heater 1990, 96–99, 197–202, 211–24; Barber 1984, chaps. 8 and 9) and service to the state, such as jury duty or national service (Gorham 1992), and the willingness to die for the state (Walzer 1971).

Although citizenship based on ancestral lineage informed the citizenship laws of ancient Greece and subject status was governed by place of birth in the feudal system and under absolutism, jus sanguinis and jus soli only became principles of state membership as the classical ideal of city-state citizenship became realized in the democratic revolutions of America and France. As the number of democratic states grew in the period between 1776 and 1930, those states adopted either the jus sanguinis or the jus soli principle of nationality, delineating which inhabitants of the state were citizens and, therefore, included in the demos.[2] Strictly speaking, jus soli and jus sanguinis refer only to ascription of nationality, whereas *jus domicili* refers to the acquisition of nationality through naturalization after a given period of residence. In practice, however, naturalization is also informed by the distinction between jus soli and jus sanguinis because the actual process of naturalization of an alien may depend on ancestral lineage, ethnic heritage, and language skills in addition to residence requirements.

As states developed nationality laws, conflicts of law resulting from the opposing principles of jus soli and jus sanguinis caused some individuals to become stateless while others received more than one nationality. Dual nationality led to serious international political, and even military, conflicts. Following the doctrine of "perpetual allegiance," Great Britain considered naturalized American sailors born in Great Britain to be subjects of the British crown and pressed them into military service, thereby triggering the War of 1812. When immigrants naturalized and became United States citizens, they often found themselves possessing two nationalities and two sets of military obligations. France, Spain, Prussia, and other German states routinely drafted naturalized Americans when they visited their homelands.

roblem of multiple military obligations associated with dual na-
...ty became a preoccupation of George Bancroft, the German edu-
cated historian who became the first U.S. ambassador to the North German
Federation in 1867 (Handlin 1984). In 1849, Bancroft argued that states
should "as soon tolerate a man with two wives as a man with two countries; as soon bear with polygamy as that state of double allegiance which
common sense so repudiates that it has not even coined a word to express
it" (Bancroft 1849). As the U.S. ambassador in Berlin, he negotiated a treaty
in 1868 with the North German Confederation in which American naturalization was recognized and German nationals secured a limited right of
expatriation. Soon thereafter, Bavaria, the grand duchy of Baden, the kingdom of Württemberg, and the grand duchy of Hesse all concluded similar
bilateral treaties with the United States (Flournoy and Hudson 1929, 660–
67). Additional bilateral treaties recognizing U.S. naturalization and limiting dual nationality were negotiated between the United States and Great
Britain, Austria-Hungary, Belgium, Denmark, Norway, and Sweden during
last few decades of the nineteenth century (Bar-Yaacov 1961, 163–66). In
total, the United States entered into twenty-six such bilateral agreements,
which collectively became known as the Bancroft Treaties. Although most
major sending states entered into agreements with the United States, some
states continued to draft naturalized American citizens when they returned
to their country of origin as, for example, Italy and Switzerland did during
World War I.

The proliferation of bilateral treaties regarding nationality during the
latter half of the nineteenth century accumulated into a set of norms against
dual nationality in customary international law. The project of codify-
ing customary international rules began in 1925 when the League of Nations began to prepare for an International Codification Conference at the
Hague. The continuing conflicts between states over their nationals during
World War I helped elevate regulation of nationality to being the first of
three issues under consideration (see Harvard Law School 1929). The conference produced the 1930 Hague Convention on Certain Questions relating to the Conflict of Nationality Laws, which stated, "it is in the interest
of the international community to secure that all members should recognize that every person should have a nationality and should have one nationality only" (League of Nations 1930a, preamble). Three protocols were
also drawn up: one dealing with "Military Obligations in Certain Cases of
Double Nationality" (League of Nations 1930b), one regulating "Statelessness" (League of Nations 1930c), and one dealing with a "Certain Case
of Statelessness" (League of Nations 1930d). The convention's recognition

of both jus sanguinis and jus soli as legitimate principles for the ascription of nationality meant that cases of dual nationality would be unavoidable (e.g., when the child of a national from a jus sanguinis state has a child in a jus soli state). To minimize the conflicts that might occur over dual nationals who involuntarily obtained two nationalities, the convention extended a right of expatriation whereby states were to accept the renunciation of their nationality by individuals residing abroad. The protocol on military obligations released individuals with two nationalities from obligations to the state in which he does not reside and has few ties.

In preparation for the 1930 Hague conference, a study by Harvard Law Research determined that seventeen states, fifteen of which were European, based nationality solely on jus sanguinis; twenty-five, fifteen of which (including Turkey) were European, primarily on jus sanguinis; twenty-six, three of which were European, primarily on jus soli; and two on an equal mixture of the two principles (AJIL 1929, 29). Several reasons have been given for the distinction between the principles of jus sanguinis and jus soli. Armstrong suggests that the principle of jus sanguinis originated with nomadic societies that stressed ancestry and kinship to delineate tribal membership, whereas jus soli originated with settled agricultural societies (Armstrong 1982, 14–53). Maxson traces the principle of jus sanguinis to rules governing membership in the families, gentes, and tribes of patriarchal societies and rules governing suffrage and rights in ancient cities, whereas jus soli emerged from the rules delineating subject status in medieval Europe. According to Maxson and Weis, jus soli persisted as part of English common law while jus sanguinis became the continental norm with the adoption of Roman law (Maxson 1930, 2–5; Weis 1979, 4). Brubaker argues that the sequencing of state formation was crucial to the development of the differing principles of citizenship—in France citizenship developed within the context of a territorially defined nation-state, while in Germany citizenship developed as a reflection of an ethno-national identity that evolved before and outside of a unified nation-state (Brubaker 1992).

Armstrong's explanation for the origin of the distinction based on the difference between settled/agricultural and nomadic/pastoral societies does not fit the circumstances in which modern citizenship emerged in the late eighteenth and nineteenth centuries, but it offers an insight into the role of migration in citizenship development. The common law/Roman law distinction provides an explanation for the differing rules in regard to the ascription of citizenship initially adopted by the American states and France during their democratic revolutions. It does not, however, account for the difference between continental European countries with Roman law traditions that extensively supplemented jus sanguinis ascription with jus soli and extended the territorial principle to naturalization (France) and those that maintained a more strict form of jus sanguinis (Germany). Brubaker's focus on state-formation sequencing explains this differentiation between France and Germany. However, his explanation cannot be generalized for the American states, which pioneered the development of modern citizenship laws, or to other continental European countries (such as Sweden and Denmark), which had territorially-defined states before they became democratic and developed modern citizenship laws, but then used the jus sanguinis principle to bound their citizenry. Together, all these conceptualizations contribute to an understanding of how this distinction developed and why states opted for one principle over the other as they became democratic in the late nineteenth and early twentieth centuries. In sum, principles of citizenship inherited from legal traditions were either strengthened or diluted by differing ideologies of national identity formation and shaped by the practicalities of the greatest human migration in history.

Rooted in the English feudal law stipulating that those born on the land of a lord were his subjects, jus soli became the primary rule for delineating who was or was not a subject of the king of England (Dummett and Nicol 1990, 24) and, thereby, became an initial qualification necessary for political participation.[3] British subjects in America who renounced their adherence to Britain nevertheless retained the common law principle of jus soli for regulating ascription of citizenship in their new states.

Following the Roman law tradition, France adopted the jus sanguinis principle for ascribing citizenship at birth,[4] which then became the norm for the rest of the European continent,[5] but rules governing ascription at age of majority and naturalization came to differ greatly. France based ascription of nationality at birth on jus sanguinis. Following its republican ideology and confident in the ability of its schools and army to turn foreigners into Frenchmen, France enacted laws in 1889 that made the French-born children of immigrants into citizens upon reaching the age of majority and, in 1927, France liberalized its naturalization rules (Brubaker 1990, 210–59).

In Germany, the principle of jus sanguinis has governed ascription and restricted naturalization until recently. German citizenship came to be understood in ethno-cultural terms because it developed in the context of defining a nation prior to a unified state. This non-territorial ethno-cultural understanding of citizenship was codified in the citizenship law of 1913, which maintained restrictions on the access to citizenship by children and grandchildren of immigrants while enabling German emigrants to maintain German citizenship and pass it on to their descendants born outside of Germany.[6]

If one follows Armstrong's line of thought that jus sanguinis is associated with nomadic life and jus soli with sedentary life, the adoption of jus sanguinis by agricultural societies in Europe during modern times must be understood in terms of an atavism. European mass migration in the eighteenth and nineteenth centuries did, however, yield a nomadic component to European societies. Whereas nationality laws in the states of the Americas developed in the context of immigration, European laws developed in the context of tens of millions of Europeans emigrating to other continents. Countries that formed through immigration—such as the United States, Canada, the Latin American countries, and Australia—tended to base nationality primarily on jus soli because it permits more rapid assimilation of immigrants. Countries experiencing great out-migration—such as Germany, the Scandinavian countries, and Italy—tended to base nationality primarily on jus sanguinis because it encourages emigrants to retain their nationality and pass it on to their children so as to facilitate—for both emigrants and their descendants—closer ties with and the return to their homeland (Hammar 1990a, 71–72; Brubaker 1990, 169–72).[7]

For example, Germans who immigrated to the United States during the nineteenth century routinely returned to Germany, particularly in periods of economic depression. It has been estimated that, in any given year, of the number of Germans who migrated to the United States, between 5 and 50 percent returned (Moltmann 1980, 386). Ironically, these Germans of the nineteenth century were much like Europe's guest workers of the post–World War II era. Likewise, Germany attempted to maintain the allegiance of its citizens who emigrated, just as sending states do today.

It is important to note that although the adoption of jus sanguinis often coincides with high rates of emigration and jus soli with immigration, principles of nationality are not solely dependent on the direction of migration. For instance, British nationality is primarily based on jus soli even though Great Britain has consistently maintained a high rate of emigration. However, in the nineteenth century Great Britain subscribed to the doctrine of perpetual allegiance whereby those born as subjects of the crown remained subjects, regardless of emigration or even naturalization. Only the children born abroad to expatriates did not gain British citizenship rights.

Germany also based its nationality laws on jus sanguinis even though it experienced large-scale immigration, primarily from Poland, starting in the 1880s and continuing until the 1920s (Bade 1980, 366–75). The issue of the ethnicity of migrants is also critical to the adoption of jus sanguinis or jus soli. At the same time that Germany was receiving many Polish immigrants, primarily from those parts of Poland that came under Prussian rule after Poland's partition, it was also receiving Germans returning from the United States along with their children born abroad. Basing nationality on jus soli rather than jus sanguinis may have facilitated the assimilation of Polish immigrants, but it would have made it more difficult to integrate ethnic Germans returning from the United States. A preference for ethnic German returnees over Polish immigrants proved decisive in the drafting of the 1913 law (Brubaker 1990, 264–304). In the case of Germany, exclusion of immigrants contributed to the adoption of jus sanguinis, but most European countries did not adopt jus sanguinis citizenship laws in order to exclude immigrants because few continental European countries other than Germany and France had significant immigrant populations at the time, especially relative to the numbers of emigrants.

Although the principles of jus soli and jus sanguinis are associated with common law and Roman law, as well as the sequencing of nation- and state-building, in practice the distinction between jus sanguinis and jus soli is, strictly speaking, a function of migration. As Brubaker notes, "In a zero migration world, they would have identical effects: every person born of citizen parents would also be born in the state's territory, and vice versa" (Brubaker 1989, 102). Once a child is born to a foreigner, or a child is born to a state's national residing abroad, a state must choose whether or not to grant its nationality to that child. This choice sets a precedent for future decisions. When the same choice is repeated, a decision rule develops that becomes codified into law.

As the Harvard Legal Research inventory discussed earlier demonstrated, however, neither principle of nationality is absolute in its application. Ascribing nationality at birth strictly by the principles of jus soli or jus sanguinis leads to practical difficulties that have prompted some moderation of each principle with certain attributes of the other. All jus sanguinis states add jus soli to govern cases of foundlings whose parentage cannot be established, and jus soli states add jus sanguinis to govern cases of children born to nationals who are temporarily abroad. Without moderating the principle of jus soli by adding a degree of jus sanguinis in naturalization, for example, an American tourist's child born in Norway could become neither a United States nor Norwegian national. In practice, the United States bestows nationality to such children through a simple act of registration upon their return to the country. Without moderating the principle of jus sanguinis in ascription, the American descendants of nineteenth-century German immigrants would continue to be not only U.S. nationals but also German nationals, regardless of whether they had any allegiance to, or even interest in, Germany. The 1913 German citizenship law revoked the nationality of German emigrants who voluntarily took on the nationality of another state or failed to fulfill military obligations but made it possible for them, or their descendants, to regain the status of German national.[8] Inclusive interpretation of Article 116, Section 1 of Germany's Basic Law[9] has, nevertheless, effectively extended citizenship in the Federal Republic to ethnic Germans from eastern Europe upon arrival in Germany, even to those descended from the Germans who settled in Hungary and Russia centuries ago.

Legal inheritance may have set out initial distinction between jus soli and jus sanguinis, and state-formation sequencing may have influenced the development of citizenship laws in a few cases; however, one can only understand the establishment of these differing principles of citizenship with reference to the demographic context of migration in which citizenship laws developed. For example, on December 6, 1921, the southern counties of Ireland left the United Kingdom and became a dominion. The Irish Free State Constitution supplemented the common law principle of jus soli governing ascription and naturalization, which it inherited from the United Kingdom, with the jus sanguinis rule that anyone whose parent was born in Ireland is entitled to Irish citizenship (Dummett and Nicol 1990, 128). This measure was motivated by the fact that a large proportion of Ireland's population had emigrated during the preceding century (Miller 1985; Jackson 1963). Given that Ireland's citizens continued to emigrate in large numbers, the Irish Nationality and Citizenship Act of 1956 strengthened jus sanguinis provisions by extending citizenship to anyone with an Irish-born grandparent.

In sum, international migration forces the issue of whether to grant citizenship to children of foreigners and expatriates. Concern for maintaining ties to emigrants and their children as well as for the preservation of ethnic homogeneity strongly influenced the drafting and revision of citizenship laws in the nineteenth and early twentieth centuries. In this way the demographic context in which citizenship laws developed played a decisive role in the choice of the jus sanguinis or jus soli principle.

Principles of Citizenship and Democratic Inclusiveness

Given that Athenian citizenship was based on ancestral lineage, the descendants of *metics* (resident aliens in Athens) could neither become citizens nor ever expect to gain political rights. Along with the exclusion of women and slaves, the situation of metics demonstrates the highly exclusionary nature of Athenian democracy (Dahl 1989, 22). Pointing out that slaves and metics often did the Athenians' dirty work, Michael Walzer paints Athenian democracy as an aristocracy of citizens ruling over the disfranchised (Walzer 1983, 53–55). The abolition of slavery and the enfranchisement of women, peasants, and the working class make modern democracies more inclusive than that of Athens; however, the nagging problem of resident aliens remains.

The problem that permanent resident aliens posed to democratic theory long remained either historical or hypothetical as long as polities that had large numbers of resident aliens were not democracies (or democracies with a demos restricted to the upper class). As the number of democratic polities increased during several "waves of democratization" (Huntington 1991) and political rights were gradually extended to all ranks of these democratic societies (Bendix 1964, 112–22; Marshall 1964, 78–105), the overall number of resident aliens living in democracies increased. Only recently, as guest workers became permanent resident aliens in established European democracies, have the inherent theoretical problems posed by resident aliens become evident in political practice (Miller 1978; Bernard 1978; Heisler and Schmitter Heisler 1985).

Political theorists who have focused on migration have explored the issues of justice that resident aliens raise (Walzer 1983; Carens 1989; Carens 1992; Schuck and Smith 1985), but the problem resident aliens pose for democracy has received relatively little attention in recent general works in democratic theory (see, e.g., Arblaster 1987; Barber 1984, Bobbio 1987; Connolly 1991; Dahl 1989; Held 1987; Keane 1988; Lijphart 1984; Mansbridge 1983; Riker 1982; Sartori 1987). This omission is understandable given that democratic theory usually assumes a bounded group of people who comprise the demos that rules (Whelen 1983). By the end of World War II, universal adult suffrage became the generally accepted standard for defining the demos in most democracies (see, e.g., Lijphart 1984, 37–39; Dahl 1989, 233–39). Once this happened, debates subsided over which parts of the population should be enfranchised and democratic theorists could focus almost exclusively on the self-government of already constituted *demoi*.

As political rights were extended in the founding of democratic polities, the demoi constituted were often bounded in an exclusive manner by citizenship laws based on ancestral lineage. As mentioned above, at the same time that the bulk of Athenian citizens became participants in Athens' democracy, citizenship was restricted to children of Athenian citizens, thereby excluding metics from the democratic polity that was being constituted.

Similarly, as participation in the decision making of early modern towns of the Holy Roman Empire and Switzerland expanded, resident aliens were excluded from membership in the associations that together composed these polities (Althusius 1964, 35; Walker 1971, 108–44; Bluntschli 1895, 160–68, 211–12; Bonjour, Offler, and Potter 1952, 103–4). The revolutionary American democracies maintained the jus soli of English common law, but the exclusion of black slaves and Native Americans from citizenship sharply restricted membership in the demos constituted, in a manner that had a practical effect similar to that of jus sanguinis. French revolutionaries criticized jus soli as being too "feudal" and "jus sanguinis was preferred for linking citizens to the state by ties more substantial than those of birthplace" (Brubaker 1990, 171). Practically speaking, large-scale demoi delineated by jus soli only came into existence beginning in the later half of the nineteenth century and the early twentieth century. This was marked by the passage of the Fourteenth Amendment to the United States Constitution, the establishment of jus soli ascription at the age of majority in France, and the development of parliamentary democracy with universal suffrage in Canada, New Zealand, Australia, and Great Britain. Even though the territorial principle of jus soli has but recently become the principle of bounding the demos in several large-scale democracies, political theorists have often assumed that the boundary of the demos coincides with the geographical boundaries of the democratic state (Whelen 1983).

Conceptualizing the demos in this way can conflate the geographic boundaries of a state with the boundaries defining membership of that state's demos. An individual joins an existing demos when he or she becomes a citizen and can exercise full political rights. One can cross the geographic borders of the state and live there for the rest of one's life without ever entering the realm of citizenship and crossing the boundary of the demos. Universal adult suffrage may establish an inclusive demos generally regarded as legitimate, but when the number of inhabitants who are denied the political rights of citizenship increases as a proportion of a democratic state's population, the legitimacy of the delineation of the demos by universal adult suffrage can be questioned.

European democracies that base citizenship on jus sanguinis, however, did not experience a significant reduction of democratic inclusiveness as long as their populations grew and emigration greatly exceeded immigration. Indeed, when the flow of migration leaves rather than enters a democratic state, and that state's emigrants do not gain citizenship in their host countries, jus sanguinis that enables political participation in the migrants' home state can maintain democratic inclusiveness. For example, hunger forces a poor citizen of a democratic state to emigrate during a famine.

Years later when conditions improve, her children wish to move back to their ancestral homeland; however, since the state's nationality laws are based on jus soli, the children are denied citizenship because they were born abroad. In contrast, a richer citizen of the same state had enough wealth to survive the famine and gave birth in her homeland, so her children were born as citizens. Here, access to political rights becomes a function of wealth. Hence, extending citizenship to poor emigrants' children born abroad could be considered analogous to extending citizenship to a segment of a democratic state's lower classes.

Given the circumstances of mass emigration, the argument could be made that jus sanguinis was compatible with liberal democracy in certain nineteenth- and early twentieth-century European states. For example, an annual average of 6.6 per 1,000 Norwegians emigrated between 1861 and 1910. "In some parts of Norway, one adult male in four had spent some time in the United States by the 1920 census" (Moch 1992, 149). By 1930 Norway was a democracy that primarily based nationality on jus sanguinis. Given the relative preponderance of emigrants leaving Norway to immigrants entering Norway, the practical effect of its jus sanguinis nationality rules was more inclusive than exclusive.

As population growth declined in western Europe and net migration reversed direction in the 1970s, the number of resident aliens increased as a proportion of the population, the gap between the citizenry and inhabitants grew, and the boundaries between the demoi and the states' geographic boundaries diverged. Nationality laws based on ancestral lineage that at one time might have promoted inclusiveness became the basis for excluding resident aliens from the demos. In this way, the changing demographics of twentieth-century European societies toward polyethnicity illuminates an inherent problem in democratic theory.

After examining the problem of inclusion, Dahl stipulates as one criterion of the democratic process that "the *demos* must include all adult members of the association except transients and persons proved to be mentally defective" (Dahl 1989, 129). Unfortunately, Dahl too casually accepts the rightful exclusion of "transients." By focusing on tourists rather than resident aliens, he neglects millions of European guest workers who share the fate of metics, a situation that, he argues, rendered Athenian democracy exclusionary. Because resident aliens are foreigners who are, technically speaking, transient, one can argue that they should be excluded from the demos. Because they are subject to the laws of a democratic polity, participate in its society and culture, contribute to its economy, and pay taxes, one can also argue that they should be included.

To illustrate the argument for the exclusion of transients, Dahl gives the example of a tourist who happens to be in Paris on election day. Even if the tourist met all the qualifications for voting, she could leave after the election and not bear responsibility for the decisions she made. Therefore, the tourist "ought to be excluded under the assumption that binding decisions should be made only by members" (Dahl 1989, 128n. 11). The problem then becomes one of defining "transient." Dahl does confess that "the definition of adult and transients is a potential source of ambiguity" (Dahl 1989, 129). He then explores the ambiguity of adulthood but drops the subject of transience and does not broach the subject of whether or not to include children born to transients.

Dahl's argument for excluding transients from the demos does not hold when those transients are temporary workers who become permanent resident aliens. One can argue that guest workers' rights to reside in host countries are of a contractual nature, in many but not all cases,[10] and that they therefore freely consented to their transient status. Walzer counters that this kind of consent is not sufficient in a democracy: "Political power is precisely the ability to make decisions over periods of time, to change rules, to cope with emergencies; it can't be exercised democratically without the ongoing consent of its subjects" (Walzer 1983, 58). Consistently subject to the laws of a democratic polity, permanent resident aliens have resided in their host countries long enough to suffer the consequences of laws they could have participated in making had they been given the political rights to do so. The analogy between resident aliens and tourists only holds for some limited amount of time.

Once resident aliens become permanent, one can make a strong argument that denying them political rights and denying their children citizenship are both unjust (Carens 1992). Walzer goes as far as generating his reconceptualization of justice by pointing out the constitutive nature of a community's decision rule regarding new members:

> The idea of distributive justice presupposes a bounded world within which distributions take place. . . . The primary good that we distribute to one another is membership in some human community. And what we do with regard to membership structures all our other distributive choices. (Walzer 1983, 31)

While welfare states achieve a high degree of equality for their members, Walzer argues that it is not the members'

> equality but their tyranny that determines the character of the state. . . . Democratic citizens, then, have a choice: if they want to bring in new workers, they must be prepared to enlarge their own membership; if they are unwill-

ing to accept new members, they must find ways within the limits of the domestic labor market to get socially necessary work done. (Walzer 1983, 61)

Questions of justice are very salient with respect to resident aliens; however, the problem of resident aliens goes beyond issues of distributive justice: the status of resident aliens can be considered a touchstone of democracy in a highly mobile world. Just as decisions that bound a community
precede distributive justice, defining a demos precedes democracy (Whelen
1983, 15–16; Dahl 1989, 193–209). For instance, the initial boundaries of
the geographical units that the established demoi of western Europe now
rule are historically given, which often means that they are given by a long
history of dynastic marriage, inheritance, and war. The geographical boundaries of these states may have bounded their demoi well enough at the time
of democracy's inception in each of these states, but these same boundaries
cannot adequately delineate the demos in the context of extensive immigration. If inclusiveness is a fundamental criterion of the democratic process, present decisions on who is allowed to join the demos are indicative
not only of how just a society is but also of how democratic a polity is.

Resident Aliens and European Democracy

Until the late 1960s, few Europeans considered the problems that resident
aliens raised for west European democracies. Many policymakers simply
thought the problem would go away as unemployment increased and guest
workers returned home. As host countries gradually accepted the fact that
guest workers and their families were becoming permanent resident aliens,
these countries developed various approaches to ameliorate the situation.
In some cases, countries encouraged naturalization (de Rham 1990); paid
guest workers to leave (Hammar 1990a, 18–19); or gave them more civil
rights (Hammar 1990b), economic rights (Vranken 1990), and even limited political rights short of the vote (Miller 1981).

Including resident aliens in the polity through rapid naturalization is the
solution most in keeping with liberal principles. Due to the prevalence of
jus sanguinis ascription on the continent inherited from the past, incorporation of migrants and their children remained difficult. As Brubaker put it,
"*Jus soli* creates and recreates a territorial community, *jus sanguinis* a community of descent" (Brubaker 1990, 168). Anyone can "become" an American or Canadian, because citizenship is the manifestation of political identity toward a territorial community and is realized through taking on new
political loyalties. In contrast, not everyone can "become" a Norwegian or

Greek in the same way because Norwegian and Greek identity are ethnically delineated.

When ascription at birth is governed by jus sanguinis, the addition of the jus soli principle to govern ascription at the age of majority includes the children of permanent resident aliens in the demos, as has been most extensively done in Europe by France. Until 1993, children of foreign parents automatically received French citizenship at the age of eighteen if the parent was also born in France (including pre-independence Algeria). A foreigner's child who lived in France for at least five years also gained citizenship at age eighteen. Legislation in 1993 required children of foreign parents to formally apply for citizenship between the ages of sixteen and twenty-one. Nationality was denied to those sentenced to six months or more in prison or could be denied to those convicted of drug dealing or terrorism (Reuters 1993; Frazer 1993). Therefore, the granting of nationality to children of foreigners born in France became more of a matter of bureaucratic discretion on a case-by-case basis, similar to applying for naturalization, rather than a practice of ascription governed only by the principle of jus soli. Shortly after coming into office in 1997, the Socialist-led government of Lionel Jospin reversed most of the 1993 legislation and reestablished jus soli at the age of majority. Despite the restrictionist interlude, postponed ascription of French nationality to the children of foreigners and relatively liberal naturalization rules governed by the territorial principle have yielded a high rate of incorporation of second-generation resident aliens into the French polity.

The role of jus sanguinis in constructing ethno-national identity can make simultaneously maintaining jus sanguinis and encouraging naturalization somewhat contradictory in both host and home countries. If foreigners are routinely naturalized in a jus sanguinis host country and their children and grandchildren become citizens by virtue of lineage, the practical distinction between jus sanguinis and jus soli dissipates and citizenship is eventually divorced from ethnicity. Difficulty of naturalization marks the degree to which jus sanguinis has an implicit ethnic content. Although some countries that base nationality on jus sanguinis, like Sweden and the Netherlands, accepted the reality of immigration and encouraged naturalization in the 1980s, others, like Germany and Switzerland, long maintained that they were not "immigration countries," discouraged naturalization, and have had relatively low naturalization rates (see table 2).

Although the 1913 German Nationality Law remained in effect, Germany changed its naturalization laws with passage of the Foreigners Act of July 9, 1990, which went into effect on January 1, 1991. Until that time,

Table 2 Persons Acquiring Nationality (in thousands) and Naturalization Rates in Selected European Countries, 1991–96 (as percentage of foreign population)

	1991	1992	1993	1994	1995	1996	Average Rates
Austria	11.4	11.9	14.4	16.3	15.3	16.2	
	2.5%	2.2%	2.3%	2.4%	2.1%	2.2%	2.3%
Belgium	8.5	46.4	16.4	25.8	26.1	24.6	
	0.9%	5.0%	1.8%	2.8%	2.8%	2.7%	2.7%
Denmark	5.5	5.1	5.0	5.7	5.3	7.3	
	3.4%	3.0%	2.8%	3.0%	2.7%	3.3%	3.0%
Finland	1.2	0.9	0.8	0.7	0.7	1.0	
	4.7%	2.3%	1.8%	1.2%	1.1%	1.4%	2.1%
France	95.5	95.3	95.5	126.3	92.4	109.8	
	2.7%	—	—	—	—	—	2.7%
Germany[a]	27.3	37.0	44.9	26.2	—	—	
	0.4%	0.4%	0.6%	0.4%	—	—	0.4%
Germany[b]	141.6	179.9	199.4	259.2	313.6	302.8	
	2.7%	3.1%	3.1%	3.8%	4.5%	4.2%	3.6%
Italy	4.5	4.4	6.5	6.6	7.4	7.0	
	0.6%	0.5%	0.7%	0.7%	0.8%	0.7%	0.7%
Luxembourg	0.6	0.6	0.7	0.7	0.8	0.8	
	0.5%	0.5%	0.6%	0.6%	0.6%	0.6%	0.6%
Netherlands	29.1	36.2	43.1	49.5	71.4	82.7	
	4.2%	4.9%	5.7%	6.3%	9.4%	11.4%	7.0%
Spain	3.8	5.3	8.4	7.8	6.8	8.4	
	1.3%	1.5%	2.1%	1.8%	1.5%	1.7%	1.6%
Sweden	27.7	29.3	42.7	35.1	32.0	25.6	
	5.7%	5.9%	8.5%	6.9%	6.0%	4.8%	6.3%
Switzerland	8.8	11.2	12.9	13.8	16.8	19.4	
	0.8%	1.0%	1.1%	1.1%	1.3%	1.5%	1.1%
U.K.	58.6	42.2	45.8	44.0	40.5	43.1	
	3.4%	2.4%	2.3%	2.2%	2.1%	2.1%	2.4%

Source: OECD 1998, 225.

Note: Acquisition of nationality includes standard naturalization, nationality recovery, and special means; naturalization rate is the number of persons acquiring the nationality as a percentage of foreigner population at the beginning of the year.

[a] Discretionary naturalizations (naturalization of nonethnic Germans), Frey and Mammey 1996, 148.

[b] Includes ethnic Germans.

naturalization required at least ten years of residence, knowledge of the German language and society, good behavior, sufficient means of support, and a naturalization fee of 75 percent of one's monthly salary. Moreover, naturalization was not considered a right but rather a matter of administrative discretion governed by the interests of the Federal Republic (Hailbronner 1989, 67–72; Hammar 1990a, 87; Brubaker 1992, 77–79). The reforms made naturalization easier for foreigners aged sixteen to twenty-three who have lived continuously in Germany for eight years. The reforms also included a temporary provision to last until the end of 1995, which stipulated that naturalization could not be arbitrarily refused to those maintaining permanent residence for at least fifteen years. In conjunction with the change in German asylum law, the 1995 deadline was lifted and extension of the right to naturalization after fifteen years of residence became permanent (Council of Europe 1995, 55–57).

In response to a groundswell of public outrage after a skinhead attack in Solingen that left five Turks dead in June of 1993, the Kohl government called for a new citizenship law to be drawn up by the end of the year to replace the 1913 German citizenship law (Sommer 1993). After several delays and the intervening 1994 parliamentary elections, the reelected Kohl government proposed much less comprehensive legislation. The proposal introduced the concept of *Kinderstaatszugehoerigkeit* (child state membership), a temporary German citizenship extended to children born in Germany to resident aliens if their parents have lived in Germany for at least ten years and one parent was born there. When reaching the age of eighteen, these third-generation resident aliens would have to accept German citizenship and give up the passport of their ancestral homeland or keep their parents' citizenship and not naturalize. In effect, the proposal introduced the principle of jus soli ascription of nationality.

In 1999, the newly elected Social Democratic (SPD)–Green coalition government led by Gerhard Schroeder enacted reforms of Germany's citizenship laws that would introduce jus soli for third-generation, and in some cases second-generation, immigrants. Beginning January 1, 2000, children born in Germany to a foreigner who was also born in Germany will receive German citizenship at birth. Children born in Germany to foreigners who legally came to the country before age fourteen will also receive German citizenship at birth. The reforms also relax naturalization rules by reducing the residency requirement from fifteen to eight years for naturalization by entitlement; spouses of German citizens must demonstrate three years of residence and two of marriage. Applicants must demonstrate that they do not receive social assistance payments, and those that have served prison sentences of nine months or more would not be eligible for naturalization. Applicants must pass a language test and sign a statement in support of the German constitution. The reforms also relax the requirement that those who naturalize to Germany as well as children born in Germany to foreigners must renounce their other nationality.

Even if a host country in which ascription of citizenship is governed by jus sanguinis adds jus soli and eases naturalization requirements, jus sanguinis principles in migrants' home countries often inhibit naturalization. Some states consider renunciation of nationality as grounds for losing more than political rights. For example, until 1995 Turks who renounced their Turkish nationality could not own or inherit land in Turkey. Similarly, some states prohibit the renunciation of nationality by emigrants attempting to naturalize in another state until they pay for the education they received and/or complete required military service. For example, male children of Greek or Iranian parents born in west European countries may also still be subject to conscription in their parents' home countries if they ever return to visit, even if they have served in the military of the country in which they were born and to which they eventually naturalized. They are then left with the choice of naturalizing to their country of birth and not returning to their parents' home country, naturalizing and serving in the military of both countries, or not naturalizing (Hammar 1990a, 8, 116–17).

Given the difficulties inherent in naturalization, some countries have opted to partially include into their demoi those resident aliens who do not naturalize. In 1975 Sweden gave the right to vote in local and regional elections to nationals of foreign countries who had lived in Sweden for at least three years. In the late 1970s and early 1980s, many European countries introduced similar proposals on local voting rights. Denmark and the Netherlands followed Sweden's example. In Great Britain and Spain, certain groups of resident aliens gained limited political rights. After Irish independence in 1949, Irish citizens retained the right to vote in Great Britain, and Commonwealth immigrants also retained voting rights. In response, Ireland gave local voting rights to foreigners in 1963 and the right to vote in national elections to British citizens in 1984. The Spanish constitution bestows voting rights to citizens of countries, which allows Spanish citizens the right to vote in their local elections and implicitly offers the same right to citizens of other countries on the same reciprocal basis. In contrast, proposals on local voting rights were stymied in Belgium, France, and Germany, often by extreme right-wing movements directed against foreigners (Rath 1990).

Contrary to the traditional norms of state practice, states may grant non-nationals rights normally associated with citizenship. As the Swedish example attests, a state may increase its democratic inclusiveness while not changing its principle of nationality by extending voting rights to non-nationals. Traditionally, citizenship requires state membership in terms of nationality, but it is theoretically possible, though seemingly incongruous, for resident aliens to receive the full political rights of citizenship without being nationals. This would happen, for example, if Sweden were to extend voting rights in national elections and eventually expand the bundle of citizenship rights extended to foreign nationals resident in Sweden until that bundle nearly equaled that of Swedish nationals. Hence, a state that bases nationality on jus sanguinis may, theoretically speaking, base citizenship on jus soli.

The understanding that democracy requires not only political rights but also the economic means necessary to realize those rights goes back to the jury pay that enabled the poorer citizens of Athens to fully participate in Athenian democracy. As Marshall pointed out, full citizenship in the modern sense entails social as well as civil and political rights. By ensuring basic economic security, the European welfare state grants the citizenry the social rights necessary to realize democracy in advanced industrialized societies (Marshall 1964).

European welfare states, however, are premised on the notion of a closed membership in which citizens are entitled to universal health care, extensive child care benefits, liberal unemployment benefits, and state-financed higher education (Freeman 1985). Closed membership could be assumed to encompass most of the inhabitants of the state as long as there was minimal migration and all migrants either did not stay permanently or were easily brought into membership. Once boundaries of the membership entitled to social rights deviate greatly from the inhabitants of the welfare state, the welfare state's own legitimizing principles are undermined. Effective and legitimate democratic welfare states that are based on closed membership may have been possible in the demographic context of increasing population growth within the established membership, but increasing proportions of resident aliens characteristic of postwar European demography have made sustaining such welfare states increasingly expensive.

As noted above, many European states were quicker to extend civil and social rights than political rights to resident aliens. European states were willing to extend social rights to young temporary migrant workers who, it was assumed, would not remain long enough to collect their pensions and health care benefits in old age. Now, as the number of permanent resident aliens grows rapidly, and these resident aliens come to include children and the elderly in addition to young productive workers, the acceptance of the extension of social rights as a fundamental principle runs headlong into fiscal constraints. Practically speaking, if citizenship is offered liberally to immigrants as immigration increases, European policymakers are confronted with a set of unattractive choices. They could increase taxes to maintain the level of social services for all residents, citizens and non-citizens alike. They could keep the same level of taxation and maintain the universality of services but decrease their quantity and quality. Finally, policymakers could forsake universality and equality in the delivery of services to all of the country's residents by excluding non-citizens from the social benefits of citizenship. The more social services that are provided on a universal basis to the members of a state, however, the more difficult it becomes to not provide similar social services to legal resident aliens (Hollifield 1992). Moreover, policymakers may wish to deny social services to asylum seekers awaiting decisions on their cases, but since these asylum seekers are legal resident aliens, such actions are constrained by the liberal constitutions and human rights conventions that European states have agreed to.[11] Policymakers are, therefore, caught in a bind between rapidly increasing budgetary outlays for migrants and liberal principles that preempt expulsion or denial of social services.

It has been argued that the extension of civil and social rights to non-nationals has "devalued" state membership itself because migrants can access the goods of citizenship without being born into the nationality of a state or naturalizing to it (Schuck 1989; Soysal 1994; Jacobson 1996). Following this line of argument, if forms of postnational membership mean that possession of a state's nationality is less important, one can question the practical importance of the distinction between the principles of jus soli and jus sanguinis that govern the ascription of nationality. The Marshallian differentiation of citizenship's component categories of civil, political, and social rights illuminates different dimensions within which exclusion and inclusion of resident aliens takes place and enables one to see how resident aliens may be treated according to the principles of jus sanguinis on one dimension, while at the same time being treated according to the principles of jus soli on another. The issue of political rights incumbent in formal state membership, however, ultimately takes precedence. With respect to the extension of civil and social rights to non-nationals, it must be kept in mind that in a democracy the "people" giveth and the "people" can taketh away. Within the bounds of international law, the rights of non-nationals are contingent on the sufferance of the demos, given that even liberal constitutions can be changed by the demos. If one is not included in the demos, opportunities to protect one's civil and social rights by political means are marginal. The 1996 Welfare Reform Act passed by the U.S. Congress demonstrates this dynamic well: it excluded legal resident aliens from various forms of public assistance. In the United States, most of those resident aliens have the option of naturalization and during 1996 the number of naturalizations doubled. Were similar legislation to pass in many European states, many resident aliens would be unable to easily attain citizenship due to more restrictive naturalization provisions. Hence, formal state membership and principles upon which it is based can easily become very important as citizenship is "revalued" through legislative action.

Inclusion and exclusion on the different dimensions of civil, social, and political rights are interrelated. For example, increasing costs involved in extending social rights prompt political pressure for restrictive redefinition of nationality laws, which in turn limits the extension of political rights to resident aliens and their children. Hence, the question of extending full citizenship, including political rights, has increasingly come to depend on the question of social rights. Given fiscal constraints, policymakers are left with balancing the social rights of present citizens with the political rights of resident aliens. Serious compromise of either can be viewed as a violation of liberal principles.

The historical development of modern nationality and citizenship laws demonstrates the importance of demographic factors such as migration to political institutions. Differentiation of one nation-state from another depended upon the articulation of norms against statelessness and dual nationality. As states articulated their nationality laws, those states experiencing extensive immigration tended to adopt nationality laws based on the territorial principle of jus soli and those states experiencing significant emigration tended to adopt jus sanguinis. This insight regarding the demographic context of the political institutions becomes useful in understanding contemporary politics.

At the same time that European demography is reverting to polyethnicity, the political institutions and political theories associated with the ideal of the nation-state remain in place. In the context of shrinking populations and increasing immigration, modern European political institutions and liberal theories confront practical problems of inclusion. With increasing polyethnicity and citizenship laws based on ancestral lineage, European societies have developed hierarchical political configurations that conflict with the liberal principles enshrined in the political institutions inherited from the era of high population growth and European emigration. The political institutions of European democratic welfare states that bounded their membership using the rule of jus sanguinis are now challenged by increasing immigration and native population decline. This challenge is not just a matter of policy, because it reaches down to the assumptions upon which the bounding of the demos and the closed membership of the welfare state are based. In turn, these questionable assumptions raise further questions regarding the realization of democracy as well as the legitimization of states by democratic processes.

CHAPTER FIVE

Political Union

*T*he political union of two or more states has been of central concern to international relations and international organization theory (see, e.g., Hinsley 1963; Claude 1964; Jacobson 1984; Suganami 1989). Examples of past political unions have been viewed as models for future unions of states that would transform international anarchy regionally, if not globally, by reducing, if not eliminating, the use of violence to resolve conflicts among those states entering in the union (Deutsch et al. 1957, 5–6). Political unions that came into being before the development of popular sovereignty differ fundamentally from the political union of democratic states with universal suffrage.

The development of popular sovereignty means that principles of citizenship impinge on the political union of democratic states due to the problem of democratic inclusiveness. Just as the demographic context conditioned the development of citizenship and the institutional arrangements of representative democracy, it served as a formative factor in political union. The demographic context of immigration conditioned the development of American democracy within a federal framework, therefore limiting the applicability of the American model to the union of European democratic states whose political institutions developed in the demographic context of emigration.

Democratization and the concomitant extension of citizenship rights fundamentally change the circumstances of political union by raising unprecedented potential conflicts between democratic inclusiveness and federation that previous acts of political union were not subject to. These potential conflicts were avoided by the early American states because the jus soli citizenship rules that they adopted facilitated subsequent political union in 1787, even in the context of extensive intra-federation migration as well as migration to the United States. In contrast, German states maintained jus sanguinis citizenship as they entered into political unions, which in turn based citizenship on jus sanguinis, thereby providing an alternative solution to the political dilemmas posed by intra-federation migration. Consideration of the contemporary EU provides the backdrop for an abstract demonstration of the theoretical conflict between democracy and federalism.

Merging Polities and Political Rights

Before the development of popular sovereignty, the act of political union entailed a merging of jurisdictions over subjects; with popular sovereignty, political union came to involve the merging of entire citizenries and the attending questions of political rights that this merger raised. Before the nineteenth century, the political union of states was often effectuated by personal unions of several sovereigns into one sovereign, usually through the institution of marriage. For example, the 1386 marriage of Jadwiga, the queen of Poland, to Jagiello, the grand duke of Lithuania, established the Polish-Lithuanian Union. Similarly, Spain was formed by the union of Aragon and Castile through the marriage of Isabella and Ferdinand in 1469 and the eventual succession of Ferdinand to the rule of Aragon in 1479. In dynastic unions, the subject inhabitants of the joined territories became subjects of the new sovereign formed through the union.

The extension of political rights to subjects within the context of constitutional monarchy and growing proportions of states' populations with political rights increased the complexities of political union. Not only did political rights in the union have to be addressed, but mutual extension of political rights in the constituent states of the union had to be dealt with as well. As was the case with both the Union of Lublin in 1569 (which transformed the personal union of Poland and Lithuania into the Polish-Lithuanian Commonwealth) and the union of England and Scotland in 1707, the nobility of each country received political rights and served in legislative capacities in the new polities formed by union. Because the Glorious Revolution of 1688 extended political rights to those of less than noble birth, in 1707 seats in the House of Commons were also reserved for Scottish representatives. Nevertheless, the political union of Poland and Lithuania involved perhaps the largest merger of political classes before the nineteenth century, given that the entire Polish-Lithuanian gentry possessed political rights and the gentry composed approximately 10 percent of the population (Jedruch 1982). A comparable proportion of the British population would not gain political rights until after the Reform Act of 1832. The political implications of even this large a merger pale before those of the nineteenth and twentieth centuries. With the move toward universal male suffrage during the nineteenth century and women's suffrage at the beginning of the twentieth century, political union increasingly meant the political merger of entire adult populations.

The political merger of entire populations of democratic states in the formation of a political union raises the question of citizenship and the rights of citizens from one state to be political participants in another. As a case in point, contemporary European political union differs from a federal union of states that defines citizenship by birthplace, as during the founding of the United States, because most EU member states base citizenship on jus sanguinis. Therefore, resident alien EU nationals, as well as their children, are more likely to be denied the political rights of citizenship than if nationality in all member states were based on birthplace. As a 1988 European Commission report noted:

> At present over four million Community citizens are deprived of the right to vote in local elections simply because they are no longer in their Member State of nationality. In a Community of Member States whose basic common characteristic is that they are all democracies, implementation of one of the four fundamental freedoms provided by the Treaty has, by virtue of national legislation, led indirectly to the loss of certain political rights. This paradox in the building of Europe cannot be allowed to continue if the principles underlying the democratic political systems of the Member States are to be respected. (European Commission 1988, 26)

Electoral laws that restrict voting rights to nationals initially give rise to this paradox, but nationality laws based on ancestral lineage perpetuate it.

The paradox noted above by the Commission is symptomatic of a deeper underlying theoretical problem: when there is migration among states entering a federal political union and those states base nationality on ancestral lineage, political union becomes incompatible with inclusive democracy. In other words, given migration and citizenship based on jus sanguinis, democracy and federalism conflict.[1] To illustrate, think of the problems that would arise in the United States if a Maryland couple moved to Pennsylvania and Pennsylvania did not grant "nationality" to them and denied their children born in Pennsylvania the rights of citizenship. Until the Maastricht Treaty went into effect in 1993, this was the case for Italians who were permanent resident aliens in Germany and vice versa.[2]

Even though this conflict among inclusive democracy, jus sanguinis, and federalism has always existed in theory, the conflict has not been addressed in general federal theory.[3] This omission is primarily due to the powerful example of the invention of modern federalism with the complementary development of democracy in the United States. The American experience inspired theorists to view democracy and federation as basically compatible (Kant 1970; Saint-Simon [1814] 1952; Tocqueville 1969; Mazzini 1864, 275; Friedrich 1968a; Duchacek 1986, 96–97). American exceptionalism, this time in its form of citizenship, was not taken into sufficient account in the process of theoretical generalization. While the propensity of migration to produce a discontinuity between demos and democracy was overcome in the development of the American, German, and Swiss federations due to the varying ways in which citizenship was institutionalized, the theoretical conflict between democracy and federalism raised by migration has remained latent in European political union.

Migration, Citizenship, and the American Federation

In contrast to the contemporary dilemmas raised by migration for European political union, America's highly mobile population did not present problems to the preservation of inclusive democracy in a federation because the states based citizenship on jus soli. One may argue that comparison between the United States and the EU is unfair because America is more culturally homogenous than Europe and the United States is a federation while the EU can at best be characterized as a *sui generis* polity between confederation and federation. This rebuttal does not hold because, first, it is not that clear whether colonial Americans had as homogenous a culture as is often assumed. Second, and more important to my argument, people who moved from one state to the other had full political rights before the U.S. Constitution was ratified. Of course, this excludes blacks, Native Americans, women, and the unpropertied. Nevertheless, the political practice of including inhabitants of other states into each state's polity increased a dimension of inclusiveness that avoided destabilizing conflicts among those who legitimately wielded political power according to the standards of the time—white, propertied males.

Although the Americans eventually accepted one another and freely extended citizenship to "foreigners" from other states, this outcome was not foreordained due to the homogeneity of the population. Rather, this fortuitous outcome rests more on the combination of English common law tradition, indigenous democratic practice that lasted more than a century, and the practicalities of extensive migration both from Europe to America and from the east coast of America to the frontier.

With respect to the assumption of colonial America's cultural homogeneity, David Fischer points out that four regional cultures developed as the result of four different migrations from various regions of Great Britain. Puritans came from East Anglia to New England (1629–41), Anglican Cavaliers and indentured servants from the south of England to Virginia (1642–75), and the Quakers from the north Midlands to the Delaware Valley (1675–1725); the predominantly Presbyterian northern Irish and lowland Scots as well as Anglican north-country English migrated to the Appalachian back country (1717–75). In addition the Dutch had previously settled the Hudson River Valley, and one-third of Pennsylvania's population was German by 1790 (Schwartz 1987, 1). Based on voluminous and meticulous documentation, Fisher makes the argument that at the time "cultural differences between American regions [were] greater in some ways than those between European nations" (Fischer 1989, 783).

After the Americans defeated the British, it was not at all clear whether conflict among them would break out and preempt any further movement to political union (Jensen 1962; Onuf 1983). With respect to the potential for religious persecution and political conflict among regions, one must pause to consider the fact that the Puritans and Cavaliers had been on opposite sides of a war in the home country. Fischer describes the animosities among regional cultures and notes that violence broke out as well:

> Fighting broke out repeatedly between Puritans and Quakers in Central New Jersey. The inhabitants of the Delaware Valley and the people of Chesapeake region met in armed combat along what is now the Mason-Dixon line. Backsettlers and tidewater folk came to blows in Virginia, North Carolina, South Carolina and Pennsylvania. North Britons fought New Englanders in northeastern Pennsylvania and the Connecticut Valley after the Revolution. (Fischer 1989, 822)

Fischer goes on to say that even more conflict had been avoided by spatial separation. He notes, however, that populations were mixed in the seacoast cities, but in the half-century before the revolution, the urban population fell relative to the rural population and "many rural parts of British America grew more uniform rather than less so" (Fischer 1989, 823).

In this context of religious and cultural diversity, the treatment of migrants from other colonies and, after the revolution, states, could have easily become a flash point for political conflict. This did not happen, mostly because the principle of jus soli citizenship had become well institutionalized in the political practices of the colonists and was retained by the newly emerging states.

According to the principle of jus soli and following electoral practices established in colonial America (Bishop [1893] 1968), property and residence entitled a free man to political rights in the early American states. Naturalization generally involved acquiring property and establishing residence for a specified period. For example, the Pennsylvania Constitution states:

> Every foreigner of good character who comes to settle in this state, having first taken an oath or affirmation of allegiance to the same, may purchase, or by other just means acquire, hold, and transfer land or other real estate; and after one year's residence, shall be deemed a free denizen thereof, and entitled to all the rights of a natural born subject of this state, except that he shall not be capable of being elected a representative until two years residence. (Pennsylvania 1776, sec. 42)

In 1781, the Articles of Confederation established equal rights for inhabitants of one state in the others:

> The better to secure and perpetuate mutual friendship and intercourse among the people of the different states in this union, the free inhabitants of each of these states, paupers, vagabonds and fugitives from justice excepted, shall be entitled to all privileges and immunities of free citizens in the several states. (Article IV in Solberg 1958, 43)

Jus soli state citizenship and equal treatment according to the Articles had been the rule except in certain less-populated territories over which the claims of states conflicted. For instance, citizenship played a crucial role in the post-revolutionary conflict between north Britons and New Englanders in northeastern Pennsylvania. The principle of jus soli governing Pennsylvania's naturalization laws was challenged by Connecticut settlers sponsored by the Susquehannah Company who moved to the Wyoming Valley in order to effectuate Connecticut's challenge to Pennsylvania's territorial claims. Maintaining their allegiance to Connecticut as expressed in their Connecticut citizenship, many settlers were not permitted to participate in local elections, partly because they refused to take Pennsylvania's oath of allegiance. Eventually, many did take the oath and their participation in Pennsylvania's general election further established Pennsylvania's jurisdiction over the territory in question (Onuf 1983, 49–73). By 1785 the decrease of wartime suspicions and resolution of conflicting territorial claims enabled jus soli to become well established as the principle governing ascription of citizenship and naturalization of citizens from other states (Onuf 1983, 64).

The establishment of jus soli in the states preempted problems at the Constitutional Convention in Philadelphia in 1787. Citizenship based on jus soli effectively eliminated problems of maintaining democratic inclusiveness while establishing a federation with a highly mobile population.

Migration, Citizenship, and the German Federation

While American states based citizenship on birthplace before federation, the principle of ancestral lineage informed the delineation of citizenship in the towns within the German states and the German states themselves, as well as in the federation formed by these states. Germanic federation demonstrates that states with jus sanguinis citizenship can enter into a successful political union. The combination of intra-union migration and jus sanguinis citizenship, however, creates problems for political unions. Jus sanguinis citizenship at the union level is part and parcel of one solution to these problems.

The exclusivity of local citizenship inhibited political integration of the individual German states and, similarly, exclusive state membership of the German states created difficulties for their federation that the American founders managed to avoid. To understand the role of citizenship in the unification of Germany in 1871, one must examine the development of citizenship in the towns of the Holy Roman Empire and the struggle between the German states and towns over citizenship during the early nineteenth century.

According to international relations scholars, the 1648 Peace of Westphalia marks the beginning of the modern international system with the solution of mutual recognition of the sovereignty of states and states' acceptance of the principle of *cujus region ejus religio,* whereby states would become either Catholic or Protestant as their inhabitants took on the religion of their rulers. While the Peace of Westphalia laid the basis for the European state system, it also served as the constitution of the *Heiliges Roemisches Reich der deutschen Nation* (Holy Roman Empire of the German Nation), upon which the larger European system rested (Walker 1971, 13). As an agreement to institutionalize the German status quo, the Peace of Westphalia involved not only a balance of power among the German princes, but also a certain balance between the princes and the towns within their territories. That is, the Peace institutionalized the particularistic and non-centralized nature of the German polity that would become the basis of German federalism.

The particularism and non-centralization of the German polity stemmed from the system of rule that emerged in the thirteenth century known as the *Ständestaat,* or "the polity of the Estates" (Poggi 1978, 36). With respect to Germany, the development of many medium-sized towns, smaller than the great commercial centers of Venice and Florence and the capital cities of Paris and London yet larger than agricultural villages, was critical to the formation of the German polity. Over the centuries these towns had secured immunities from territorial rulers over a wide variety of matters, particularly those connected with commercial and productive pursuits. These were rights that were corporate in nature, meaning that they applied only to individuals inasmuch as these individuals were members of communities. In this way the towns carved out a sphere of self-government that was based on the unit of a cohesive community.

The combination of the corporate nature of town rights and requisites of self-government necessitated a delineation of membership. During the early stages of the growth of the towns in the eleventh and twelfth centuries, the rule *Stadtluft macht frei* meant that rural immigrants who lived in the towns for a year and a day became free men. This rule would seem to imply that membership in the subsequent town communities would be based on residence, but it did not. Although the towns received rural migrants to sustain their populations, these migrants did not necessarily become members of the corporate community. As the townsmen gradually came to rule themselves within the context of the *Ständestaat* that had become prevalent by the thirteenth century, membership involved increasing participation and obligations and became ever more exclusive as a result.

Whereas absolutist rule developed in France, Spain, and Prussia in the seventeenth and eighteenth centuries, the political fragmentation of the Holy Roman Empire enabled towns to retain a high degree of autonomy in much of Germany well into the nineteenth century. Since that autonomy was primarily centered on economic activity, membership in the community was largely a function of guild membership. It was generally quite difficult for children of members of one occupational guild to become members of another due to higher membership fees. It was even more difficult and expensive for someone who was not of any of a town's guilds to become a member. Only after becoming a member of a guild, attaining the age of majority, and gaining the assent of the community did one receive citizenship rights. Moreover, someone marrying an outsider or entering certain occupations, such as the army or the civil service, could lose community membership. Walker notes:

> The community was a *Bürgergemeinde* of citizens, not an *Einwohnergemeinde* of inhabitants. Simply living in the town space did not confer membership rights. Often outsiders were forbidden to own immovable property in the town, and citizens were forbidden to sell such property to non-citizens (or even rent living quarters to them without special permission), so that physical property itself, while not held in common, had a strong communal cast. (Walker 1971, 140)

The bearing of migration on citizenship in the towns was not just a matter of excluding outsiders who moved into the towns but also one of retaining existing members. Due to the value placed on participatory membership by the community (and the future taxes a citizen would pay), the costs involved in renouncing citizenship were high. Emigration taxes were about 10 percent of the citizen's property (Walker 1971, 140). Also, in the pre-1750 demographic context of low population growth and the constant threat to urban population presented by epidemics, communities could hardly afford to lose skilled and wealthy members. Hence, urban communities exhibited a somewhat mercantilist position on the question of migration. Community rules encouraged skilled members to stay while enabling outsiders with sufficient wealth and skills to reside in the town as "tolerated residents" (Walker 1971, 29). Given that citizenship signified corporate membership, it was both hard to attain and hard to lose.

In contrast to the towns in which citizenship was neither a function of residence nor just birth in the town, territorial rulers claimed as their subjects all those who inhabited and were born in their realms. Hence, citizenship in German towns came to be governed by the principle of ancestral lineage while subject status in German states came to be governed by the principle of birthplace. The autonomy of town communities over economic organization combined with the restrictive delineation of membership in these autonomous communities conflicted with the prerogatives of the territorial ruler whose laws were ostensibly to have direct effect on and be uniformly applied to all subjects. This conflict became evident as territorial rulers sought to effectuate freedom of movement within their realms while towns resisted state encroachment on the control of their borders as well as on their right to exclude the non-citizen poor from municipal relief.

In the process of effectuating internal free movement, states more clearly delineated who belonged to the state itself so as to differentiate internal from interstate migration. If, in an effort to coordinate membership and poor relief in all of the towns in a state the state were to oblige the towns to accept the migrant poor, it had to ensure that only migrant poor from within that state's borders were included. Otherwise, towns in neighboring states could unload their poor on towns whose membership the state had pried open. Hence, effectuating freedom of movement within the state prompted the state to favor measures minimizing interstate migration. In this way states not only established formal state membership but also adopted exclusive citizenship laws that forestalled the dumping of migrant poor from other states (Grawert 1973, 71–77; Brubaker 1990, 145–47).

In the wake of the French Revolution and the collapse of the Holy Roman Empire in 1806, reformers in the German states of the west and southwest abolished guilds and freed peasants from local restrictions on movement. Following the doctrine of popular sovereignty and the French model of a "national" citizenship, reformers devised the category of state citizen (*Staatsbürger*) and applied it to the inhabitants of their state, peasant and burgher alike. Even as the individual German states developed their own state citizenship laws during the early nineteenth century, the state citizenship that developed still excluded fellow Germans (Lee 1980, 28–29; Sheehan 1989, 441–43). Similarly, the 1842 laws on Prussian subject status both delineated formal state membership and based Prussian state membership (*Staatsangehörigkeit*) on the principle of ancestral lineage. In effect, state citizenship and state membership were like local citizenship, just projected up one level. To facilitate freedom of movement among the states, they negotiated bilateral treaties among themselves during the early nineteenth century. "They abolished controls on exit but not entry. Persons had the right to leave any state without obtaining special permission or paying the traditional exit fees, but they could settle elsewhere only if the new state were willing to accept them as a subject" (Brubaker 1990, 147).

Moreover, as the nineteenth century progressed, migration among German states was often a mere step toward emigrating out of Germany, usually to the United States. Although the German states gave up on charging emigrants exit fees, many states did not consider the fact of emigration as being sufficient for loss of citizenship. For that matter, neither was the happenstance of birth abroad. This became somewhat problematic when emigrants naturalized and became United States citizens or had children born as American citizens. These new Americans found themselves possessing two citizenships, which meant two sets of rights as well as obligations, including military obligations. In this way, emigrants from Baden, Bavaria, Hesse, or any other German state would be encouraged to maintain contact with their home state to make it easier for them or their children to return. As discussed above, the basing of citizenship on the principle of lineage in this manner led to increasing cases of dual nationality, which were only reduced by subsequent bilateral treaties whereby German states recognized U.S. naturalization.

The adoption of ancestral lineage at each higher level of the German polity was partly due to an effort to maintain claims on emigrants and connections to their offspring born abroad, partly the expression of ethnonational identity, but also partly the outcome of ancestral lineage governing membership on the lower level. That is, exclusive town citizenship rules led to a struggle between the towns and the states over internal migration, and this struggle was resolved by a uniform state membership that was itself based on ancestral lineage. As states developed exclusive forms of membership, resident aliens from fellow German states were excluded. The liberal solution, embodied in the 1849 constitution, was to conceptualize liberal democracy within the boundaries of a German people.[4] In this way liberals essentially projected the boundaries of community from the local to the national level. Conservatives eventually gave up their predisposition to local particularistic memberships and adopted the nationalism of the liberals in the latter half of the nineteenth century. Once they did so, a "common nationality" governed by the principle of jus sanguinis was adopted in the Reich Constitution of 1871 (Article 3, reprinted in Hucko 1987) and the process of creating a national citizenship unified the German states into one polity. While citizenship in Germany was initially local, particularistic, corporate, and exclusive in nature, it made German unification more difficult than it might have been had citizenship been understood more in terms of a bundle of rights possessed by an individual. Had citizenship been more general and abstract in nature, it would have been easier to extend to foreigners, whether from a neighboring town or a fellow German state.

As the problems raised by migration among towns and among states were central to the institutionalization of citizenship and thereby problematic in political unification, on the state as well as federal level, citizenship and migration were also central to the question of democracy. Althusius conceptualized the self-government of the towns in terms of popular sovereignty, but that sovereignty was embedded in a multilayered corporatist matrix of association in which exclusive citizenship was part and parcel of this conceptualization (Althusius 1964, chap. 9). Inasmuch as one might consider German towns in democratic terms, the demos was a *Gemeinschaft*, or community, rather than a *Gesellschaft*, or society (Tönnies 1887). As Walker notes, "Hometown equality and hometown democracy meant the subjugation of everybody in the community to everybody, to limits set by the whole community" (Walker 1971, 134). Membership rules are critical to the differentiation between this communitarian form of democracy and modern liberal democracy. Migration shaped the membership rules in this community of mutual subjugation, and the issue of free movement provided a dividing line for the differentiation between these types of democracy.

Communitarian democracy of citizen elites governing themselves was sustainable with moderate flows of outsiders concomitant with the demographic context before 1750. From the standpoint of liberal political philosophy, the rapid increase in German population and the increasing flows of poor migrants challenged the exclusivity of the citizenship on which this communitarian democracy was based. Hence, liberal theory justified state intervention in town citizenship and, under the formula of enlightened despotism, the state became the fount of liberalism. From one point of view, the attempt of monarchical states to abridge the rights of towns to define their membership threatened what little democracy that existed in eighteenth-century central Europe. From another point of view, the exclusiveness of the towns was a barrier to the realization of liberal democracy at the state and federal levels. In the context of mass population movements, however, within Germany democrats could only conceptualize a form of membership that was liberal in nature.

In the context of migration, exclusive citizenship and the local communitarian democracy based upon it conflicted with the political integration of a collection of associations into states. Similarly, when the individual German states did manage to gain effective internal sovereignty and institutionalized forms of state membership, adoption of citizenship based on lineage by the states presented a similar challenge to the states' formation of a political union. The solution to this dilemma proved to be a reconceptualization of belonging internally along liberal lines of citizenship as a bundle of rights paired with a reconceptualization of identity that involved projecting the bounds of community to the German people as a whole. The German people were not a territorial category at the time, but in fact included an ever growing diaspora of millions of emigrants. Therefore, this reconceptualization of identity was expressed in the institutionalization of a nationality based on ancestral lineage and codified in the German Nationality Law of 1913.

Migration, Citizenship, and European Federalism

The idea of European unification was first enunciated in a series of peace plans offered by Pierre Dubois, George Podebrad, the Duc de Sully, Emeric

Cruce, William Penn, and the Abbe de Saint Pierre (Hinsley 1963). These early peace plans provided inspiration for modern federalism in that they advocated a European *foedus* (treaty) among European sovereigns that would become the foundation of a European peace. Much as in the case of political unions between two states that took place before the development of popular sovereignty, only the European elites were relevant actors in such schemes. In that a European *foedus* could become the basis for a European political union, the authors of the peace plans envisioned the development of federal political institutions for the representation of the constituent states. While considering the problems involved in representing the states and members of European elites in the federal government, they ignored the problem of merging entire populations because the bulk of European states' inhabitants did not have political rights well into the latter half of the nineteenth century.

As popular sovereignty raised the question of merging populations in the nineteenth century, the American model provided a ready answer to the problems raised and became the basis for general theoretical considerations of international federalism as well as post–World War II visions for European political union. Although these efforts yielded an impressive body of federal theory, traditional theories of European federalism are inadequate for conceptualizing the novel dilemmas of political rights prompted by intra-European migration, and traditional federal models do not easily accommodate the political union of democratic states that base citizenship on ancestral lineage.[5] Federal theorists shared the commonly held assumption that intra-European migration furthers political integration and did not take into account the potential negative consequences of member state nationality for maintaining inclusive democracy in the end state of political union.[6]

The theoretical problem at hand can perhaps best be approached by examining Carl Friedrich's understanding of the relationship between democracy and federalism. Friedrich identified "absolutist democracy" as unrestrained majority rule and acknowledged that it "is incompatible with federalism because it does not permit an effective division of power" (Friedrich 1968a, 197). He credits this incompatibility for part of the opposition to a European federation among radical democrats, but then argues:

> These difficulties can be resolved, if a constitutional democracy, instead of an absolutist one, is taken as the basis of theoretical analysis and of practical operation. All that is required is to recognize that every member of the inclusive political order is part of, that is to say, a citizen of, two communities operating on two levels, the regional and the national (federal). A given group of

persons, A1, A2, A3 . . . , and another group, B1, B2, B3, "belong" not only to community A or B, but also to community AB, which includes them both and is therefore a composite community. The participating decisions of these persons, their "will" in the old-fashioned terminology, shape communal decisions of AB as well as either A or B. The inclusive community as well as the included community being politically organized, democracy, far from clashing with federalism, now is seen to require it whenever a composite community exhibits more than one level of effective communal existence in terms of distinctive values, interests, and beliefs. (Friedrich 1968a, 197)

This argument only holds universally if there is no migration between A and B. For example, if B3 migrates to A, four alternatives exist:[7] B3 is denied citizenship of A and loses citizenship of B by virtue of leaving B; B3 cannot become a citizen of A but retains citizenship of B; B3 becomes a citizen of A and loses citizenship of B; B3 becomes a citizen of A but also retains the citizenship of B.[8]

All four alternatives can occur at the level of A and B within the context of the formation of the composite community AB, but only the third alternative (B3 becomes a citizen of A and loses citizenship of B) enables the formation and functioning of AB to develop as Friedrich describes. For B3 to be able to become a citizen of A, however, the citizenship of A could not be based exclusively on jus sanguinis. At a minimum, naturalization rules in A would have to be governed by the territorial principle with a relatively short period of residency. In the context of migration, Friedrich's argument only holds if citizenship in A and B are based on jus soli with a liberal naturalization policy.

With alternative two (B3 stays in A but cannot become a citizen of A), B3 becomes a permanent resident alien excluded from A's electorate and, thereby, B3's status challenges the inclusiveness of democracy in A.[9] If in addition to basing citizenship on jus sanguinis community A permitted dual nationality, it would not significantly increase democratic inclusiveness because B3 could only take advantage of dual nationality if he or she was a descendant of community A citizens. Only if naturalization is based on the territorial principle and requires just residence, without additional requirements of descent and ethnicity, does the permission to maintain dual nationality increase inclusiveness.

Alternative one (B3 cannot become a citizen of A and loses citizenship of B) would effectively leave B3 "stateless." This situation would challenge the inclusiveness of democracy in A and B.

Alternative four (B3 becomes a citizen of A but also retains the citizenship of B) is as inclusive as alternative three, but only if the migration flow is from B to A. Were A3 to migrate to B when citizenship in B is based on jus sanguinis and citizenship in A on jus soli, A3 could not become a citizen of B. Only when both A and B base citizenship on jus soli can inclusivity be assured.

Alternative four introduces the possibility of multiple membership not only in terms of the individual belonging to both community A and the federal composite community AB, but also at the level of A and B. Given that citizenship is a bundle of civil, political, and social rights and often includes obligations, such as jury duty or compulsory military service, the permutations of multiple membership can vary greatly along these dimensions. Dual nationality (i.e., de jure full citizenship status in both A and B) is at one end of the spectrum of variation. At the other end of the spectrum of variation in multiple membership is reciprocity of rights beyond that customary of international relations, for instance, a set of mutual guarantees against discrimination based on nationality in employment, remuneration, and work conditions (i.e., Articles 7 and 48–49 of the Treaty of Rome). Forms of multiple membership between these extremes include social rights (such as mutual provision of social security, health benefits, and transferable pensions) as well as political rights (such as permitting one another's citizens to vote and run in labor union elections and the partial inclusion of one another's citizens in the electorate). Just as there is great variety in the forms of dual membership, the practical consequences of dual membership for political integration can also vary.

Although political union is a long-standing institution going back to the dynastic marriages that formed the Polish-Lithuanian Commonwealth as well as Spain, democratization and the concomitant development of modern citizenship as membership in the state transformed political union into an act of political merger of entire populations. The migration of citizens of one of the merging political units to the other raises challenges to the maintenance of democratic inclusiveness in the process of federation. By virtue of their uniform jus soli citizenship laws, the American states managed to avoid a latent theoretical dilemma that member states of the EU face due to the prevalence of jus sanguinis citizenship in Europe.

With no migration, citizenship based on jus sanguinis, inclusive democracy, and federation are compatible because the practical distinction between jus sanguinis and jus soli would dissolve and the entire adult population could vote in all elections. Everyone subject to national and federal laws and policies, as well as decisions of joining and leaving a federal union, would have a say in their making. With large-scale migration, however, a federation of states that base citizenship on jus sanguinis may be possible, but the inclusiveness of these states' democracy or consanguinity of their citizenship or the traditional federal structure would have to be compromised. This dilemma will be explored in more detail through an analysis of EU citizenship.

Part 3

Migration, Citizenship, and the Emerging European Polity

CHAPTER SIX

European Union Citizenship

*T*he political consequences of migration for European integration generally eluded extensive examination until the collapse of the Berlin Wall suddenly made migration an important foreign policy issue. Migration to the EU presents greater challenges of social assimilation and political incorporation than immigration from fellow EU countries and has, rightfully, received more attention by policymakers and scholars alike. If my contention that increasingly polyethnic social structure conflicts with political institutions inherited from a previous demographic context is correct, then theoretical anomalies and practical problems should arise even from the polyethnicity brought about by migration within the EU. I first examine the harder case of intra-EU migration in this chapter before going on to analyze migration to the EU. I argue that migrants from fellow EU member states have rights under EC law and, therefore, the problems raised for liberal theory go beyond domestic political practice and become problems for the international relations between liberal democratic states and the process of political integration of such states.

This political dilemma is illuminated by the Treaty on European Union, which went into effect on November 1, 1993, and included new provisions establishing EU citizenship. By extending partial political rights to resident alien EU nationals (nationals of one member state who reside in another member state), EU citizenship supplements the civil and social rights that were established by the Treaty of Rome and expanded by the Single European Act as well as associated decisions of the European Court of Justice. The extension of civil, social, and partial political rights to resident alien

113

EU nationals demonstrates how EU member states' nationality and citizenship that had previously coincided has been gradually separated. This disaggregation of nationality and citizenship blurs the boundaries of the units of the classical European state system and restructures the European demos in a way that invites unconventional political conflicts that, in turn, illuminate the theoretical incompatibility between inclusive democracy and federation.

EU rules governing migration within the EU constitute an intra-EU migration regime, which impinged on the sovereignty of EU member states and became the basis of EU citizenship. Intra-EU migration fostered legal integration while raising questions regarding political rights of EU nationals. Given that the majority of EU member states based citizenship on jus sanguinis, resident aliens from fellow EU member states were often excluded from the demos in which they lived, even after their residence became permanent. In this way, inclusive democracy, forms of citizenship based on lineage, and European political union conflict. To have all three, there must be a compromise of democratic inclusiveness, or jus sanguinis, or the traditional federal political structure. This conflict has become evident in the compromise solution adopted to mitigate it, namely EU citizenship and its concomitant restructuring of the European demos. As the Amsterdam Treaty reaffirms that EU citizenship should complement but not replace member state nationality, EU citizenship reflects increasing multiple political identification exhibited by Europeans while constituting a novel polity characterized by increasing complexity and political contestation.

Evolution of European Citizenship and the Intra-EU Migration Regime

The evolution of EU citizenship took place in the context of steps toward deeper economic integration and the development of an intra-EU migration regime (Plender 1988a, chap. 6; Evans 1984; Magiera 1991; Meehan 1993, chaps. 3 and 7). In conjunction with the principle of free movement of goods, capital, and services, the Treaty of Rome enunciated the freedom of movement of economic agents. Freedom of movement within the European Community was not conferred on individuals as citizens of member states, but rather as "workers" and recipients of services (Articles 48–59). Subsequent regulations realized the principle of free movement of workers in terms that were generally applicable and binding on the member states. A 1961 regulation enabled workers from one EC member state to take a position in another member state if a suitable worker from that state could not be found within three weeks, a 1964 regulation removed the need to search for local workers and augmented rights of family reunification, and a 1968 regulation stipulated that workers from another member state had "the right to take up available employment in the territory of another Member state with the same priority as a national of that State" (European Commission 1961, 1964, 1968; Boehning 1972, 11–19). The 1986 Single European Act (SEA) enshrined the free movement of persons as one of the core principles of the Single Market. Throughout this entire period, the European Court of Justice rigorously applied prohibitions against discrimination based on nationality and secured the Treaty of Rome's guarantees through decisions on civil and social rights (Johnson and O'Keefe 1994).

The issue of free movement within the European Community spurred the de facto development of European citizenship conceived as a bundle of social and economic rights. Member states, however, were reluctant to consider the elimination of border controls within the framework of European citizenship because such controls were considered more central to state sovereignty than work and residence rights. A 1975 Commission report, "Towards European Citizenship," first called for the elimination of border controls (European Commission 1975). Border controls became the subject of intergovernmental negotiations among justice and interior ministers within the intergovernmental frameworks of European Political Cooperation (EPC), the "Trevi" group created in 1975 by the European Council, and after 1986 an ad hoc group of ministers responsible for immigration within the Trevi framework (den Boer and Walker 1993, 6). The group of ministers examined questions of migration that would arise with the reduction of border controls within the EU. They addressed visa policy coordination, asylum application abuse, and the development of a common external border to complement the relaxation of internal border controls.

Reluctance by the United Kingdom to lift border controls and conflict between the United Kingdom and Spain over Gibraltar, however, sidetracked any agreement. While the prospects for EC-wide cooperation appeared dim, a protest by truck drivers tired of long lines at internal borders prompted France and Germany to lift controls between them. A year later, the Benelux countries (which had lifted border controls among themselves in 1960) joined France and Germany at the town of Schengen in Luxembourg to sign an agreement to allow unimpeded travel and erect common external border controls. Parties to the 1985 Agreement signed a Convention in 1990 to which Italy, Spain, Portugal, Greece, and Austria subsequently joined. As members of the Nordic passport union, Denmark, Sweden, Norway, Finland, and Iceland joined Schengen in 1996, non-EU

Table 3   Resident Aliens in the European Union from Other EU Member States (in thousands)

	1987	1988	1989	1990	1991	1992
Belgium	495	474	446	497	551.5	554.6
Denmark	21	21	22	19	27.6	28.4
Germany	1,437	1,325	1,375	1,417	1,439.1	1,487.0
Greece	12	14	11	14	54.1	61.5
Spain	55	59	57	60	272.9	158.3
France	1,386	1,397	1,360	1,347	1,311.7	1,311.8
Ireland	60	65	62	61	68.5	73.3
Italy	—	—	—	—	149.4	111.2
Luxembourg	88	88	91	98	102.7	114.6
Netherlands	168	174	182	175	168.4	176.1
Portugal	10	12	11	13	28.7	30.0
UK	812	764	803	732	781.0	770.5
Total EU 12	4,544	4,393	4,420	4,433	4,955.6	4,877.3

Source: 1987, 1988, 1989, 1990: Eurostat 1993b, selection 2.2.1.5, statistics for Italy not reported; 1991: Eurostat 1993a; 1992: Eurostat 1994.

member states have been included as well. A year later, the Amsterdam Treaty incorporated the Schengen Convention into the EU treaty framework, while permitting the United Kingdom and Ireland, as island nations, to remain outside.

As the above developments indicate, member state cooperation on intra-EU migration was often driven by spillover from one area of functional cooperation to another. The goal of the free movement of workers in practice entailed member state cooperation on free movement of spouses and dependents. As the criteria for subjects of the principle of free movement expanded, liberal interpretation of these criteria in the adjudication of discrimination cases prompted expansion of the free movement principle to EU nationals in general. Once member states agreed on the objective of realizing the free movement of persons within the Community and defined free movement in terms of a frontierless area, it also prompted cooperation on external border controls. In this way, member state cooperation in labor policy has been linked to cooperation in the very different realms of foreign policy on refugees and policing.

It was widely expected that relaxation of barriers to labor migration within the EU would lead to increased migration, especially with the accession of less developed member states such as Spain, Portugal, and Greece. Contrary to the expectations of the European Commission (1985), the SEA did not greatly increase intra-EU migration (see table 3). The removal of barriers to labor mobility did not increase the migration of industrial workers within the EU, in large measure due to the substitution of intra-EU capital mobility (Molle and Mourik 1988; Straubaar 1988; Werner 1993). It remains to be seen, however, if migration increases within other segments of the EU population as more barriers to movement drop. By separating the right to residence from employment, EU citizenship expands the potential pool of intra-EU migrants beyond that of traditional labor flows. By stipulating mutual recognition of professional credentials, the 1988 General Systems Directive (Orzack 1991) not only enables professionals to work anywhere in the EU, it frees students from career limitations imposed by academic degrees from other countries, and allows professionals nearing retirement to purchase homes abroad yet still practice part time. Also, the "Europeanization" of member state businesses facilitated by the SEA has also led to a restructuring of firms and redeployment of personnel that fosters migration of highly skilled corporate employees (Salt 1992). At this point, however, the overall effect of changes in rules governing intra-EU migration on migration rates has been marginal (Hovy and Zlotnik 1994).

Changing rates of intra-EU migration should not be equated with the strength or weakness of the intra-EU migration regime, because migration rates are not really indicative of state compliance with the regime. The objective of the regime is the elimination of barriers to free movement and the elimination of member state discrimination against EU nationals, not increased intra-EU migration itself. The issue is not the behavior of individuals but rather the behavior of states.

The strength of the intra-EU migration regime could be better assessed by examining member state discrimination against resident aliens from fellow EU member states. The fact that migrant workers from fellow EU member states keep their jobs despite persistent record-setting unemployment rates is testament to the strength of the intra-EU migration regime. Nevertheless, actions directed explicitly at foreign workers from EU member states do occur, and member states have violated the rule of non-discrimination. Such member state actions, however, spur resolution of conflicting policies through either new rounds of harmonization or adjudication by the Court. Not only has adjudication provided a means of gaining member state compliance, the Court has consistently reaffirmed the principle of free movement and rules of non-discrimination (Johnson and O'Keefe 1994).

Given that a frontierless area for free movement of persons was the objective stated in the SEA, the existence of border controls experienced by EU nationals is another good measure of regime compliance on the part of member states. On this front, the EU was not successful in achieving the

SEA's stated goal given that internal border checks were relaxed more than two years later than initially projected and then only among the Schengen countries.

Strictly speaking, it can be argued that the delayed and incomplete removal of border checks indicates a lack of free movement and a retention of sovereignty by member states (Anderson, den Boer, and Miller 1994, 104–6). However, defining free movement in terms of an absence of border checks and defining sovereignty in terms of border control is misleading. For example, automobiles are stopped at the California-Arizona border and checked for contraband fruit and vegetables, and the Pennsylvania State Police routinely stop automobiles crossing from New Jersey that are suspected of bringing in cheap New Jersey booze (Pennsylvania maintains a state monopoly on the sale of wine and liquor). Yet these border checks do not mean that free movement has not been realized within the United States nor that California and Pennsylvania have retained their "sovereignty." A passport check at an internal EU border may slow a properly documented, law-abiding EU national crossing the border; however, it does not stop that person from entering another member state or residing there because he or she has a legal right to do so.

With the Schengen group's acceptance of multinational mobile patrols to conduct internal checks, the nature of unimpeded movement among signatory states has also been significantly redefined. While this can be viewed as another de facto setback in the realization of an "area without internal frontiers," widespread institutionalization of multinational police units represents further functional integration through intersectoral spillover that has important implications for the sovereignty of Schengen states. For example, one could easily imagine a situation in which a Spanish police officer confronting an armed suspect in France has authority to use deadly force against a French citizen. On the one hand, one could argue that such internal checks are practically equivalent to border checks and that member states have in fact retained sovereignty with respect to internal borders. On the other hand, extending jurisdiction and policing powers to other states could easily be viewed as an even greater abdication of sovereignty than removing border checks.

Migration, Citizenship Rights, and Political Integration

Empirically speaking, one might argue that the political significance of resident alien EU nationals is marginal because, at 5.5 million, they constituted only about 1.5 percent of the 369 million total population of the fifteen EU member states in 1993 (Eurostat 1996b). However, this is more than the total population of Luxembourg, Ireland, or Denmark. Moreover, resident aliens from non-EU member states constitute only 3.2 percent of the total population (Eurostat 1996b), yet few political scientists would quibble over the political impact of these migrants. Unless one demonstrates that some threshold exists between 1.5 percent and 3.2 percent of a population at which point political circumstances become significant, one must look beyond the magnitude of migration flows alone.

To begin with, intra-EU migration has played a pivotal role in legal integration and legal integration has been critical to maintaining the movement toward political union. Burley and Mattli point out that integration theorists overlooked the process of legal integration as they focused on economic integration leading to political spillover (Burley and Mattli 1993). It was legal integration, however, that quietly continued after de Gaulle stymied political integration in the 1960s and the oil-shock recession stalled economic integration in the 1970s (Stein 1981; Mancini 1991; Weiler 1991). The landmark *Van Gend en Loos* decision was critical to this process of legal integration because it conferred rights under EC law to member state citizens (ECJ 1963). Individual rights under EC law multiply the political significance of intra-EU migration because, in constitutional terms, the circumstances of resident alien EU nationals take on meanings of a somewhat absolute nature. Denying civil, social, and political rights to five million EU citizens is not "less unconstitutional" than denying rights to fifty million. It only takes discrimination against one individual to bring forward a case that sets a legal precedent.

Even the relatively small movement of people within the EU has prompted decisions in test cases regarding the status and rights of EU member state citizens in other member states. For instance, in the 1985 *Gravier* judgment, the European Court of Justice held that the Belgian policy of charging a French vocational student registration fees that Belgian students did not have to pay constituted discrimination and violated Article 7 of the Treaty of Rome (ECJ 1963). In the 1989 *Cowan* judgment, the Court held that a British citizen who had been assaulted after leaving a French metro station should receive compensation for damages entitled to French citizens because he had received a service and, therefore, for France to deny his case standing because he was not a French citizen would violate the nondiscrimination provisions of Article 7 of the Treaty of Rome (ECJ 1989).

Intra-EU migration facilitates the process of legal integration by creating circumstances leading to legal conflicts between resident aliens and the member states in which they reside. Grievances emerge from these conflicts that enable individuals to evoke EC law for remedy in member state courts. Decisions in cases such as *Gravier* and *Cowan* have not only affirmed certain social and civil rights, they have effectively enabled virtually any citizen of a member state to claim rights through a de facto expansion of the definition of rights bearers under the treaty from "workers" to those receiving services as commonplace as purchasing a metro ticket.

The circumstances of these cases provide *topoi,* or what Cicero called "seats of arguments," that "not only establish 'starting points' for (legal) arguments, but locate the issues of debate in a substantive set of common understandings" (Kratochwil 1989, 214, 219). Moreover, the selection of *topoi* is a means of characterizing an act (e.g., riding the metro is receiving a service). Such characterizations in large measure determine which set of rules (e.g., Article 7 of the Treaty of Rome) should be applied to the case at hand (Kratochwil 1989, 212–48). Essentially, the social and economic interaction of citizens of one member state who are in another member state produce concrete cases that without intra-EU migration would not occur.

Decisions rendered by the Court regarding the status and rights of citizens of one EU member state who are in another proved pivotal in using the Treaty of Rome's provisions for free movement to help transform the treaty into a constitution (Mancini 1991, 186). In a similar manner, the U.S. Supreme Court utilized the Constitution's interstate commerce clause to enforce civil rights and, in the process, strengthened the federal government relative to the states.[1] In general, protection of member state citizens' civil and social rights in other member states has become a vehicle of legal integration (Frowein, Schulhofer, and Shapiro 1986; Garth 1986) that has helped build a legal framework essentially federal in nature (Capelletti, Seccombe, and Weiler 1986; Weiler 1991).

Economic integration not only raised questions about free movement across borders and prompted legal integration, it also entailed citizenship issues that went beyond economic and social rights for those living abroad to include the question of political rights. As increasing numbers of member state nationals took advantage of the right to work and live in fellow member states, a particular kind of democratic deficit emerged. As the Commission pointed out, many resident alien EU nationals were effectively disfranchised by moving. This loss of political rights violated the principle of equality for those member state nationals who availed themselves of the opportunities in other member states made possible by the SEA and was itself a barrier to movement (European Commission 1986). Integration of the European labor market not only led to a loss of political rights, it was also argued that the loss of political rights inhibits the formation of a single European market and, therefore, hinders integration.

The drive for political rights began with the European Parliament's 1960 draft convention on direct elections to the Parliament (van den Berghe 1982; Magiera 1988, 475–80). The draft called for a uniform electoral system across member states that enabled member state nationals to vote and run in elections in the member state in which they resided. The proposal did not garner sufficient support in the Council and progress on political rights was postponed until the 1970s. Member states first considered extending voting rights to EC nationals at the 1974 Paris Summit and instructed the Commission to prepare a report on the subject. The report stated that full political rights at all levels of member state government would be "desirable in the long-term from the point of a European Union" (European Commission 1975, 28). In the meantime, the Commission advocated local voting rights and participation in European Parliamentary elections as an interim solution. Even this limited proposal died. In the first parliamentary election in 1979, some states allowed resident aliens from fellow member states to vote in their place of residence and some states did not. Some provided consular voting facilities for their nationals in other member states, some did not (van den Berghe 1982, 133). The issue of political rights arose again in the context of the relaunching of European integration in the 1980s. Anticipating that the SEA's goal of eliminating barriers to movement would eventually increase international population mobility within the EU, the Commission's Committee on a People's Europe, chaired by Pietro Adonnino, called for expanding political rights for resident aliens in both European Parliament and local elections (European Commission 1985, 1986, 1988). Members of the Council did not act on the Commission's initiative until 1990, when Kohl and Mitterrand led the drive to convene an intergovernmental conference on political union (Belgium 1990). The Spanish government drafted the language on European citizenship (Spain 1991), and EC member states established EU Citizenship within the Treaty on European Union signed at Maastricht.

The Maastricht Treaty and the Dimensions of EU Citizenship

Written as a separate part of the Treaty (Part 2, Articles 8–8e), EU citizenship entitles every national of a member state to citizenship of the European Union. This citizenship provides the right to move and reside within the Union, the right to vote and stand for election in local and European Parliament elections in the citizen's place of residence, the right to diplomatic and consular protection of fellow member states in countries in which the citizen's member state is not represented, and the right to petition the European Parliament and the right to register complaints to Community institutions (except the Court) with an ombudsman. With its provision of local and European parliamentary voting rights, EU citizenship decreases, but does not eliminate, a particular form of the "democratic deficit" resulting from the combination of migration and jus sanguinis citizenship.

The Maastricht Treaty stipulated that detailed arrangements for European Parliament elections were to be adopted by the Council before December 31, 1993, and arrangements for local voting rights by December 31, 1994. With a Council directive issued shortly after the Maastricht Treaty went into effect in November 1993, resident aliens from fellow member states were able to vote in the June 1994 European elections in their member state of residence (European Commission 1993). The December 1994 Council directive on local voting rights, which included a controversial derogation for Belgium, began the process of realizing local voting rights for resident aliens from fellow member states through transposing the directive into member state law (European Commission 1994b). As of January, 1, 1997, only eight member states had fully done so and the Commission decided to take action against France, Greece, Belgium, Spain, Sweden, Austria, and Finland. (Austria and Finland have partially implemented the directive and all foreign residents have been able to vote in Swedish local elections.) Participation of non-national EU citizens in European parliamentary elections was low, with an average turnout of 11.81 percent, and only one non-national candidate, a Dutch citizen named Wilmya Zimmermann, was elected in her member state of residence, Germany. Non-national EU citizens have participated in local elections in Luxembourg, Italy, Germany, Austria, Finland, and the United Kingdom. At this point, assessing participation in local elections is difficult because turnout rates are incomplete and not systematically gathered, but in Bavarian elections non-national voter turnout was between 21 and 25 percent and in Vienna it was 35.5 percent (European Commission 1997a). Low participation has primarily been attributed to the fact that EU citizens lacked knowledge of their political rights at the time (*Eurobarometer* 1994).

Maastricht also extended the right of diplomatic and consular protection to nationals of one member state from any of the fourteen other member states when traveling or residing in a third country in which their member state is not represented (European Commission 1995a). This represented a clear break with the traditional convergence of nationality and citizenship (O'Leary 1995, 523). The EU's extension of a right of citizenship impinges on traditional member state obligations in terms of extraterritorial protection. As the practice of reciprocal protection among EU member states becomes established, it reduces the need for member states to open new consulates in states in which other member states already have consulates. It also increases the incentives for states with dwindling foreign ministry budgets to close consulates in more peripheral areas, because their nationals will still be protected by fellow EU member states. If member states do reduce their overall diplomatic presence around the world, it would decrease the number of classic signifiers of sovereign statehood maintained by member states and, at the same time, increase the practical importance of EU citizenship in the lives of member state nationals.

For some, Maastricht's citizenship provisions do not go far enough. Hans Ulrich Jessurun d'Oliveria, for example, called EU citizenship "nearly exclusively a symbolic plaything without substantive content" and argued that Maastricht added little "to the existing status of nationals of Member States" (d'Oliveria 1995, 82–83). The Commission essentially concurred with d'Oliveria (although in more diplomatic language). It concluded its 1995 assessment of EU citizenship by noting that it had "immense potential" but had not yet lived up to expectations, mainly as evidenced by slow progress toward the abolition of border controls (European Commission 1995b, 21–22).

These criticisms, whatever their particular merits, deflect attention from the historical shift represented by the creation of EU citizenship. The extension of civil and social rights within the EU, and even partial political rights to resident aliens from fellow member states, demonstrates a gradual separation of nationality status and citizenship rights—categories that had previously coincided. This growing disjunction between nationality and citizenship blurs the boundaries of European nation-states and is indicative of a transformation of Europe into a new form of political organization.

Citizenship, Legitimacy, and Identity

The establishment of Union citizenship has been central to the Commission's efforts to build up the EU's legitimacy. The purpose of Union citizenship, it argued, was to "deepen European citizens' sense of belonging to the European Union and make that sense more tangible by conferring on them the rights associated with it" (European Commission 1995b, 21). To what extent has European citizenship successfully addressed the legitimacy issue? If legitimacy is conceived in normative terms as the presence of democratic and representative institutions, that impact has been rather limited. To the extent that EU citizenship extends the political rights of EU nationals living in fellow member states and allows them to participate in European Parliament elections, it addresses the EU's democratic deficit. Given their modest numbers and the still circumscribed competencies of the European Parliament, the impact of EU citizenship on democratic legitimation should not be overestimated. If legitimacy is conceived not just in terms of representation, however, but also in terms of recognition—as support for and identification with the EU—the effects of EU citizenship appear more extensive. To the degree that the extension of citizenship leads more Europeans to recognize the EU as a legitimate framework for political contestation, it promotes the legitimation of the integration project.

Assessing the contribution of EU citizenship to legitimacy through opinion polls is fraught with difficulty. Even though many of the rights associated with EU citizenship existed in various forms since the Treaty of Rome, citizenship was only formally established with the Maastricht Treaty. Moreover, many of the provisions of the treaty are not yet fully incorporated into member state law and policies. As a result, many Europeans seem to know little of EU citizenship itself. For example, while 77 percent of EU citizens surveyed in 1996 knew that they had the right to live anywhere in the Union, only 46 percent knew that non-nationals had the right to vote in European Parliament elections in their state of residence and only 38 percent knew that non-nationals had the right to vote in the local elections of their state of residence (*Eurobarometer* 1996b, 92). Furthermore, little systematic study of the influence of EU citizenship on changing attitudes has taken place. However, two kinds of evidence illuminate actual and potential implications of EU citizenship for legitimacy. The first concerns levels of public support for the different dimensions of European citizenship, while the second concerns the compatibility of different kinds of identity, European and national, within the EU.

Public opinion reveals growing support for EU citizenship and each of its dimensions—an indication of its promise as a legitimacy-building strategy. One of the most controversial provisions of EU citizenship concerns the lowering of borders to the free movement of EU citizens. While the free movement provisions of the Maastricht Treaty and the removal of border controls for signatories of the Schengen Convention have compromised a major aspect of member state sovereignty, proponents of European integration argued that free movement within the EU was one of the practical benefits that citizens would experience and anticipated that it would lead to greater popular support for integration. Public opinions taken shortly after the implementation of the Schengen Convention in March of 1995 were, on balance, negative, with 46 percent considering removal of border controls a "bad thing" and 41 percent calling it a "good thing" (Eurostat 1995a). Within a year, however, only 40 percent thought removing border

Table 4   Popular Support for Extending Rights in Local Elections to Resident Aliens from
Fellow Member States (percentage of sample)

	Fall 1993 (EU 12)	Spring 1994 (EU 12)	December 1994 (EU 12)	Spring 1995 (EU 15)	Fall 1995 (EU 15)	Spring 1996 (EU 15)
Right to vote	47	53	56	54	54	56
Right to be a candidate	39	42	46	45	45	n/a

Source: *Eurobarometer* 1995a, 75 (released spring 1995; includes figures for fall 1993 and spring 1994); *Eurobarometer* 1995b, 36 (released autumn 1995); *Eurobarometer* 1996a, 71 (released April 1996); *Eurobarometer* 1996b (released December 1996).

controls was a bad thing and 43 percent considered it a good thing (Eurostat 1996c). When EU citizens were asked in an April–May 1996 survey if they thought it was important to be able to travel anywhere in the EU without border formalities, 74 percent said it was important and 19 percent said in was unimportant (*Eurobarometer* 1996b, 93).

A similar pattern of growing support is evident in the context of voting rights. Although the extension of local voting rights generated some opposition from several member states during the Maastricht ratification debates, opposition faded in years after the treaty took effect. In 1993, only 47 percent of a sample of member state nationals said they were prepared to give local voting rights to nationals of fellow EU member states. In a spring 1996 survey, 56 percent thought it was important that EU citizens from fellow member states have the right to vote in local elections and 30 percent thought it was unimportant (*Eurobarometer* 1996b, 93) (see table 4).

Overall, then, these figures point to growing support for the different dimensions of EU citizenship. Europeans appear increasingly willing to accept a level of citizenship above the level of the nation-state. Moreover, many not only accept EU citizenship but also think that it is necessary. In a 1996 *Eurobarometer* survey, respondents were asked, "Do you think that, to make progress in building Europe, it is necessary to have a European citizenship in addition to your (national) citizenship?" In response, 50 percent said that European citizenship was necessary, 37 percent said it was not necessary, and 14 percent said that they did not know (*Eurobarometer* 1996b, 87).

A parallel pattern is evident at the level of identities. Here, as in the case of citizenship, the national level takes precedence over the European—but both exist side by side. In a 1990 *Eurobarometer* survey, 48 percent of re-

Table 5   Responses to National Identity/European Identity Survey (in percentages)

Q: "In the near future do you see yourself as . . . ?"	Fall 1993 (EU 12)	Fall 1994 (EU 12)	Fall 1995 (EU 15)	Spring 1996 (EU 15)	Spring 1997 (EU 15)	Spring 1998 (EU 15)	Fall 1998 (EU 15)
Nationality only	40	33	40	46	45	44	43
Nationality and European	45	46	46	40	40	41	43
European and nationality	7	10	6	6	6	6	7
European only	4	7	5	5	5	5	4
Do not know	4	4	3	3	4	4	3

Source: Eurobarometer 1995a, appendix 9.5 (includes figures for fall 1993); *Eurobarometer* 1995b, B14; *Eurobarometer* 1996a, B22–23; *Eurobarometer* 1998, 41; *Eurobarometer* 1999, 59.

spondents felt attached to the European Community and 47 percent to Europe as a whole, while 46 percent said they did not feel attached to the EC or Europe as a whole. In contrast, 88 percent felt attached to their country, 87 percent to their region, and 85 percent to their locality. Growing numbers of Europeans have little trouble identifying with Europe, their nation-states, and their subnational regions and localities. Although the coexistence of political identities, one "nested" in the other, appears at first glance to be a new phenomenon, it is perhaps better understood as a return to patterns of political identification characteristic of premodern European polities and premodern polities in general (Ferguson and Mansbach 1996).

The compatibility of European and national identity is also reflected in more recent *Eurobarometer* surveys on the compatibility of different kinds of identity within the EU. In a 1990 *Eurobarometer* survey, 63 percent viewed European identity as compatible with national identity, while only 23 percent thought their national identities would disappear over time (Reif 1993, 138–41). Although the degree of national and European identification has fluctuated, a minority of this sample of Europeans consistently identified themselves as nationals only (between 33 and 46 percent) and a higher proportion (46–56 percent) identified themselves as some combination of national and European identities (see table 5).

Recently, *Eurobarometer* has changed the question to prioritize responses and asked respondents if in the near future they see themselves above all else as citizens of the EU, citizens of their member state, or citizens of their regions, and then asked for second and third preferences. This survey also demonstrates the persuasiveness of multiple identities, including European identity (see table 6). Only 11 percent of respondents did not express a third preference and only 6 percent also failed to specify a second preference. If we assume that those without second and third preferences gave citizen of country as their first preference and that those without a third preference gave citizen of country or citizen of region as their first and second preferences, then at least 89 percent of those asked saw themselves as EU citizens to some degree. There is no clear causal link between EU citizenship and shifting conceptions of identity. It is striking, though, that efforts to construe European and national citizenships as compatible find parallels at the level of identity. EU citizenship constitutes a new layer of political identity alongside existing national ones.

The interplay between citizenship, identity, and legitimacy was also evident amid the struggle over Maastricht ratification. In most of the member states, ratification of the treaty—and its citizenship provisions in particular—occasioned little controversy. An examination of the three states where the ratification battle was most divisive—Denmark, Britain, and France—reveals both the salience of the citizenship issue and some of its implications for legitimacy. In all three states, Maastricht's opponents construed EU citizenship as a threat to national sovereignty and identity. In the British and Danish debates, EU citizenship's symbolic infringement on national sovereignty and identity proved most salient. In France, by contrast, the issue of extending political rights to non-nationals became a highly contentious constitutional issue as well. By giving nationals of one member state who are permanent resident aliens in another the right to vote and run for office in local and European Parliament elections, Maastricht challenged notions of popular sovereignty. It called into question the delineation of the demos that is to be sovereign, traditionally defined in terms of nationality.

British and Danish Euroskeptics seized upon the symbolic implications of European citizenship in their efforts to defeat Maastricht. Perceived

Table 6   Responses to Feelings toward Citizenship Survey (in percentages)

	First Preference	Second Preference	Third Preference
Citizen of EU	16	21	56
Citizen of country	61	32	4
Citizen of region	22	42	30
Do not know	0	6	11

Source: Eurobarometer 1996b, 86.

threats to national identity and British sovereignty figured prominently in
the rebellion of members of the Conservative Party against the government's
efforts to ratify the treaty signed by John Major (Baker, Gamble, and Ludlam 1994). Early in the campaign against Maastricht, Margaret Thatcher
directly linked sovereignty to citizenship in her criticism of the Maastricht
Treaty: "We should cooperate more closely together as nation-states. I don't
think it does anyone any good to try to dissolve twelve countries, twelve
different languages into something called European citizenship. We do it
better [when] confident in our own nationhood, confident in our own parliament, confident in our own nationality" (Reuters 1992b). During the
House of Lords debate on ratification of Maastricht, Thatcher argued that
EU citizenship was unprecedented, created a legal and political entity toward which citizens may shift their loyalties, and gave the EU a fundamental attribute of a sovereign state. "If there is a citizenship, you would all owe
a duty of allegiance to the new Union. What else is citizenship about? There
will be a duty to uphold its laws. What will happen if the allegiance to the
Union comes into conflict with the allegiance to our own country? How
would the European Court find them? The Maastricht Treaty gives this new
European Union all the attributes of a sovereign state" (Thatcher 1993,
564). The first vote in the House of Lords on Maastricht was on an amendment to remove aspects of EU citizenship from the ratification bill. As the
government beat back the Euro-rebels by a vote of 242 to 248, it became
clear that their last stand would fail (Herald 1993). The House of Lords
motion for a referendum on ratification was defeated by a majority of 269,
clearing the way for the Maastricht bill to become law in July 1993.

Much of the Danish electorate echoed Thatcher's assessment; opposition
to EU citizenship proved one of the main reasons that most Danes voted
against ratification in the first referendum in May 1992. Ironically, Denmark had already extended local voting rights to resident aliens from fellow member states as well as non-member states. Moreover, the Danish
government had been among the strongest supporters of efforts to introduce European citizenship into the Maastricht Treaty (Denmark 1990).
During the ratification debate, however, many Danes apparently viewed EU
citizenship as a replacement for Danish citizenship, while others simply
considered it an affront to national sovereignty, which grated against the
Danish sense of national identity. In response to the referendum, the other
eleven member state governments addressed the concerns of the Danish
government at the Edinburgh Summit and agreed to opt-outs for Denmark
on monetary union and common defense policy as well as to recognize
a Danish "Unilateral Declaration on Citizenship of the Union." Although
Denmark accepted voting rights for nationals of other member states in Eu-

ropean Parliament and local elections (which they already had), the Declaration states:

> Citizenship of the Union is a political and legal concept which is entirely different from the concept of citizenship within the meaning of the Constitution of the Kingdom of Denmark and of the Danish legal system. Nothing in the Treaty on European Union implies or foresees an undertaking to create a citizenship of the Union in the sense of citizenship of a nation-state. The question of Denmark participating in any such development does, therefore, not arise. (European Council 1992, Annex 3)

Only after receiving the opt-outs and recognition of the Danish interpretation of EU citizenship at Edinburgh did the Danish government submit the treaty to a second referendum in which it was ratified.

The symbolism of EU citizenship also played a key role in the French referendum debate. During the campaign leading up to the September 1992 vote, some resident aliens in France voiced their demands for political rights, while French center-right and right-wing parties opposed extension of voting rights as a threat to French sovereignty and identity. Prompted by the interpretations of anti-Maastricht politicians, many came to associate EU citizenship's reduction of barriers to free movement with migration of undesirables rather than professionals, students, and retirees (Buchan 1992; Laxer 1992). Michel Poniatowski, interior minister from 1974 to 1977 and a close associate of Valery Giscard d'Estaing, warned of "a free market in immigration, drugs and crime" (Criddle 1993, 232). A National Front candidate even argued against EU citizenship by calling attention to the threat posed by the British who had moved to France's Dordogne region, one of the most contested regions during the Hundred Years' War (Pfaff 1992). While the Maastricht referendum passed by a slim margin, exit polls listed "loss of French sovereignty" as the number one reason for voting "no" (Criddle 1993, 238).

In the French case, Maastricht's citizenship provisions also raised sensitive constitutional questions. Since the French Parliament had to approve an amendment to the French Constitution allowing voting rights for resident aliens from fellow member states, EU citizenship became a pivotal issue in the ratification process (Hoffmann 1993, 71). When the Treaty on European Union was signed, the Gaullist Rally for the Republic (RPR) Party's General Secretary Alain Juppe said that EU citizenship was "unacceptable" and that his party would oppose changing the constitution to give non-citizens the vote (Agence France Presse 1991). Another Gaullist, Charles Pasqua, even charged that such constitutional revision meant renouncing sovereignty and amounted to "treason" (Reuters 1992a). The party sponsored an amendment in the senate that denied resident aliens from fellow member states the right to vote, but it was rejected. To avoid an impasse, Socialist Prime Minister Pierre Beregovoy, eager to secure the necessary constitutional changes, endorsed a compromise bill stating that "eligibility and the right to vote *may* be granted to citizens of the Union residing in France" and that "the citizens cannot exercise the function of mayor or deputy mayor, nor take part in the appointment of senatorial electors or the elections of senators" (Agence Europe 1992; emphasis added).

On the face of it, the degree of public controversy surrounding Maastricht ratification in all three states undermines any link between EU citizenship and legitimacy. The controversies demonstrate the potential for EU citizenship to arouse opposition and actually detract from the legitimacy of the integration project. Three points are worth noting, however. First, Maastricht did eventually pass in all three countries. The legitimacy problem did not bring the treaty down. Second, opposition to its citizenship provisions was often based on a misunderstanding of their content. To the extent that Europeans learn about what EU citizenship actually entails, they appear likely to become more supportive of the integration process. Third, the French ratification process demonstrated the successful—if contested— incorporation of EU citizenship provisions into a national constitution. It is difficult to imagine a clearer demonstration of the compatibility of European and national citizenship.

Controversy surrounding European citizenship parallels other areas of EU politics. While Europeans increasingly acknowledge the EU as a framework for politics, they differ over its institutional makeup and appropriate policy competencies. Given the fluid, unfolding nature of the EU polity, such contestation is inevitable. But a focus on conflict obscures broad recognition of—and identification with—the reality of the European polity. In the case of citizenship, Europeans increasingly recognize the existence of political rights in their possession as members of a European political community. Many are ready to embrace a European identity alongside national and subnational ones. As the ratification controversies demonstrated, political conflicts over European citizenship are more about its content than its existence. Those conflicts are bound to continue, but they are not necessarily an indication of an intractable legitimacy problem.

EU Citizenship and the Constitution of a European Polity

While EU citizenship is not analogous to member state nationality, it nevertheless is an institution that sets out legal relationships that together constitute a novel form of membership in an equally novel form of polity. A quintessential characteristic of a federation is dual state/suprastate citizenship, which makes it fundamentally different from a confederation. In a federation, Kenneth Wheare has argued, "general and regional governments both operate directly upon the people; each citizen is subject to both governments" (Wheare 1964, 2). Drawing on this definition, Richard Nathan (1991) views the European citizenship that developed out of the right of free movement and the direct effect of European legislation a primary reason to consider the EU a federation. However, EU citizenship renders the emerging European polity rather different from the traditional models of federalism followed in the United States or Germany.

Federalism denotes the division of powers between a general government and the governments of the federation's constituent geographical subunits (Wheare 1964, 2; Riker 1964, 11). In the traditional model, each level of government has a different electorate, but the electorate is layered telescopically. Every member of the electorate of a smaller subunit is a member of the larger unit to which it geographically belongs. EU citizenship bounds political units so that the composition of European Parliament and local electorates would vary from the national and regional electorates— depending on the level of intra-EU migration. For example, a German national from Frankfurt living in London for more than five years may vote in elections for the London city council, the Hesse *Landtag,* the German *Bundestag,* and the member of the European Parliament from the London district in which she lives. With zero migration there would be no practical difference politically between traditional federal systems and the EU. With migration, the EU's segmented citizenship constitutes an equally segmented electorate and a much more complex polity.

Some day Europeans may establish a form of EU citizenship that gives full political rights to residents of one EU member state who move to another. The German who moved to London could then also vote for a member of the British Parliament. Hence, the European demos would more closely resemble traditional federal models and its complexity would be reduced.

Although French opposition to local voting rights received much attention due to the razor-thin margin of the French referendum on the Maastricht agreement, it is doubtful that a traditional federal system granting full political rights to migrants from fellow EU member states would currently be much more acceptable to other EU member states. One need only look at Sweden, in this respect the most liberal jus sanguinis European country. Resident aliens are permitted to vote not only in local elections but in regional ones as well. The Swedish Parliament, however, rejected resident alien voting rights in national parliamentary elections (Rath 1990). The absence of full political rights for resident aliens in any EU member state combined with the necessity of unanimity for treaty revisions means that for the foreseeable future, the chances are rather remote for EU constitutional development to follow the traditional model of federalism. If the traditional model of federalism is not on the horizon, EU citizenship's restructuring of the European electorate leads to new forms of inequalities between member state citizens, changes the political dynamics of accession, and complicates any future act of secession.

Although EU citizenship narrows the gap in political rights possessed by a resident alien EU national and the nationals of the member state in which he or she resides, it also introduces new inequalities among resident alien EU nationals across the EU. For example, the new electoral system arising from EU citizenship may provoke problems based on the differences between the EU member states that are unitary democracies (France) and those that are federal (Germany). Resident aliens from France voting in local elections in Germany would participate in setting the agenda and, if part of a majority, rule on issues within the local subunit's jurisdiction. Resident aliens from Germany voting in local elections in France, however, even if part of a majority, would have relatively less power because local governments primarily implement national laws rather than craft laws to implement policies originating at the local level.[2]

A similar difference arises between electoral systems utilizing proportional representation (e.g., Spain) and first-past-the-post (e.g., Great Britain). With proportional representation, minorities have a greater chance of electing their representatives (or representatives sensitive to their particular concerns) and minority parties have greater access to power within governing coalitions than with first-past-the-post systems. Therefore, the 86,100 British resident aliens in Spain would have a greater potential for articulating their particular interests and attaining political power on the local level than the 29,000 Spanish resident aliens in Great Britain (Eurostat 1993a, 6–7).

The new European citizenship is a form of "deepening" the EU that may preclude some "widening." Granting full EU membership to countries such as Poland, Romania, or Turkey would entail giving the vote in local elections in EU member states to Polish, Romanian, or Turkish resident aliens, whose aspirations for rights (the least of which being the right to stay) have already triggered nationalist reactions in many EU member states. With EU citizenship, accession takes on a new meaning that, in turn, changes the

terms of debate on accepting new members in the domestic politics of current EU member states. EU citizenship would also have ramifications for
the domestic politics of countries aspiring to EU membership. For instance,
if Poland became a member of the EU, resident aliens from Germany would
be able to vote in local Polish elections. By altering the framework of domestic politics regarding accession, within both EU member and applicant
states, EU citizenship changes the dynamics of accession to the EU and,
therefore, also changes the context of EU relations with the rest of Europe.

The potential of member state secession from the EU is more politically
explosive. In a discussion of EU federalism, James Buchanan argues, "There
must also be some explicit acknowledgment, in the contract of establishment, of the rights of citizens in the separate units to secede from union,
upon agreement of some designated supra-majority within the seceding
jurisdiction" (Buchanan 1990, 7). The mechanics of secession, however,
could be bedeviled by EU citizenship due to the question of participation
of resident alien EU nationals. For instance, a majority of a member state's
citizens might vote for secession in a national referendum. In contrast, if all
its "European citizens" (the member state's citizens plus resident alien EU
nationals and their descendants) were allowed to participate in the referendum, a majority vote for secession might not be attainable.

Although the potential for enfranchised residents from fellow EU member states swinging the vote in such a hypothetical referendum may seem
small, one should bear in mind, for instance, the slim margin of victory in
the French referendum on the Maastricht Treaty. With a 69.8 percent turnout, the "yes" vote was 13,172,716 (51.05 percent) and the "no" vote was
12,632,816 (48.95 percent)—a 539,900 vote margin of victory (Criddle
1993, 228). At the time, there were 1,311,700 resident alien EU nationals
in France, or approximately 2.5 percent of the total population (Eurostat
1993a, 6–7).

Hence, the outcome of potential referendums and votes on secession in
the EU could hinge on the definition of citizenship delineating who could
participate, as was the case in 1860–61 when America's southern states se-
ceded and formed the Confederacy. Given that Blacks constituted a high
proportion of the population of southern states (Archdeacon 1983, 25) but
were not citizens, it is questionable whether majorities in favor of secession
would have been attainable in many of the southern states.[3]

In general, a political union of states that bases citizenship on ancestral
lineage may be possible, but the inclusiveness of these states' democracy,
consanguinity of their citizenship, or the traditional federal structure of the
political union would have to be compromised. If jus sanguinis is main-

tained and the national electorates become increasingly exclusive, the legitimacy of democracy can be challenged, with the boundaries of each political subunit being contested and the potential for conflict within the federation increasing. If democratic inclusiveness is maintained by giving up jus sanguinis, the ethnic delineation of political identity must erode as well and new foundations of identity must be developed. Conversely, both jus sanguinis and a large measure of democratic inclusiveness could be maintained if the traditional federal model is abandoned for some alternative form of federal organization. The following three theoretical solutions are ideal types, none of which are meant as descriptions of the current situation in the EU or prescriptions for its future. Rather, these ideal types should be understood as points between which actual European practice lies, and that, together, provide a framework for understanding future developments in European citizenship laws.

Implicit in the initial comparison between the United States and the EU, the American solution would entail uniform adoption of jus soli by all the member states. The status of resident alien would be voluntary on the part of migrants from fellow EU member states. That is, they could easily naturalize in their member state of residence and exercise full political rights at all levels of government. This solution has been the Commission's stated goal, toward which granting local voting rights is a first step.

Since most EU member states base citizenship on jus sanguinis, the American solution would require a realignment of political identity formation across the EU. Even in France, where naturalization is most in keeping with the territorial principle of jus soli, the dynamics of political identity formation would have to change since naturalization would be less a matter of taking on a new national identity and more of a routine procedure of voter registration. If such a reorientation of political identity could be achieved, inclusive democracy could be maintained in a future EU federation. To maintain inclusive democracy in a future EU federation, EU member states that conceive of themselves as not being "immigration countries," such as Germany, could alter this self-conception and the principle of nationality it engenders. Germany's loosening of naturalization rules with the 1990 Foreigners Act and 1999 reforms indicates that a move in the direction of the American solution, however unlikely, is still possible.

If the "non-immigration" EU member states could at least include the citizens of other member states, the solution of European jus sanguinis could develop. This would be analogous to the nineteenth-century solution of German unification. As discussed above, German states essentially based subject status or citizenship on jus sanguinis before unification in 1871 and after unification Germany did so as a whole. The difference between the historical German case and a future form of European jus sanguinis is that the German solution of uniting jus sanguinis states into a jus sanguinis union occurred in the context of net emigration and included more emigrants than it excluded immigrants. The EU will most likely experience net immigration for the foreseeable future so the net effect would be more exclusionary.

Practically speaking, to realize European jus sanguinis EU member states would initially permit dual nationality for citizens of fellow EU member states but not for citizens from non-EU member states. They would treat each other's citizens according to both jus soli and jus sanguinis while treating citizens from non-EU member states according to only jus sanguinis. All those born to nationals of one EU member state would have full citizenship in all of the others. They would vote in their place of residence in all elections, regardless of their member state of birth. All those not descended from nationals of EU member states would be excluded. At the same time, this solution would also require member states that base nationality on birthplace (the United Kingdom, Ireland, and Portugal) to treat migrants from outside of the EU according to jus sanguinis. Otherwise, non-EU migrants could gain access to European citizenship through the jus soli laws of these member states and European jus sanguinis would no longer hold. On the one hand, the potential resistance to such a restriction of citizenship in these member states augers against this option. On the other hand, increasing anti-foreigner sentiment across Europe makes a uniform change in nationality laws in the direction of European jus sanguinis more politically possible than uniform jus soli because it realizes the objective of a European citizenship with full political rights while justifying the exclusion of "non-Europeans."

Finally, jus sanguinis and inclusive democracy may coexist with a different form of federal political organization, for example, non-territorial federalism (Renner 1918) or federalism combined with consociationalism (Althusius 1964; Lijphart 1985; Elazar 1987, 18–26; Taylor 1990). Drawing an analogy from the political structure of the Netherlands, Belgium, and Switzerland in a form of European federalism combined with consociationalism, the European electorate would be divided along ethno-national as well as territorial lines and non-territorial representation would be institutionalized at all levels of the political structure of the EU. For example, in addition to geographically delineated electoral districts, overlapping at-large districts could be constituted for elections to regional legislatures and national parliaments in a way somewhat akin to New Zealand's system for

Maori representation (Lijphart 1984, 18; Roy 1983). Children of resident aliens who were not born into the nationality of their member state of residence due to jus sanguinis laws as well as resident aliens who were not eligible to naturalize could then vote for such at-large representatives.

On the face of it, this solution appears very complex, impractical, and, therefore, unlikely. However, EU member states have demonstrated a willingness to accept the complications inherent in the Maastricht Treaty's compromise version of Union citizenship. Member state toleration of constitutional and political complexity was reaffirmed by the Amsterdam Treaty, which emphasized that "Citizenship of the Union shall complement and not replace national citizenship" (Amsterdam Treaty 1997). Given this tolerance for complexity and given the political challenges involved in changing member state nationality law in order to realize uniform jus soli among EU member states or to achieve a European jus sanguinis, the most likely scenario for the near future may be the continuation of an ad hoc evolution of political union toward some form of European consociationalism. Such European consociationalism is characterized by multiple overlapping demoi, multiple access points of interest articulation at all levels of governance, and an EU citizenship that remains in a permanent state of tension with member state nationality.

This tension may well be sustainable. To imagine its persistence is to imagine the continued evolution of the EU outside established statist categories. Along these lines, Joseph Weiler suggests considering the constitutive dimension of a Union citizenship that separates citizenship from nationality and contemplating it outside of a state-centric constitutionalism. "On this view, the Union belongs to, is composed of, citizens who by definition do not share the same nationality. The substance of membership (and thus of the demos) is in a commitment to the shared values of the Union as expressed in its constituent documents, a commitment, inter alia, to the duties and rights of a civic society covering discrete areas of public life, a commitment to membership in a polity which privileges exactly the opposites of nationalism—those human features which transcend the differences of organic ethno-culturalism" (Weiler 1997, 119). EU citizenship embodies both a type of general European "constitutional patriotism" (Habermas 1992) and the delineation of rights and duties in the discrete jurisdictional spaces allocated between member states and the EU by treaty. Political identification with the values embodied in the EU's constitutional documents represents one potential source of legitimacy, while another source is found in the politically contested practical realization of the rights and duties of citizens within the jurisdictional spaces created.

Rather than conceiving democracy as only possible within nation-states, the emerging European polity can be better thought of as a site for the practice of democracy on several levels by overlapping demoi as constituted by the combination of member state nationality and European citizenship (Koslowski and Wiener 1998). To the extent that Europeans view the EU as a diverse polity with a common democratic foundation, the EU can perhaps dispense with projects to develop a common identity defined in cultural terms—on the model of the nation-state. "On this reading, the conceptualization of a European *demos* should neither be based on real or imaginary trans-European cultural affinities or shared histories, nor on the construction of European 'national' myth of the type which constitutes the identity of the organic nation. The decoupling of nationality and citizenship opens the possibility, instead, of thinking of co-existing multiple *demoi*" (Weiler 1997, 119). While the institutional framework for such coexisting multiple demoi in which to practice democracy may still be inchoate, it is important to remember that democracy originated in city-states; it was only the invention of representation that permitted the practice of democracy in much larger nation-states—the kind of democracy we now consider normal—and it is quite possible that new institutions of transnational democracy are currently developing (Dahl 1994). Much as citizenship was constitutive of the state known to Aristotle and national citizenship was constitutive of democratic nation-states, the emergence of EU citizenship marks the contemporary transformation of democracy in Europe. Even if EU citizenship is not greatly expanding the means of representation associated with the practice of democracy in nation-states, that does not necessarily mean that EU citizenship is not grounding new processes and institutions of democratic legitimation.

The international relations theorist Raymond Aron argued that European states might have been willing to extend economic rights to non-nationals, but political rights were another matter:

> Neither in theory nor in fact do any properly *political* rights—the vote, freedom of speech, freedom to hold office, etc.—now extend beyond the borders of the old states. Perhaps, on the day that a European Assembly is elected by universal suffrage, a Frenchman will be able to be nominated for office in West Germany or a German in France. Yet how many people would avail themselves of such a right? (Aron 1974, 647)

Five years after Aron's article was published, Europeans directly elected the European Parliament; twenty years later, Germans living in France voted for members of the European Parliament from the French delegation and, something Aron did not foresee, Germans living in France are voting in local French elections. Aron considered this kind of multiple citizenship a "contradiction in terms" that is incommensurate with the logic of the state system. From his perspective, given the institutions of the nation-state and the state system, multiple citizenship should not exist and when it does exist, it is unsustainable. But if one accepts the reality of such multiple citizenship, it becomes clear that it is the system of nation-states that is changing in Europe.

EU citizenship is constitutive of the emerging European polity. EU citizenship decreases a particular form of the "democratic deficit," but it does not eliminate it. The extension of voting rights in local and European Parliamentary elections has been viewed by the European Commission as a step toward full political rights for resident alien EU nationals. Should full political rights be extended to resident alien EU nationals and the bundle of citizenship rights of resident alien EU nationals equal that of member state nationals, then even while some member states would continue basing nationality on jus sanguinis, they would grant citizenship to resident alien EU nationals according to jus soli. Such an action would constitute de facto, if not de jure, change in the nationality laws of member states. Because EU citizenship complements rather than replaces member state nationality, it renders the European polity and its form of political membership unique.

In practice, EU citizenship has encouraged the articulation of compatible identities within Europe and become the object of growing societal acceptance. Not only does EU citizenship provide an institutional object of identification at the European level, but the acceptance of a form of multiple state membership by EU member states legitimates the expression of multiple identities possessed by individual nationals of those member states. In a sense, then, the incomplete and fragmented European citizenship criticized by the Commission is simply a reflection of the fragmented identities of European citizens who do not accept political identification as an either/or proposition. Popular toleration of such complexity—of a new relationship between nationality and citizenship—reflects a broad recognition and acceptance of the EU as an evolving polity without precedent that stretches the conceptual categories of international politics, comparative politics, and political theory.

CHAPTER SEVEN

Dual Nationality

Growing numbers of dual nationals that make up expanding border-spanning diasporic communities are anomalies in the system of nation-states that challenge assumptions of the convergence of political identity, territory, and sovereignty as well as the state-centric worldview that is built upon that convergence. Dual nationality has significant practical consequences for individuals, given that dual nationals may take advantage of the resulting conflicts of laws between states or suffer the consequences. Dual nationality often gives individuals full access to two labor markets, complete property rights that are often reserved for nationals, and certain tax shelters; however, it also raises the potential of double income or inheritance taxes. Extending the political rights of citizenship to emigrants abroad or permitting newly naturalized immigrants to keep their first nationality may strengthen ties to the homeland polity or facilitate immigrant political incorporation. At the same time, the resulting dual nationality may also raise the dilemmas of double voting and multiple political loyalties. Individuals with two passports may find international travel easier; however, dual nationals may also have multiple military obligations and risk being drafted on trips to their ancestral homeland. In facing these practical problems, jurists have traditionally argued against dual nationality.[1] Most states do not, in principle, endorse dual nationality and, as discussed above, some states have entered into multilateral agreements aimed at international cooperation on naturalization and expatriation policies in order to minimize dual nationality.

In the post–World War II era, international cooperation to reduce dual nationality by treaty continued in the United Nations;[2] however, codification of international norms against dual nationality increasingly centered on regional efforts, most extensively in Europe. According to the 1963 Council of Europe's Convention on the Reduction of Cases of Multiple Nationality (Council of Europe 1963) a national of one participating state who gains the nationality of another should lose his or her previous nationality and an individual with nationalities of two participating states should be able to renounce one state's nationality. France, Austria, Denmark, Germany, Italy, Norway, Luxembourg, Sweden, and the Netherlands ratified the Convention while the United Kingdom, Ireland, and Spain agreed only to Chapter 2 of the Convention, "Military Obligations in Cases of Multiple Nationality."

The development of a set of international legal norms against dual nationality over the past century helped delineate which parts of the world's population belonged to which states—in effect, they grounded a demographic boundary maintenance regime. More and more states, however, are changing their laws to explicitly permit dual nationality, newly formed states are adopting the principle into their nationality laws, and other states whose laws ostensibly forbid dual nationality often tolerate it in practice. For the most part, domestic politics rather than the international environment is driving these changing state practices that have undermined the demographic boundary maintenance regime and led to growing numbers of dual nationals. The phenomenon of dual nationality challenges traditional notions of political identity, and increasing cases of dual nationality challenge basic assumptions of the classical European state system.

Understanding Changing State Practices

Thomas Franck has interpreted changing state practices to tolerate, if not embrace, dual nationality in terms of the emergence of a "new personal right to compose one's identity" in which "self-determination evolves from a plural to a singular entitlement, from a right of peoples to one of *persons*." He argues that loyalty has become more a matter of personal choice and "enlightened legal systems" are increasingly permitting it (Franck 1996, 359–60, abstract). While this is a very good first cut at explaining the phenomena, its subtext is the triumph of liberalism—with the expansion of personal rights recognized by increasing numbers of enlightened legal systems. This depiction is somewhat problematic because the norms against dual nationality were in large measure the outcome of, first, a compromise between American liberals and conservative German nationalists to coordinate their nationality laws so as to reduce the numbers of dual nationals and, then, the codification of international law to minimize conflicts between states over their nationals that embodied the liberal ideal of rule of law in the international realm.[3] In the nineteenth and most of the twentieth century, the political actions of liberals produced norms against dual nationality; at the end of the twentieth century, the liberal position is increasing in favor of permitting dual nationality. The liberal embrace of dual nationality perhaps says more about the evolution of liberalism than the spread of liberalism means for states' embrace of dual nationality.

A very different way of explaining these changing norms and state practices is to understand them in terms of the formation of a "security community" (Deutsch et al. 1957). That is, due to the development of postwar European integration, North Atlantic security structures, and now with the end of the Cold War, their extension to the east, there is a decreased probability of war within Europe and North America. Therefore, the probability of multiple loyalties being put to the test in war has decreased, and the problem of dual nationality lessened. Moreover, since the end of the Cold War several states are considering, or have announced, that they are abandoning conscription in favor of all-volunteer military forces, thereby reducing the instances of multiple military obligations. The permissive context of a security community provides additional insight into understanding these changes, but a security driven explanation is insufficient in and of itself. Most of those states that have relaxed their prohibitions on dual nationality have done so for nationals of all states, not just those from states within the security community. Indeed, French practice negates this security community thesis. France as a party to the 1963 Council of Europe Convention and, in accordance with its treaty commitments, does not permit dual nationality for nationals from the other signatory states (who are all members of NATO and/or the EU). However, France does permit dual nationality to nationals from all other states (Council of Europe 1995, 47).

If spreading liberalism or decreasing security threats do not sufficiently explain changing state practices and international norms on dual nationality, then what does? Unfortunately, international relations scholars must enter the messy realm of domestic politics to understand these changes, and there are at least four domestic political factors contributing to changing state practices, depending on the state concerned.

A major factor for increasing cases of dual nationality is the postwar rise of women's movements (Hammar 1985). In the development of nationality law in the nineteenth and early twentieth centuries, states that followed the principle of jus sanguinis generally followed the additional practice of paterlineal ascription. That is, legitimate children received the father's nationality and illegitimate children received the mother's nationality. This practice reduced the number of dual nationals because the child of a marriage between nationals of two jus sanguinis states would then have the father's nationality and, if born out of wed-lock, the mother's—but not both. Essentially, the pervasiveness of paterlineal ascription yielded an informal coordination game among states. This informal coordination was effectively sanctioned by the 1930 Hague Convention on Nationality, given that attempts to institutionalize a principle of gender equality in nationality laws failed (Brown Scott 1931). Nevertheless, in response to widening women's suffrage and subsequent movements for equal treatment of women under the law, many states gradually abandoned paterlineal ascription in favor of gender equality in the transmission of nationality to children. The more states that ascribe their nationality to children of mixed marriages, regardless of the citizen parent's gender, the greater the possibilities that children of mixed marriages will be born with dual nationality. Although the struggle for women's equality can be viewed as a chapter in the triumph of liberal ideology, the actual increase in cases of dual nationality arising from mixed marriages was not a matter of the state's acceptance of the individual's right to choose dual nationality because the ascription of nationality is not a matter of choice. Rather, the increase in dual nationality in such circumstances is the unintentional outcome of declining informal international coordination of nationality laws.

The second domestic political factor is primarily operative in migrant-sending states such as Colombia, the Dominican Republic, Ecuador, Turkey, Italy, and Mexico. Most of these sending states recently changed their policies to permit emigrants to maintain their nationality after naturalizing to another state, in large measure due to the lobbying of emigrants who wish to retire or invest in the homeland and as a means of retaining emigrant identity. In many cases, sending states are permitting dual nationality among their emigrants in the hope that as citizens of host countries, they might form stronger ethnic lobbies that can work to change host country foreign policies in favor of the home states' interests (Dillon 1996; Özdemir 1996). Thus, policy change from singular state loyalty to dual nationality is understandable from the perspective of both emigrants pursuing their interests and a state's desire to achieve its political objectives.

Similarly, historic sending countries of Europe often maintained postcolonial ties by explicit agreements on dual nationality with former colonies or through more informal toleration of the practice. For example, in 1949 the United Kingdom changed its law to permit dual nationality, thereby permitting its nationals to gain the nationality of Canada, Australia, and New Zealand after these former colonies established their own citizenship laws (Goldstein and Piazza 1996, 521). Similarly, between 1958 and 1969 Spain negotiated a series of bilateral agreements permitting dual nationality for nationals of Chile, Peru, Paraguay, Nicaragua, Guatemala, Bolivia, Ecuador, Costa Rica, Honduras, the Dominican Republic, and Argentina (Council of Europe 1997a).

New states emerging from the collapse of the Soviet Union and Yugoslavia also opted to permit dual nationality, if only as a possibility for emigrants and their descendants. As the Soviet Union collapsed, twenty-five million Russians found themselves outside of Russia. Russian politicians quickly championed the cause of Russians in the "near abroad" and ensured that the new Russian citizenship law permitted dual nationality (Council of Europe 1997a, 142). Members of the "Croatian nation" who do not reside in Croatia may acquire Croatian nationality without renouncing their existing nationality, and Slovenia permits dual nationality for Slovenians who naturalize elsewhere (Council of Europe 1997a, 30, 151).

The third domestic political factor is primarily operative in states experiencing net immigration, that is, receiving states. Many receiving states have relaxed their prohibitions on dual nationality to facilitate political incorporation. In 1977, Canada changed its law to explicitly permit dual nationality for immigrants who naturalize as well as for Canadian nationals who naturalized elsewhere. Australia does not require renunciation of previous citizenship for those who naturalize; however, Australians who naturalize elsewhere automatically lose their Australian nationality. The U.S. government officially "discourages" dual nationality but permits it in practice because it is restrained by Supreme Court decisions striking down involuntary expatriation as a violation of the Fourteenth Amendment. Also, naturalized Americans routinely keep their previous nationalities and passports because the renunciation clause of the oath of allegiance is not strictly enforced (Goldstein and Piazza 1996; Spiro 1997). Switzerland stopped requiring renunciation of previous nationality of those who naturalize in 1990 (OECD 1995, 163, 165), and the Netherlands changed its policies in 1991 so as to permit those who naturalize to retain their previous nationalities in certain circumstances (Council of Europe 1996, 22).

A co-related fourth domestic political reason for loosening restrictions on dual nationality is operative in countries that have historically been net migrant-sending states and have recently become net receiving states. Permitting dual nationality among emigrants undermines laws that do not permit it for immigrants. For example, Switzerland's removal of its renunciation requirement was not just a matter of the desire to increase naturalization rates. Switzerland has long maintained a policy that Swiss nationals residing abroad who naturalize in their host state do not lose Swiss nationality. Given that approximately 70 percent of the five hundred thousand Swiss nationals residing abroad maintain dual nationality (*Neue Zuercher Zeitung* 1993), it became difficult for Swiss politicians to argue in principle against dual nationality on the grounds of divided loyalties without alienating a significant constituency (D'Amato 1997).

Changing state practices to permit dual nationality are primarily driven by domestic politics; however, these changes are facilitated by a permissive international security context. Increasing gender equality has probably been most responsible for the growing numbers of dual nationals over the past few decades, although recent changes in expatriation policies by sending states and the elimination of renunciation requirements in receiving states has drastically increased the potential pools of dual nationals.

Erosion of International Norms against Dual Nationality

Although international norms intended to decrease cases of dual nationality had been most fully developed within the Council of Europe, by the beginning of the 1990s it became clear that increasing migration had put them under significant pressure (Hailbronner 1992, 92–98). Migration places political pressures on receiving states by increasing the number of people who find themselves caught between two states and suffering adverse consequences because of it. As migration increases the number of permanent resident aliens, growing proportions of a state's inhabitants are excluded from the polity and thereby undermine its democratic inclusiveness. While liberal principles call for inclusion of permanent resident aliens into the polity, international norms against dual nationality constrain states into requiring renunciation of previous nationality for those who naturalize. In Europe, such renunciation policies have yielded relatively low naturalization rates (Hammar 1990a, 84–105) and have therefore become central to immigrant incorporation efforts (Council of Europe 1996, 20). Whereas norms against dual nationality minimize conflict between states, in the context of increasing migration these norms can become a point of conflict within democratic polities between liberals, who are unwilling to compromise on the inclusiveness of their democracy, and conservatives, who place a higher value on maintaining a citizenry with undivided loyalties to the polity and view dual nationality as a threat to this value.

Despite such conservative proclivities, international norms against mul-

tiple nationality in Europe are being increasingly undermined by state practice. Belgium, Greece, Ireland, Portugal, and the United Kingdom do not require renunciation of previous nationality for those who naturalize (OECD
1995, 163, 165). Although the 1990 change in Swiss policy has been depicted as a harbinger of changing European norms, this policy change did
not directly challenge the existing international regime against dual nationality in Europe because Switzerland did not sign and ratify the Council of
Europe's 1963 convention. In contrast, France is a signatory state, yet since
French policy only requires renunciation of previous nationality by nationals from fellow signatory states, France has exploited its strict interpretation of the Convention to the effect that well over a million naturalized
French citizens maintain dual nationality (Hammar 1990a, 111). More direct challenges to the regime were posed by two signatory states. The
Netherlands liberalized its policies in 1991 to permit those who naturalize
to retain their previous nationalities in an increasing number of circumstances (Council of Europe 1996, 22), and Italy enacted a new set of nationality laws that included provisions permitting dual nationality in 1992
(Council of Europe 1995, 73).

These ostensible "violations" of the 1963 Convention were not considered particularly problematic given that the Council of Europe, itself,
began to reconsider the 1963 Convention after being prodded by a French
parliamentarian's concern for a constituent's ambiguous legal status (Miller
1989, 949). Interestingly, "French efforts were driven by government officials and French emigrant groups who bemoaned the inequities of the legitimate dual national status of a Franco–non-European, such as Franco-
Algerians, and the problematic dual national status of a Franco-European,
such as a Franco-German, whom they considered 'culturally closer'" (Feldblum 1998, 237). It was not until after the Netherlands and Italy changed
their policies, however, that the Council of Europe diluted the 1963 Convention with a 1993 protocol that permits dual nationality in certain cases
"to facilitate the acquisition by one spouse of the nationality of the other
spouse and the acquisition by their children of the nationality of both parents, in order to encourage the unity of nationality within the same family"
(Council of Europe 1993a, 2).

On May 14, 1997, the Council of Europe's Committee of Ministers took
a further departure from the 1963 Convention with the adoption of a new
European Convention on Nationality that was opened for signature on
November 7, 1997. The convention states:

A State Party shall allow: a) children having different nationalities acquired
at birth to retain these nationalities; its nationals to possess another nation-

ality where this other nationality is automatically acquired by marriage [Article 14]. . . . The Provisions of this Convention shall not limit the right of a State Party to determine in its internal law whether: a) its nationals who acquire or possess the nationality of another State retain its nationality or lose it; b) the acquisition or retention of its nationality is subject to the renunciation or loss of another [Article 15]. . . . A State Party shall not make the renunciation or loss of another nationality a condition for the acquisition or retention of its nationality where such renunciation is not possible or cannot reasonably be required [Article 16]. (Council of Europe 1997c)

It is important to note that the 1997 Convention does not reverse the 1963 Convention. The attached explanatory report explains that the convention simply allows states to permit dual nationality or not to permit it, require renunciation or not require it. Indeed, Article 26 explicitly states that the new convention does not abrogate treaty commitments made in 1963[4] and the explanatory report notes, "States which are bound by Chapter I of the 1963 Convention will not, as regards their respective nationals, be able to allow more than a limited number of cases of multiple nationality" (Council of Europe 1997b, 32).

The 1993 Protocol and the 1997 Convention provide evidence for changing European norms on multiple nationality. As the new Convention is being signed and ratified by member states, the change in norms is being codified. That change, however, is neither a wholesale reversal of the 1963 Convention nor a blanket endorsement of the principle of dual nationality. Moreover, the central norm against multiple nationality remains in place as long as the new 1997 Convention remains largely unratified by the negotiating parties[5] and as long as signatory states of the 1963 Convention do not avail themselves of the prerogative to take advantage of the changes embodied in the 1993 Protocol. In fact, most parties to the 1963 Convention still retain prohibitions against dual nationality in their nationality laws. Also, the laws of most EU member states still required renunciation of first nationality by naturalization applicants in November 1997 when the European Convention on Nationality was signed. (The Netherlands changed its policy back to requiring renunciation on October 1, 1997.)[6] Even though European norms on dual nationality were changing at the time, they remained, on balance, tipped against dual nationality, both in terms of effective international legal instruments and in terms of prevailing domestic law—that is, until recent developments in Germany.

As far as the future of international norms against dual nationality are concerned, Germany is crucial because Germany hosts Europe's largest population of permanent resident aliens. Of the parties to the 1963 Council of Europe Convention, Germany has perhaps most strenuously resisted relaxing the prohibition against dual nationality. Until its defeat at the polls in September 1998, Germany's Christian Democratic Union (CDU) led government rebuffed calls by political leaders from opposition parties as well as from dissenters within coalition ranks to eliminate the renunciation requirement.

Nevertheless, actual state administrative practices often deviate significantly from existing formal principles of individual states' nationality laws. If one looks beyond the legislative battles of the 1990s into Germany's administrative practices, a different picture emerges. For example, ethnic Germans from eastern Europe and the former Soviet Union are considered German nationals according to Article 116 of the Basic Law. Since these *Ausseidler* are simply claiming their existing German nationality, they are not required to renounce their previous nationality. Also, many children of mixed marriages are born with dual nationality and are not necessarily required to surrender one. Finally, Germany's renunciation policy includes loopholes permitting dual nationality for foreigners whose country of origin arbitrarily refuses release of previous nationality or, in the case of draft-age foreigners who received the majority of their schooling in Germany, if the home country requires military service for release from its nationality. These loopholes meant that dual nationality was tolerated in 13,082 of 29,108 discretionary naturalizations (44.9 percent) in 1993 (*Ausländer-beauftragte* 1997, 33).

Moreover, after years of urging Germany to permit dual nationality, Turkey changed its laws in 1995 to permit emigrants who renounce their nationality for purposes of naturalization to reapply shortly thereafter.[7] Given that dual nationality was tolerated for over a third of the Turks who naturalized in 1993 (*Ausländerbeauftragte* 1997, 33) and that those who did renounce their Turkish nationality were permitted to get it back, it is fair to say that a majority of the Turks who naturalized in 1993 most likely now have both German and Turkish nationality. Cornelia Schmalz-Jacobsen, the former *Ausländerbeauftragte* (Federal Government's Commissioner for Foreigners' Affairs), estimated that already in 1995 there were over two million German citizens with dual nationality (TWIG 1995). In practice, Germany has followed the example of France and violated the spirit, if not the letter, of the Council of Europe 1963 Convention.

In January 1999, the Social Democratic (SPD)–Green coalition government proposed changes to Germany's citizenship law to relax naturalization rules by eliminating the renunciation requirement. Soon after the government announced the proposals, the CDU-CSU (German Christian

Democrat Union–Bavarian Christian Social Union) launched a petition campaign targeting the provision that permitted dual nationality in order to mobilize the electorate in upcoming *Länder* elections. With a CDU victory of 44 percent to the SPD's 39 percent of the votes cast in the Hesse election on February 7, a Christian Democrat–Free Democrat (CDU-FDP) coalition replaced Hesse's eight-year-old SPD–Green coalition government and the petition campaign was credited as the primary reason for the upset (Rheinische Post 1999). Having lost Hesse in the upper house of the German Parliament, the Schröder government had little alternative to modifying its reform plan to embrace an earlier FDP plan to accept dual nationality but limit it (FAZ 1999).

In May 1999, both houses of the *Bundestag* approved reforms to Germany's citizenship law that went into effect on January 1, 2000. Dual nationality is now permitted to those born of foreign parents; however, they must choose between German nationality and their other nationality by the time they become twenty-three years old. As was already the case, if a state will not release a dual national from his or her non-German nationality, he or she may retain that nationality. As Germany relaxes its renunciation requirement, whatever is left of the international norm against dual nationality becomes a somewhat moot point because an overwhelming majority of Europe's population of resident aliens are becoming able to maintain a second nationality.

Formal international norms are gradually, but persistently, following changes in domestic laws and administrative practices. Changing nationality laws, evasive treaty interpretations, and contradictory administrative practices on the part of European states undermined these norms and have led to the deterioration of Europe's demographic boundary maintenance regime. Not only does this decline of international cooperation on nationality law contrast with increased international cooperation on border control and asylum policies, it has somewhat paradoxical implications for sovereignty. By following the dictates of domestic politics and unilaterally changing their naturalization policies instead of strictly adhering to international norms, the Netherlands and Italy exerted their sovereignty vis-à-vis the other Council of Europe member states. By permitting dual nationality, these European states have also changed the act of naturalization from one of loyalty transfer and migrant recognition of sole authority of a state over him or herself to an act that reflects much more complex political identities. They have thereby contributed to a transformation of the very meaning of sovereignty in Europe today.

Dual Nationality and Political Identity

It is tempting to interpret the meaning of dual nationality in terms set out by Zygmunt Bauman's suggestion that "if the modern 'problem of identity' is primarily how to construct an identity and keep it solid and stable, the postmodern 'problem of identity' is primarily how to avoid fixation and keep options open" (Bauman 1997, 18). That is, modern states try to construct solid and stable identities for individuals while postmodern individuals "keep their options open" by acquiring a second nationality. In many cases this depiction of the situation may be quite appropriate; however, it falls short as a general rule.

Part of the problem is that dual nationality is not simply a matter of individual choice, but rather the confluence of state laws and policies regarding the ascription, acquisition, and renunciation of nationality. The fact that states are increasingly permitting dual nationality may have quite different implications with respect to policymakers' expectations or concerns regarding individual political identification. Likewise, the act of migrants and their descendants taking on or retaining two nationalities may have different meanings to each individual. Dual nationality may be indicative of a step in political identity transfer from home to host state, retention of home state identity, a desire to maintain multiple political identities, or a reluctance to choose a political identity, or it may have nothing to do with political identity at all.

Even when dual nationality is accepted in principle by states, it has been commonly viewed as a marginal and transitory feature of migration and naturalization rather than an ongoing condition of a changing international order. This view is largely based on the classical model of assimilation as it relates to the nineteenth-century immigration experience of countries such as the United States, Canada, and Australia, in which the political identity of immigrants and their descendants was understood to shift in one direction—from home country to host country. It was generally assumed that eventually, the immigrants' descendants, if not the immigrants themselves, would come to consider the host country to be their home country and they would lose interest in the politics of the ancestral homeland. The transfer of immigrants' political identity from one country to another was usually marked by the act of renouncing home country citizenship and taking an oath of allegiance during naturalization.

Sending countries often view such assimilation in terms of a demographic and national "loss." In response, countries experiencing great out-migration tended to base nationality primarily on jus sanguinis because it encourages emigrants to retain their nationality and pass it on to their children so as to facilitate—for both emigrants and their descendants—closer ties with and the return to their homeland (as discussed in chapter 4). The tug of war between receiving and sending states over the political identity of migrants increased the instances of dual nationality, whereas the norms against dual nationality helped make citizenship in the host or home country a clear line of distinction of political identification.

Interestingly, receiving states that expect the permitting of dual nationality to increase naturalization are also permitting residual homeland political identification, thereby making the act of naturalization no longer one of political identity transfer. Apparently, the hope is that homeland political identity would fade with time after naturalization. In contrast, sending states hope that emigrants will maintain strong homeland political identities despite their newly acquired nationality. That is, states may permit individuals to "avoid fixation and keep options open" but do so with the objective of furthering their modernist projects of constructing stable identities. Contrary to the designs of sending and receiving states, the migrant's act of taking on two nationalities may be indicative of neither assimilation nor homeland political identification, but rather of multiple political identities, an ambivalent political identity, or even an apolitical identity.

The same migrants who express their feelings of political identification with the ancestral homeland often voice similar feelings toward their new country of residence when on visits "back home." Such expressions may be a manifestation of a strong desire to maintain a multiple political identity— to simultaneously be both a "good American" and "good Cuban," a "good Canadian" and "good Italian," and so on. The political identity of migrant communities and individual migrants may even switch back and forth over their lifetimes as expressed in the objectives of their political actions—at one time focused on the host country and at the other on the home country (see, e.g., Blejwas 1995). The internal logic of nationalism may militate against the notion of political identification with two nation-states; nevertheless, individuals defy this logic by expressing multiple political identification through their actions (including voluntary military service to both states). Hence, an individual who maintains or acquires dual nationality may do so as an act of multiple political identification.

An ambivalent political identity can be thought of in terms somewhat similar to multiple political identity; however, individuals may be less proactive in efforts to maintain and express both host and homeland identities and more reactive to their host and home country environments. For example, the immigrant who actively tries to leave his or her homeland behind may feel spurned by host country social and political associations and then defensively retreat toward a halfhearted affiliation with homeland political organizations. Similarly, the migrant who returns to the homeland may identify with his or her new country of residence, not because he or she wishes to actively maintain that identity, but because homeland compatriots may not fully accept, or may even reject, the emigrant's expressions of homeland identification. When migrants feel rejected by both host and homeland societies, the retention of dual nationality may be much more the expression of indecision between political identities rather than the affirmation of both. Retention of dual nationality may also be a self-protective move based on fear of rejection after renouncing one of the two nationalities.

While many (whether fearful conservatives or hopeful multiculturalists) may equate dual nationality with multiple political identities, the individual's act of acquiring or retaining a second nationality may have no deep political significance at all. Dual nationality is often viewed in utilitarian terms as having a second passport for easier travel and gaining access to business and employment opportunities for which citizenship is required. For example, Dominica sells its citizenship for cash contributions of $50,000.[8] St. Kitts, Nevis, the Cape Verde Islands, and Belize offer similar programs, while Ireland and Portugal have offered investment-linked citizenship programs in the past. When individuals treat citizenship as a commodity through the purchase of a second passport in this manner, the resulting dual nationality is apolitical, if not anti-political, in nature.

The apolitical meaning of dual nationality need not be as blatant. Increasing dual nationality among nationals of certain states with decreasing rates of political participation may simply be indicative of more general trends of decreasing interest in politics. Dual nationality may also simply be a manifestation of ignorance or apathy. Many individuals do not know that they became dual nationals at birth, as is frequently the case for children of Greek or Turkish parents born abroad. They often only become aware of their dual nationality after receiving a draft notice from their ancestral homeland. Even if they do discover that they are dual nationals, many, especially those who do not face complications with military service obligations, simply do not bother to renounce one of their two nationalities.

Multiple, ambivalent, and apolitical identities are just as much a part of diasporic existence as strong homeland identities or the transfer of political identity to host states. These alternative political and apolitical identities can also be considered part and parcel of the economic and political dynamics of globalization. As such, we can expect that as the economic and technological processes of globalization intensify and states increasingly permit dual nationality and other forms of multiple membership, members of diasporas will increasingly sustain such alternative transnational identities that transcend undivided loyalties, assumed to exist with singular nationality in sharply delineated nation-states.

Multiple Loyalties and Changing Patterns of Authority

Raymond Aron dismissed multiple citizenship by arguing that, historically, the nation-state informed the development of citizenship and that it was unlikely that the practice of citizenship, including both the exercise of political rights and the fulfillment of duties such as military service, could ever take place outside of the singular relationship between the individual and his or her state (Aron 1974). Aron argued that European institutions of democracy, military service, and the principle of equality were all organized around the nation-state. Citizenship is the connection between individual and state, whereby with popular sovereignty, citizenship defined the state and, as a fundamental aspect of sovereignty, the state determined who its citizens were and obliged them to fulfill the duties incumbent in their exercise of rights. Along such lines of thinking, multiple citizenship is theoretically inconsistent.

The theoretical contradiction, however, only rings true given the history of a set of actors' practices that have settled into institutions. For their reproduction these settled practices depend on constitutive and regulative norms. As discussed above, the differentiation of the world politics into an international system of states is made possible by constitutive norms like those against statelessness and dual nationality. Changes in state practices can lead to changes in constitutive norms, which in turn reconstitute the international system itself. Since reproduction of the practice of international actors (i.e., states) depends on the reproduction of the practices of domestic actors (i.e., individuals and groups), changes in domestic politics can transform international systems.

Dual nationality is an "abnormality" within the classical state system because it contradicts the system's constitutive norms. If the incidence of dual nationality increases because domestic politics forces state practice in the international arena to depart from the constitutive and regulative norms of the existing international system, these new state practices can either be dismissed as being anomalous and ephemeral or viewed as precedents in the establishment of a new set of international norms and indicative of the transformation of the international system. Aron viewed EU member state practices of extending civil and economic rights to non-nationals as anomalous and unlikely to expand into the political realm. One can similarly dismiss the increasing practice of permitting dual nationality among European states as anomalous and likely to be reversed. In contrast, one could view the combination of changes in the Council of Europe in 1997 and the lifting of prohibitions against dual nationality by European states as part and parcel of the development of a new set of constitutive norms incumbent with the replacement of the classical European state system and the emergence of a new European polity. What kind of polity could a new norm of permitting dual nationality indicate?

When considering the potential alternative to the contemporary state system, Hedley Bull described a "new medievalism" or "a system of overlapping authority and multiple loyalty" (Bull 1977, 254). By blurring the boundaries of authority of states over their subjects and increasing the potential for multiple loyalties, increasing dual nationality may be indicative of one dimension of a transformation of the international system in Europe toward such a new medievalism. Gidon Gottlieb (1993) furthers this reconceptualization of international society by advocating that the existing territorially delineated international system be adjusted for overlapping authority and dual loyalties through international recognition of nonterritorial political associations. Gottlieb distinguishes citizenship that is tied to the state from nationality that is tied to the nation and advocates the idea of a "national home" distinct from the state, to which nationals could belong regardless of their residence. Given that a state's acceptance of dual nationality legitimates migrants' residual political identification with another state, the acceptance of dual nationality on the international level would be a first step to international recognition of national homes and an international system of what Gottlieb calls "states plus nations."

This formulation of "states plus nations" conjures the image of a matrix of homeland nationality superimposed onto territorially organized citizenship, as with the classical European state system. Within this matrix, individuals would have dual nationalities in which the rights and duties of homeland citizenship would become recessive upon naturalization in a new state, whose citizenship would then be active. Should those who naturalize return to their "national homes" the process would reverse. Although overlapping authorities and multiple loyalties would proliferate, the breakdown of undivided loyalties, assumed to exist with singular nationality in sharply delineated nation-states, need not result in loyalties that are uniformly divided between two states. That is, much as in medieval Europe, authorities and loyalties could easily become functionally differentiated (Guetzkow 1955). Sets of rights extended by the home state and duties owed it may be quite different than rights and duties of the state of naturalization that, in turn, may be quite different from the rights and duties incumbent with European citizenship.

Such disaggregation of unitary nationality and citizenship that the plurality of nationalities incurs is indicative of a parallel disaggregation of unitary authority into a set of overlapping authorities. In this sense, the movement toward a norm permitting dual nationality can be considered part of what Ole Waever calls "a collective redefinition of sovereignty." As Waever points out, at one time sovereignty "meant the ability to decide the religion of one's subjects. Although this is no longer included in sovereignty, states have not become less sovereign. Religion and the state have both changed" (Waever 1995, 417–18). Likewise, sovereignty once meant the ability to unilaterally determine who one's subjects were and then extend rights to and impose duties upon them. In the context of increasing migration, the development of popular sovereignty, and the articulation of constitutional rights as well as international human rights, state sovereignty in the determination of nationality and the content of citizenship rights and obligations is being redefined. As European norms governing nationality are changing so as to exclude certain unilateral prerogatives, nationality and the state are both changing as the classical European state system transforms into today's new European polity.

After World War II, Europe took the lead in adopting regional conventions against dual nationality. European states are now among those permitting dual nationality and thereby undermining the demographic boundary regime. Although dual nationality can easily be interpreted in postmodern terms as the avoidance of fixation and the desire to keep options open, this interpretation only captures one possible interpretation of the increasing cases of dual nationality in regard to political identity. Dual nationality may just as easily signify the retention of homeland political identity as political incorporation into the host society, just as easily signify the possession of multiple political identities or the lack of any political identities at all. The bearing of dual nationality on international politics becomes clear if one is willing to consider the constitutive nature of citizenship and accept the role of nationality law in bounding states. Given that international norms against statelessness and dual nationality were constitutive of an international system of nation-states, the decline of the demographic boundary maintenance regime and the concomitant increase in cases of dual nationality are indicative of a transformation of the international order toward a new medievalism, particularly in Europe.

CHAPTER EIGHT

Border Control and State Sovereignty

O ver the past decade increasing migration flows into western Europe have led to public perceptions of growing foreigner populations as cultural, economic, and security threats. Extremist right-wing parties and movements have capitalized on such perceptions, which has in turn prompted governments led by mainstream parties to respond with policy changes. To varying degrees and in varying proportions, European governments have adopted a two-pronged set of policies—incorporation into the host society and polity of those migrants who have already become permanent resident aliens, and stricter asylum policies and tighter border controls to stem further increases in the number of foreigners within their borders.

As explained above, efforts to increase naturalization by permitting dual nationality have raised serious questions regarding the delineation of nation-states and nature of their sovereignty. Similarly, increasing EU co-operation on border control and asylum policy may become an important component of sovereignty transforming political integration. Although the most significant policy changes concern intra-EU migration of EU member state nationals, recent agreements signal the integration of member state migration policies governing migration to the EU itself. Given that integration of policies governing migration to the EU has mostly involved tighter border control and restriction of further immigration, it may be tempting to interpret these changes as a reassertion of state sovereignty. This is misleading because regardless of the purpose, policy integration transforms member state sovereignty. Moreover, EU integration has transformed the sovereignty of states that are not even members of the EU. Applicant states from central and eastern Europe are changing their border control and asylum policies to meet EU norms, despite the economic and political sacrifices entailed in doing so. Finally, the increase in smuggling of clandestine migrants into the EU raises new challenges for border control and European cooperation.

The Emerging Regime Governing Migration to the EU

In contrast to the classical immigration states such as the United States, Canada, and Australia, most EU member states do not have a tradition of immigration and the rapid transformation of permanent residents into citizens. Rather, the relatively recent net migratory flows into the EU have primarily been composed of guest workers, their families, individuals from former colonies, co-ethnics with citizenship rights (e.g., ethnic Germans from Poland and the former Soviet Union), and asylum seekers. Temporary labor migration and migration from former colonies predominated in the 1960s and early 1970s, family reunification predominated in the latter 1970s and early 1980s, and refugee flows have come to the fore over the last decade. During the late 1980s and early 1990s, increasing migration of co-ethnics and political refugees primarily from eastern Europe drove up the total number of resident aliens in the EU from non-EU member states (see table 7).

Individual member states attempted to restrict entry of non-EU nationals by tightening visa policies and reducing support to asylum seekers. Although such unilateral actions may have decreased the number of asylum seekers, they diverted the flows to other countries and asylum seekers turned away from one country simply reapplied in the next (Funk 1995; Santel 1995). As unilateral measures proliferated, the extent of the marginal reduction in refugees experienced by one member state increasingly depended on other member states not enacting even more restrictivist policies.

In response to increasing numbers of refugees, and given the concern on the part of foreign policymakers that the collapse of communism would unleash mass east-west migration, EU member states intensified their cooperative efforts (Papdemetriou 1996; Ucarer 1997). The 1990 Schengen Convention harmonizes asylum application procedures and mandates that asylum seekers may only apply in one country. It also calls for a common visa policy, harmonization of polices to deter illegal migration and an automated information system so as to coordinate actions regarding individ-

Table 7   Migration to the EU (in thousands)

	1988	1989	1990	1991	1992	1993
Total net migration[a]	+622.5	+1,017.4	+1,076.1	+1,054.4	+1,344.5	+1,037.6
Non-EU resident aliens[b]	7,911.3	8,487.2	9,542.9	10,438.9	12,098.3	12,251.2

[a]Total net migration is the total of net migration of the fifteen EU member states. "Net migration is the difference between the total population on January 1 and December 31 of the same year, minus the differences between births and deaths and including corrections (due to population censuses, register counts, etc., which cannot be classified as births, deaths or migrations)" (Eurostat 1995b, 4, table A-1). Figures are for EU 15, including Sweden, Austria, and Finland.

[b]Source for stock statistics on resident aliens in the EU from non-EU member states (Eurostat 1995b, 12, table A-5.1). Figures are for EU 15, including Sweden, Austria, and Finland. Stock statistics do not directly demonstrate migration flows but rather present yearly snapshots of the numbers of non-EU nationals resident in the EU on January 1 of each year. Stocks may decrease due to the death or naturalization of non-EU nationals and increase due to births in countries in which the children of resident aliens do not gain citizenship.

uals who have been denied entry. The 1990 Dublin Convention (which was ratified and went into effect in 1997) provided rules for determining which member state had jurisdiction in asylum applications, governed by the principle that the state of entry would be responsible for any given application. If that state rejected the application, the asylum seeker could not then apply in other member states. The objective was to eliminate "asylum shopping"—abuse of member state asylum laws through multiple applications. In addition to the principle that the state of entry should process asylum applications, the Edinburg Council of 1992 introduced the norm that asylum seekers should "be encouraged to stay in the nearest safe area to their homes" (European Council 1992, 44). Given that newly democratic east-central European countries bordering member states were deemed to be "safe countries," the criteria became a basis for rejecting asylum claims of those who crossed the EU frontier from these states (Neuman 1993).

Title VI of the Maastricht Treaty formalized the process of intergovernmental cooperation among the member states in regard to migration. Cooperation in the fields of Justice and Home Affairs (JHA) formed one of three "pillars" of the EU along with the original European Community and Common Foreign and Security Policy (CFSP). The pillar structure effectively kept most policies regarding migration to the EU outside of the Community legal order. As Maastricht's "Third Pillar," Title VI does not promulgate specific rules to govern migration policy but designates matters for common interest, including asylum policy, rules governing the crossing of external borders, and policies regarding third country nationals (Article K.1); stipulates compliance with the European Convention for the Protection of Human Rights (Article K.2); and sets up a coordinating committee of senior officials (Article K.4). A common visa policy was inserted in the EC Treaty itself (Article 100c).

Strengthening the Third Pillar became a central priority of Germany's ruling coalition government after its 1994 reelection (CDU/CSU/FDP 1994) as well as one of four top priorities announced by the German and French governments in advance of the 1996–97 Intergovernmental Conference (IGC) on revising the Maastricht Treaty (Kohl and Chirac 1995). Although the 1996–97 IGC was intended to make institutional changes to prepare for enlargement, the centerpiece of the Amsterdam Treaty was a strengthening of the Third Pillar with the "Progressive Establishment of an Area of Freedom, Security and Justice," which included a new title in the TEC on "Free Movement of Persons, Asylum and Immigration" (Amsterdam Treaty 1997). Not only does this new title incorporate the Schengen Convention into the EU, over the five years following ratification, it is to bring important aspects of common policy on external border controls, asylum and immigration into the EC treaty and the community legal framework.

For the most part, member states have not utilized the new framework to go beyond previous intergovernmental cooperation until quite recently. The JHA Council agreed to its first legally binding joint position at its November 1995 meeting when it stipulated a common definition of "refugee." Based on a strict interpretation of the 1951 Geneva Convention that defines a refugee as someone with a well-founded fear of being persecuted for reasons of race, religion, nationality, membership in a particular social group, or political opinion, the new common EU definition effectively excludes those who flee civil wars, generalized armed conflict, and persecution by "non-state agents," such as armed militias and insurgent groups. Before the common definition was issued, Germany, France, Italy, and Sweden were the only member states that did not define those persecuted by non-state agents as refugees. The UNHCR criticized the common position as contrary to the spirit of the 1951 Convention and as a step backwards that could imperil refugee protection throughout the world (ANP 1995; European Insight 1995).

To understand why the regime governing migration to the EU became increasingly restrictive, it is important to point out that member states avoided transferring authority in this area to the supranational institutions of Commission and Court, working instead through the intergovernmental institutions of EPC and the Council of Ministers[1] as well as through extra-Community multilateral forums such as Schengen. In the late 1980s and early 1990s, liberal economic precepts held by center-right governments in Germany and Great Britain as well as the free market-(re)oriented Socialist government of France called for realization of the SEA's provisions for a frontierless labor market. At the same time, the lack of government response to growing public perceptions of migration as a threat played into the electoral designs of right-wing movements that challenged those governments. Given the collective action problems involved in unilateral restriction of entry and asylum application, cooperation became imperative. However, the lowest common denominator of agreement was cooperation on policing and assignment of asylum application responsibility, rather than on the more comprehensive cooperation advocated by the Commission in the areas of trade policy, foreign policy, and development—areas aimed at the root causes of migration, such as human rights abuses and civil war (particularly in the former Yugoslavia), economic disparities, population growth, and environmental degradation (European Commission 1994a, 13–19).

Also, member state cooperation developed within the context of a growing web of multilateral forums and an explosion of international conferences and meetings on migration in the European region during the late 1980s and early 1990s. In addition to the EU and Schengen frameworks, member states participated in meetings organized by the UNHCR; International Organization for Migration (IOM); Council of Europe; Organization for Economic Cooperation and Development (OECD); International Labour Office (ILO); the Inter-Governmental Consultations on Asylum, Refugee, and Migration Policies in Europe, North America, and Australia (often referred to as the "informal consultations"); the Berlin Process; and the Organization for Security and Cooperation in Europe (OSCE). During the first half of 1993 there were approximately 80–90 such meetings, twice the number taking place two years before (Council of Europe 1993b, 2). As use of the Schengen forum demonstrates, with a multitude of forums, multilateral cooperation can take the path of least resistance to the lowest common denominator of agreement and then become the basis for subsequent negotiations involving more participants and greater scope in issues. However, the basic norm of the regime is usually set in the initial agreement to which subsequent member states accede.

The characteristics of EU migration regimes can be further understood by considering the work of individuals and NGOs that have reached across state borders in common cause regarding a particular issue area. Such transnational efforts to gather information and publicize particular problems help place issues on the agenda of foreign ministries (Risse-Kappen 1995). Moreover, provision of technical analysis and expert opinion by "epistemic communities" informs the terms of debate in multilateral negotiations.[2] The development of the regime governing migration to the EU was influenced by the agenda setting of dueling epistemic communities— academic experts and NGOs committed to protecting human rights versus transnational networks of police dedicated to using migration control to fight crime.

The many meetings and conferences on European migration brought officials from the EU and other international organizations together with academics and NGO representatives who presented demographic analyses and predictions as well as offered policy analysis and prescriptions.[3] Moreover, NGOs have an important role in standard setting, promoting ratification (Niessen 1994), and monitoring state compliance. The epistemic community committed to protecting human rights became particularly influential in the formation of policy proposals by the Council of Europe, European Parliament, and the European Commission.

In contrast, transnational networks of police professionals that developed through contacts made under the auspices of Interpol and Trevi were crucial to setting the agendas for member state cooperation by linking the problems of international crime and illegal immigration. As Monica Den Boer and Neil Walker put it, "The consistent association of the different themes in the language and practice of politicians and professionals has created a mutually reinforcive 'internal security ideology.'"[4] This internal security ideology came to inform the development of the intergovernmental institutions that dealt with migration, most noteworthy being the Third Pillar of the TEU that lumped immigration and asylum policy together with drug addiction and international fraud. In member state negotiations within the Third Pillar framework, migration is not addressed in terms of human rights but rather in terms of internal security; resolutions focus on the instrument of policing rather than foreign policy, trade, and development (Funk 1995). In this sense, the tug of war pitting the Commission and Parliament against the Council for authority over EU migration policy is also a contest in the battle of ideas.

Since the objective of the emerging regime governing migration to the EU is not free movement but rather reducing illegal migration and eliminating asylum abuses, cooperation should reduce migration flows. Illegal migration is difficult to measure, but figures for asylum seekers in the EU since the 1990 signing of the Schengen and Dublin Conventions are very enlightening. Although the number of asylum seekers continued to increase during the first two years after the agreements were signed, they dropped in the third as member states, most notably Germany, put stricter asylum policies into place (see table 8). Still, absolute decreases in migration flows cannot be the sole criteria for regime effectiveness, because without whatever cooperation that did exist, migration rates could have been even higher, especially since the primary objective of cooperation was to eliminate abuses of asylum application procedures, rather than arbitrarily limit the number of political refugees accepted into the EU.

Germany accounts for close to, if not more than, half of the EU's asylum seekers in any given year, and changes in the overall EU number reflect German trends. The drop in the number of asylum seekers in Germany during the mid-1990s can be attributed to the introduction of a new asylum law that went into effect July 1, 1993, and stipulated that asylum seekers entering Germany from countries that offer asylum should make their application there and that those coming from countries considered "safe" would have to provide evidence of selective individual persecution.

Strictly speaking, Germany's action was unilateral in nature;[5] however, it is better understood in the context of the changing European norms enunciated in the Dublin Convention and the Edinburgh Summit Declaration. The emerging EU migration regime was useful to the CDU/CSU/FDP governing coalition in justifying a restrictivist policy that required constitutional amendment. As Chancellor Helmut Kohl put it, "The new regulation of the right to asylum of 1 July was an important precondition for the fact that Germany can fully participate in a common European asylum policy."[6] Moreover, given that Schengen rules generally give responsibility for asylum seekers without visas to states of first entry (even if illegally), Schengen put additional pressure on member states with external borders to maintain strict border controls and adopt restrictive asylum policies lest they bear a disproportionate burden of asylum seekers (Neuman 1993). Hence, Germany's accession to the Dublin and Schengen Conventions provided international legitimization as well as a practical incentive for domestic political action.

Generally speaking, even though all EU member states have not signed the Schengen convention (e.g., the United Kingdom and Ireland) and even before the Dublin Convention went into effect in September 1997, these agreements had an indirect effect on migration rates through anticipatory changes in the asylum policies of individual member states. Given that efforts to enact restrictivist migration policies are hampered by domestic economic interests and human rights concerns, changes in international norms

Table 8   Number of Asylum-Seekers in Each EU Member State, 1989–98

	1989	1990	1991	1992	1993	1994	1995	1996	1997	1998
Belgium	8,188	12,945	15,444	17,675	26,717	14,340	11,409	12,232	11,575	21,965
Denmark	4,588	5,292	4,609	13,884	14,347	6,651	5,104	5,896	5,100	5,699
Germany	121,318	193,063	256,112	438,191	322,599	127,210	127,937	116,367	104,353	98,644
Greece	4,033	10,569	5,944	3,822	862	—	—	—	—	—
Spain	4,077	8,647	8,138	11,712	12,645	10,230	5,678	4,730	4,973	6,639
France	61,422	54,813	47,380	28,872	27,564	26,044	20,170	17,153	19,983	22,375
Ireland	36	62	31	—	91	355	1,752	573	1,712	4,626
Italy	2,240	3,570	24,490	2,589	1,323	1,834	—	—	—	6,939
Luxembourg	87	114	238	120	225	—	—	—	—	—
Netherlands	13,898	21,208	21,615	20,346	35,399	52,576	29,258	22,857	34,443	45,217
Austria	21,822	22,789	27,306	16,238	4,744	5,082	—	—	—	13,805
Portugal	116	61	233	655	2,090	614	—	—	—	—
Finland	179	2,743	2,137	3,634	2,023	849	854	771	973	1,272
Sweden	30,335	29,420	27,351	84,018	37,581	18,640	9,047	5,753	9,619	12,844
UK	16,775	38,200	73,400	32,300	28,500	41,000	55,000	27,875	32,502	58,000
Total	289,174	403,496	514,428	674,056	516,710	305,259	266,709	214,147	225,232	298,025

Source: 1989–94: Eurostat 1996, 2–3; 1995–98: Secretariat of the Inter-Governmental Consultations on Asylum, Refugee and Migration Policies in Europe, North America and Australia, <http://www.igc.ch/>.

within an international migration regime are useful in changing domestic policies. In this case, multilateral cooperation can be viewed as part of a "two-level game" (Putnam 1988) in which states justify the curtailment of certain rights and increased state interference in the domestic economy in terms of prevailing international norms and adherence to multilateral commitments,[7] much in the way leaders in developing states who wish to effectuate painful economic reforms find it politically useful to blame the International Monetary Fund (IMF) for their actions.

Sovereignty

While member states appear to have transferred an aspect of sovereignty to the EU with respect to the migration of EU nationals within the Union, it also appears that they have resisted a similar transfer of sovereignty over the migration of non-EU nationals into the Union. Generally speaking, one could argue that member state sovereignty had for the most part been retained with respect to external border control, illegal migration, and asylum policy because some member states have either not become parties to certain agreements (e.g., Schengen) or when member states did negotiate and sign agreements in these areas, they did so primarily in multilateral state-to-state forums or in intergovernmental institutions of the EU. Cooperation agreements in these areas remained outside of the Community legal order and the jurisdiction of the European Court of Justice. Sovereignty with respect to migration to the EU, however, is much more complex and requires further clarification here.

First, cooperation in Justice and Home Affairs may be separated from the community framework, although the separation is not complete. The Commission is associated with the work in this area (Article K.4) and shares a right of initiative with the member states (Article K.3). The Council may also apply Article 100c of the EC Treaty to actions in the area of migration (Article K.9), in effect "communitarizing" parts of the Third Pillar.

Moreover, the 1997 Amsterdam Treaty has set the stage for a large-scale communitarization of the migration, asylum, and border control policies. At the outset of the 1996–97 Intergovernmental Conference (IGC), there were early indications that a majority of member states favored a communitarization of parts of the Third Pillar (Agence Europe 1995). British protest over the EU's ban on beef suspected of infection with "mad cow disease" stalled IGC negotiations on cooperation in Justice and Home Affairs, and it was primarily British resistance that blocked wholesale communitarization of the Third Pillar. In the face of British intransigence, Germany and France formed a coalition that struck a bargain for communitarization of migration and asylum policy with opt-outs available for the United Kingdom and Ireland (Gaunt 1996).

The Amsterdam Treaty sets out a plan for the incorporation of the Schengen Convention into the EU treaties and calls for common policies and joint actions on visas, asylum, immigration, and external border controls to be put under Community procedures and into the Community legal framework (see Article 73 TEC as amended at Amsterdam). Aside from common visa policies, the Council is to decide by rule of unanimity which migration polices are to move from intergovernmental Third Pillar to the First Pillar and be governed by Community procedures. This process is projected to take place over a five-year period beginning when the Amsterdam Treaty entered into force on May 1, 1999. During this transitional period, both the Commission and member states have the right to initiate legislation and the Council may only act unanimously after consulting the European Parliament.

At the end of the five-year transition period, the member states may decide to move to qualified majority voting and co-decision with the Parliament. Since the German Constitutional Court's ruling that upheld Maastricht ratification reinforced the role of the German *Länder* in German-EU relations, the *Länder* (particularly Bavaria) were able to apply sufficient political pressure on Helmut Kohl to make him insist that the shift to qualified majority voting on immigration and asylum policy, scheduled to take place five years after the Amsterdam treaty went into effect, could only come after a unanimous vote of the member states (see *FT* 1997).

Hence, the institutional and legal framework set up by Title VI of the Maastricht Treaty is actually a mixture of simple intergovernmental cooperation and integration within the Community. With the ratification of the Amsterdam Treaty, that mixture is becoming less intergovernmental. Should a significant portion of immigration and asylum policies come under the qualified majority voting rules at the end of the five-year transitional period, these policy areas will become fully integrated within the community framework. Therefore, member state sovereignty is currently much more compromised than in other multilateral forums dealing with migration, and it may become even further compromised in the not-too-distant future.

Second, the common practice of determining the location of sovereignty by drawing a sharp line between the community legal order and international treaties resulting from multilateral or intergovernmental negotiations is somewhat problematic. Theoretically speaking, one can say that member states retain their sovereignty when signing multilateral or intergovernmental agreements because there is no legal enforcement mechanism similar to the European Court of Justice and these agreements are not binding, since they can ultimately be broken by states. As pointed out at the outset of this book, however, this traditional definition of sovereignty as complete state autonomy to act as it will does not even really hold for international relations outside the European Community. Member states may retain sovereignty by negotiating intergovernmental agreements on migration instead of utilizing the Community legislative process to do so; however, it does not necessarily mean that member states will comply any less with the agreements made.

Finally, one must be careful not to confuse restrictivist common policies with retention of sovereignty. It is very common for scholars to argue that EU member states have not "lost" sovereignty because they are collectively tightening their border controls. For example, Gary Freeman argues that one reason for not viewing recent developments in EU migration polices as "a stunning case of voluntarily relinquished sovereignty" is that "the cooperation that has been achieved has been motivated by a desire to enact restrictivist measures. Cooperation, in other words, has been the means of enhancing traditional state attempts to bar entry to unwanted migrants and to limit state obligations to asylum seekers" (Freeman 1998, 91). In a similar vein, Gallya Lahav argues that EU member states are not "'losing control' or abdicating sovereignty. . . . European states are increasingly delegating policy elaboration and implementation to third party actors—especially the European Union itself—as a means to increase policy effectiveness" (Lahav 1998, 675–76).

When individual states step up border checks and deport rejected asylum seekers and those who overstay their visas, these states demonstrate their sovereignty through these exercises. However, when a group of states cooperate to harmonize their migration policies, or integrate their migration policy-making institutions, they cede some sovereignty regardless of whether the objective of that cooperation or integration is to restrict immigration or encourage it. Cooperation is cooperation; integration is integration. A restrictivist common policy might enable a participating state to assert its sovereignty in the particular area in question, as with the still unratified Dublin Convention that facilitated change in Germany's asylum law in 1993. The cooperation required to enact that common policy, however, itself constrains the range of state actions and can require states to do what they would not otherwise do had the cooperation agreement not been in place. Hence, states may actually sacrifice sovereignty in one dimension to exercise it in another.

A hypothetical example may help to clarify this point. If almost all EU member states agreed that the goal of cooperation should be a common policy that opened their common external border and encouraged migration to the EU but one member state refused to cooperate and stepped up border controls, clearly that one state would be demonstrating its territorial sovereignty as well as retaining its sovereignty in relation to the other members of the EU. If almost all states agreed to the goal of a restrictivist common policy but one state refused to cooperate and eliminated border checks at its portion of the common external border, that state may be abdicating territorial sovereignty with respect to controlling migration but would also be retaining its sovereignty in relation to the other EU member states. Although this hypothetical example may seem farfetched because few, if any, individual EU member states have recently encouraged immigration, one could easily see how a very restrictivist common policy on migration would infringe on an individual member state sovereignty in the area of nationality and citizenship.

With the institution of EU citizenship, the nationality laws of one EU member state effectively become the boundaries of residence and employment rights of all member states. For example, free movement in the EU was effectively extended to ethnic Germans from Poland, Romania, Russia, and Khazakhstan because the expanded understanding of German citizenship as delineated in Article 116(1) of the German Basic Law is in effect for community purposes (Plender 1988a, 198). A Pole of German ancestry who speaks fluent English, but little German, could claim German nationality, retain his or her Polish nationality, and, as an EU citizen, have the right to reside and work in the United Kingdom. Similarly, an American who has an Irish-born grandparent may claim Irish nationality, gain EU citizenship, and have the right to live and work in Austria. Due to special bilateral agreements between many Latin American states and Spain, Latin Americans have been able to gain access to the EU labor market through special accelerated naturalization provisions in Spain.[8] Nationals of Portuguese-speaking countries and individuals of Portuguese descent can be exempted from Portugal's residency requirements for naturalization, and those who do not have the requisite ancestry, at one time, were able to accelerate naturalization by virtue of purchasing property.[9]

If internal free movement is paired with a highly restrictivist common policy on asylum and external border control, which effectively cuts potential migrants' existing points of entry to the EU, potential migrants would have greater incentives to gain access by acquiring a member state national-ity. Much as differing asylum policies of individual member states prompted "asylum shopping," differing nationality laws could prompt "citizenship shopping" among member states. If EU member states were to respond by harmonizing their nationality laws, states with relatively open access for particular categories of third-country nationals would be pressured to change their nationality laws. Fellow EU member states have already pre-vailed upon Portugal to curtail easy naturalization of foreigners who pur-chase property (O'Nes 1990, 109), and Spain has been under pressure to stop preferential treatment of Latin Americans because of the immigration of members of Colombian drug cartels (Starchild 1993, 19). Inasmuch as sovereignty means that a state can, for the most part, make anyone it chooses a citizen, such harmonization represents a loss of sovereignty in re-lation to other member states.

These complexities of state sovereignty reflect the fact that the member states of the EU have taken international cooperation on migration further than any other states in the world. Member state cooperation on migration not only exceeds that of international cooperation on a global level, it also goes beyond that of other regional organizations of comparable advanced industrialized states. For example, the North American Free Trade Agree-ment (NAFTA) does not directly impinge on member state actions that regulate migration, aside from cooperation on the mobility of managerial staff associated with foreign direct investment. In contrast to the Treaty of Rome, NAFTA does not affirm the principle of free movement of work-ers.[10] Canada and the United States consciously looked to the Dublin Con-vention as a model when they were engaged in negotiations on an agree-ment that would enable one state to return asylum seekers who entered via the other (Neuman 1993, 504).

Unlike international cooperation on migration among other states, EU member state relations are conditioned by a multitude of principles, norms, rules, and decision-making procedures that have become institutionalized in the course of over four decades of practice. In William Wallace's memo-rable words, the EU "is less than a federation, more than a regime" (Wal-lace 1983). Likewise, EU regulation of migration can be characterized as not quite that of a federation but also more than that of an international regime. Member state sovereignty with respect to migration within and to the EU is just as ambiguous: the EU is not quite sovereign over intra-EU mi-gration but more sovereign than the member states; member states are for the most part sovereign over migration from outside of the EU but not as sovereign as non-EU member states due, in large part, to the constraints of EU membership and the demands of continuing integration in general.

Migration Regimes and EU Enlargement

The Amsterdam Treaty not only "deepened" European cooperation and integration with respect to migration, the emerging EU migration regime is set to be "widened" over the coming decade. At the time that the Amsterdam Treaty was signed, Cyprus, Turkey, and the ten central and east European countries (CEECs)—Bulgaria, the Czech Republic, Estonia, Hungary, Latvia, Lithuania, Poland, Romania, Slovakia, and Slovenia—were queuing up for membership negotiations. In July 1997, the Commission issued its opinion that only the Czech Republic, Estonia, Hungary, Poland, and Slovenia, in addition to Cyprus, were ready for negotiations. The Council agreed with the Commission's assessment at the December 1997 Luxembourg Summit and only invited the six countries to begin accession negotiations in March 1998. The eventual membership of the state waiting the longest, Turkey, was essentially put off indefinitely. Although official EU statements referred to Turkey's poor human rights record as a justification for the action, the political, economic, and social challenges raised by the prospect of free movement from an Islamic country remains an unspoken subtext of Turkey's stalled application process.

The criteria for EU membership are a democratic government, a market economy, rule of law, respect for human rights, and the ability and willingness to take on the obligations of membership that have accumulated over time, the *Acquis Communitaire*. The *Acquis* has been expanded by the Amsterdam Treaty with the incorporation of the Schengen Convention, and each new member state is expected to accept this expanded *Acquis* at the time of accession (see, e.g., European Commission 1997b). Enlargement of the regimes governing migration within and to the EU will have a significant impact on existing EU cooperation and integration and will entail major changes in the migration policies of the new member states. Moreover, the very prospect of enlargement has given the norms of EU migration regimes an influence beyond the current boundaries of the EU itself, with significant implications for the sovereignty of applicant states.

Although EU enlargement presents some potential advantages to the further development of European cooperation on migration (e.g., more comprehensive migration regimes based on an EU institutional framework), it presents very serious challenges as well. The Dublin Convention, the Edinburgh declaration that east-central European states like Poland, the Czech Republic, and Hungary are "safe"; Germany's revision of its asylum law to invalidate asylum applications of those who passed through these countries in effect made east-central Europe into the EU's immigration buffer zone. Estonian, Hungarian, Slovenian, and Polish membership would eliminate this buffer zone and expand the EU's borders to Croatia, Serbia, Romania, and Russia—large and potentially very large migrant-sending countries. With enlargement, the costs of the EU's increasingly restrictionistic common asylum policies will be less easily externalized and, given the incorporation of the Schengen Convention into the EU treaty that east-central European states are aspiring to join, free movement within the EU could some day begin just west of Minsk. Through increasing JHA cooperation and incorporation of the Schengen Convention into the EU treaty framework, the Amsterdam Treaty poses challenges to widening the EU to include new members and ratchets up the membership criteria that applicants must meet.

Given that the leading candidates for EU membership are more likely to have been net emigration rather than immigration countries, they have not yet developed the administrative structures necessary for the implementation of the laws, rules, and regulations of the Union that they are joining. This fact of life will diminish confidence among current members in the ability of applicant states to fulfill their obligations, such as external border control. Such lack of confidence does not bode well for further deepening cooperation on migration after widening the Union. Moreover, it is clear that aspiring member states will have to meet increasingly strict criteria for cooperation in Justice and Home Affairs in order to join the EU and that these criteria have already had a significant impact on the migration policies of the applicant states.

According to the guidance of the Commission's plan for enlargement contained in *Agenda 2000,* criteria for JHA cooperation include: Council of Europe membership and ratification of its human rights conventions; ratification of the Geneva Convention on the Status of Refugees and the 1967 New York Protocol; adoption of the Dublin Convention and the JHA *Acquis* at the time of enlargement, including the Schengen Convention; and the development of an independent judiciary and the administrative apparatus to implement JHA policies (see European Commission 1997b). All applicant states have become members of the Council of Europe, and the first group of applicants from central and eastern Europe are all signatories of the Geneva Convention. Hungary has a geographic reservation that restricts application of the Geneva Convention to European refugees. A new asylum law intends to remedy this deficiency. Although the Dublin Convention is not open to non-EU member states, the Czech Republic is revising its asylum laws to include the "safe country of origin" and "safe third country" principles; Estonia only ratified the Geneva Convention in February 1997, although the implementing legislation includes EU requirements; Hungary is preparing a new asylum law to update administrative procedures; the Polish legislature is working on an Aliens Act that would address existing deficiencies with respect to the "safe third country" principle; and Slovenia is preparing a new asylum law, although the Commission has voiced concerns that the proposed legislation might not include all the legislation necessary to fully meet the JHA *Acquis*. The Czech Republic, Estonia, Hungary, Poland, and Slovenia all have bilateral readmission agreements with most of their neighbors. Estonia and Slovenia use the EU list for determining visa requirement; however, the Czech Republic, Hungary, and Poland allow visa-free travel (with invitations) for nationals of the New Independent States (NIS), including Russia (European Commission 1997c,d,e,f,g).

While aspiring members have worked diligently in adopting treaties and passing legislation to meet EU norms, the major challenges appear to be primarily in the development of judicial and administrative infrastructures that are up to the task of implementing the adopted laws and regulations. Commission assessments of the ability to assume the obligations of JHA membership (in the order of best performance) indicate that the Czech Republic is likely to meet the JHA *Acquis* within the next few years, although it needs to improve its communications systems for border control and develop more effective means to fight organized crime; Hungary's legislation is "on track" to meet the JHA *Acquis*, but the Commission is concerned about the potential abuse of the immigration permits given to ethnic Hungarians and the possibility that the facilitation of travel by ethnic Hungarians may interfere with external border control; Slovenia should meet the EU's legal requirement, but needs to develop its judicial system and be able to fully implement its new asylum law; Poland faces "significant challenges" with "border management, migration, and transnational crime" and "could" meet the JHA *Acquis;* Estonia needs a "sustained effort" in both passing legislation and improving its administration of asylum policies (European Commission 1997c,d,e,f,g).

Much as southern European states have been developing migration policies that are influenced by northern European norms (Baldwin-Edwards 1997), central and east European states are trying to follow the moving target of EU norms. While the existence of an EU migration regime and the question of member state sovereignty over migration is debated by academics, the actions of aspiring member states to conform to EU norms is a testament to the regime's existence. When applicant states change their migration policies to satisfy the EU despite preexisting national interests to maintain the status quo, we also see how the norms of the emerging EU migration regime impinge on the sovereignty of the states that are not even members. For example, as EU officials were criticizing Poland's porous borders in Birmingham, Polish officials began tightening rules for travelers from Belarus and Russia while, at the same time, worrying that the EU wanted new visa requirements in place by the end of 1998 (Barker 1998). Traders from Belarus and Ukraine generate a significant amount of business in Polish bazaars, and Polish officials are concerned that the recently enacted travel restrictions may hurt regional economies (Barker 1998). Similarly, EU concerns may prompt Hungary to abandon aspects of its policy toward Hungarian co-ethnics from neighboring states.

Here, a common policy bent on restricting migration is not reinforcing the sovereignty over borders of the states participating in that common policy. Rather, states with more open migration policies are voluntarily constraining their freedom to decide who may enter their countries. They do so not because they are compelled by the rulings of supranational court, but because they wish to be members in good standing of Europe's international migration regime.

Balkan Refugee Crises

While some countries east of the EU have been working hard to meet the criteria to join, others to the southeast have produced sudden refugee flows that have presented major challenges to EU cooperation in both foreign and home affairs. The collapse of Yugoslavia, the Bosnian War, and the Kosovo crisis have not only tested European cooperation, they have also vividly demonstrated the consequences of migration for international politics. Readers who have not been fully persuaded that migration is central to international politics in the post–Cold War world should just consider the latest episode. The NATO air strikes that began on March 24, 1999, were in large measure prompted by the Serbian repression of Kosovo Albanians that, in the preceding fifteen months, had driven out over one hundred thousand asylum seekers, eighty-five thousand of whom went to the EU (UNHCR 1999a). As over eight hundred thousand refugees poured out of Kosovo in the wake of the NATO bombing campaign, the shaky consensus within the alliance to continue bombing solidified around the objective of returning the refugees. In addition to the generation of refugee flows to the EU, demographic factors played a key role in the outbreak of ethnic conflicts within Yugoslavia, and emigrants had a hand in the breakup of Yugoslavia itself as well as in the Kosovar bid for independence from Serbia.

As mentioned in chapter 3, the west European ideal of representative democracy within states delineated along national lines flew in the face of eastern Europe's demography, and the dispersal of ethnic groups was perhaps no place as extensive as in Yugoslavia. Although Tito's death and attempts at reform within the League of Yugoslav Communists in the mid-1980s opened an opportunity for the entire country of Yugoslavia to join fellow east European countries in the march toward democracy, the potential for exploiting cleavages among Yugoslavia's nationalities proved too tempting for unscrupulous politicians. The gray communist *apparatchik,* Slobodan Milosevic, transformed himself into a populist when he mobilized Kosovo's Serbian minority by fanning fears of rapid Albanian population growth relative to the Serbs and vowing to protect the Serbs from the Albanian threat. As the utility of nationalism quickly became evident to Milosevic, his propagation of a Serbian nationalist movement short-circuited liberal reform within Yugoslavia and prompted Croatian and Slovenian communists to form their own reform parties, pursue separatist agendas, and develop their own nationalist movements.

Milosevic found a Croatian alter-ego in the nationalist Franjo Tudjman, who wanted an independent state for Croatians and refused to guarantee equal rights for Croatia's Serbs. However, the Croatian movement for national self-determination was not just a home-grown affair. Croatian emigrants supported Croatia's bid for independence from what they perceived as a Serb-dominated Yugoslavia, to the point of attempting to smuggle millions of dollars worth of weapons to Croatia (Swardson 1993). Before non-communist political parties were even legalized in Yugoslavia, Tudjman's Croatian Democratic Union (HDZ) and other newly created Croatian parties raised funds from the diaspora in western Europe, the United States, Canada, and Australia. It has been estimated that as much as 80 percent of the money spent by political parties in the 1990 elections came from Croatian emigrants and their descendants.[11] The lion's share, at least $4 million, went to Tudjman's HDZ (Glenny 1992, 63). These funds were primarily raised by Canadian Croats led by Gojko Susak, a refugee who came from Herzegovina in 1967 and became successful in the pizza business. After Tudjman won the election and Croatia declared independence on June 25, 1991, Tudjman appointed Susak defense minister. Susak's so-called "Herzegovina lobby" pushed for Croatian intervention in Bosnia-

Herzegovina to support ethnic Croats and prompted Tudjman to suggest the partition of Bosnia-Herzegovina between the Croats and Serbs (Zimmerman 1996, 181).

The Croatian diaspora also played an important role in Croatia's diplomatic recognition by the international community. Croats who originally came to Germany as Yugoslav guest workers lobbied German political parties, particularly the Bavarian Christian Social Union (CSU) and helped establish back-channel contacts between Tudjman and the Kohl government before Croatia declared independence. Then, in demonstrations during May 1991, thousands of Croatians called on Germany to recognize Croatian sovereignty. These activities helped place the question of self-determination—long championed by West German politicians for eastern Europe, particularly for East Germany—squarely before the German public and thereby contributed to forming a consensus among German political parties to recognize Croatia despite the protests of their fellow EU members, particularly Britain and France (Crawford 1996, 503). While the activities of Croatian emigrants were not, in and of themselves, decisive factors in German recognition of Croatia, German recognition proved decisive for the breakup of Yugoslavia in that it forced the rest of the EU to recognize Croatia as well. Although Bosnian Muslim leaders had publicly announced their objective of Bosnian sovereignty, as soon as the EU recognized Croatia, Bosnian Muslim leaders argued that Bosnia could not survive in a Serbian-controlled Yugoslavia (Zimmerman 1996, 177) and led their country out of Yugoslavia and into civil war.

Germany's unilateral recognition of Croatia nearly aborted the EU's Common Foreign and Security Policy; the feeble European response to the Bosnian War left it stillborn. As EU diplomats and peacekeepers proved incapable of stopping the "ethnic cleansing" of one ethnic group by the other, by October 1992, some seven hundred thousand Bosnians fled their country to neighboring states and the EU and more than two million became internally displaced.

The flight of Bosnians abroad raised a dilemma as articulated by Sadako Ogata, United Nations High Commissioner for Refugees: "To what extent do we persuade people to remain where they are, when that could well jeopardize their lives and liberties? On the other hand, if we help them to move, do we not become an accomplice to 'ethnic cleansing'" (Ogata 1992). Ogata advocated a more comprehensive approach to asylum that combined "preventative protection" within areas of origin and "temporary protection" for those who could no longer remain in their home country. Although asylum is ostensibly temporary by nature, the innovation of extending temporary protection to the Bosnians was intended to both expedite the reception of large numbers of refugees and provide UNHCR reassurance to receiving states that those who came would also leave once the conflict subsided. Given that the 1990 Dublin and Schengen conventions already set the stage for slowing, if not restricting, the asylum application process of EU member states, temporary protection was perhaps just as much a practical necessity.

EU member states did not in fact extend asylum with permanent residence permits to most Bosnians, but rather provided temporary protection that expired once peace was restored. As of the beginning of 1995, Germany provided temporary protection to 345,000 Bosnians, over three times as many as the rest of its fellow EU member states combined (UNHCR 1995, fig. 2.1). The disproportionate numbers prompted eighteen months of negotiation among EU member states on "burden sharing" that, in the end, produced a very weak agreement (MNS 1995a). After Srebenica fell to the Serbs in July 1995 and Serbs stepped up the shelling of Sarajevo in August, the UNHCR asked the EU to accommodate an additional 50,000 Bosnians. EU member states balked at taking in more, hoping instead that NATO military intervention would lead to a resolution of the crisis (MNS 1995b). The Bosnians were supposed to return after the November 1995 Dayton Accord stopped the fighting; however, given the widespread destruction of homes and the reluctance of the Bosnian Muslims to return to areas controlled by Serbs and Croats (and vice versa), the process of repatriation has been slow and difficult. By November of 1998, of the 345,000 Bosnians in Germany, 265,000 had returned or gone to a third country and 80,000 remained (MNS 1998i).

The experience of EU member states with Bosnia in many ways shaped their approach to Kosovo. Still dealing with the repatriation of Bosnians, the EU avoided offers of temporary protection to Kosovo Albanians and instead enunciated a policy of providing assistance to the displaced within Yugoslavia and to refugees in neighboring countries (MNS 1998h). Having accepted the bulk of those fleeing the Bosnian civil war, and unable to get a burden-sharing agreement from its fellow EU member states, Germany refused to provide temporary protection to the Kosovo Albanians (MNS 1998e) and Austria followed suit (MNS 1998f). After failing to effectively coordinate their actions in Bosnia, EU member states also accepted that they could not deal with Kosovo without the United States and NATO. After watching the atrocities in Srebenica as Dutch peacekeepers were rendered helpless, EU member states were also more inclined to use NATO air power and target Belgrade.

The Kosovo crisis revolved around a protracted struggle involving an Albanian majority versus a Serb minority in Kosovo, within the larger context of a Serb majority and Albanian minority in what was left of Yugoslavia. To this mix, one must add the rapidly growing diaspora of Kosovo Albanian emigrants who played a crucial role in the Kosovar self-determination movement. By the end of 1998 there were an estimated 600,000 ethnic Albanians in Europe and 300,000 in Canada and the United States who contributed to establishing independent education, social services, and public administration in Kosovo (Hedges 1999). Led by Ibrahim Rugova, this non-violent movement to establish a civil society was similar to previous resistance to totalitarian regimes in the 1970s and 1980s in other parts of eastern Europe. After the 1995 Dayton Accords led to EU recognition of Yugoslavia without having addressed the plight of Kosovo's Albanian majority, the more radical Kosovo Liberation Army (KLA) initiated attacks against Serbian police and eventually forged a political role that overtook the efforts of Rugova and other moderates. The KLA maintained a military command in Kosovo and a coordinating and fundraising operation in western Europe (Hedges 1999). To fund its activities, the KLA successfully managed to divert emigrant contributions for social services to military purposes and raise money directly—contributions to one KLA fund in Germany almost reached $1 million per month (Drozdiak 1998). The KLA also imposed "taxes" on Kosovo Albanian migrant workers who had hoped to remain less generous to the cause (Murphy 1998). Many Albanian emigrants and their children born abroad joined the KLA and returned to Kosovo to fight, as Serb police and paramilitary groups intensified attacks on Kosovo Albanian villages in the wake of NATO bombing.

Soon after the NATO bombs began falling, Serbian police and paramilitary groups stepped up attacks on Kosovo Albanian villages, refugee flows accelerated rapidly, and Macedonia closed its borders and threatened to keep them closed to refugees if they did not have a second country of asylum. In response, a special JHA Council meeting on April 7, 1999, reaffirmed that those displaced persons in need of protection should receive it within the region. The Council argued that long-term accommodation outside the area would only consolidate displacement and help Serbian leaders achieve their objectives of cleansing Kosovo of Albanians. Finally, the Council cited stress on emigrant-receiving states in the region, such as Macedonia, as a justification for individual member states to offer temporary protection (JHA 1999). Member states not only offered temporary protection but also organized an evacuation of refugees from Macedonia.

Germany had agreed to take up to 40,000; Greece 5,000; Italy, the Netherlands, and Ireland several thousand each and the United Kingdom announced that it would be taking in 1,000 refugees per week within a month. By the end of April 1999, European states allocated a total of 85,000 slots for the entry of Kosovo refugees (UNHCR 1999b).

The unprecedented evacuation did not proceed without its fair share of strife. Within ten days of announcing its offer of temporary protection, Germany evacuated 10,000 refugees. By the beginning of May, however, some *Länder,* particularly those with CDU and CSU led governments, refused to take in more refugees unless other EU member states fulfilled their pledges (MNS 1999a). Former German Chancellor Kohl said that it was "scandalous" that most EU states were reluctant to take in Kosovo refugees, and although he did not name the United Kingdom, it had only evacuated 330 refugees by that time (MNS 1999b). Jack Straw, U.K. Home Secretary, responded to criticism by pointing the finger at the UNHCR, which did not have the United Kingdom on the list of countries given to evacuation applicants. This was the case because, unlike other countries, the United Kingdom never gave a fixed quota to fulfill (MNS 1999c). By June 15, EU member states had evacuated over 50,000 Kosovo Albanians from Macedonia with Germany taking in over 14,500 and the United Kingdom receiving over 4,000 (UNHCR 1999c). By mid-June, Serb forces had also withdrawn from most of Kosovo and the net refugee flow reversed direction. Despite NATO requests that they wait until mines were first cleared, tens of thousands of refugees returned in the first few days after NATO deployed its forces in Kosovo.

The Bosnian and Kosovo refugee crises were challenges to EU cooperation that demonstrated the limits of restricting migration flows through tougher asylum policies at the same time that they exemplified refugee politics becoming "high politics" in post–Cold War Europe. Despite increasing EU cooperation that reduced the number of asylum seekers, commitments to human rights meant that EU member states, particularly Germany, could not shut the door to the hundreds of thousands of Bosnians who fled ethnic cleansing. EU member states, having provided temporary protection once before, would, or so the Serbian leadership in Belgrade may have surmised, eventually take in the Kosovo Albanians who were driven from their homes. Increasing refugee flows, however, can give moralistic humanitarian intervention an additional *realpolitik* justification of national interests, as President Clinton's rationale for invading Haiti in 1994 made quite clear. If EU member states were to avoid "another Bosnia" of daily atrocities on the evening news and waves of refugees that would be politically unfeasible to turn back, then, as diplomacy failed, military intervention became the only option. NATO miscalculated in thinking that a show of resolve would bring a quick diplomatic resolution to the crisis and in not anticipating the Serbian expulsion of Kosovo Albanians. The Serbian leadership miscalculated in thinking that massive refugee flows generated by ethnic cleansing would be tolerated by NATO's European members as well as had been the case with the Bosnians. Instead, "return the refugees" provided NATO the clear military objective that it had heretofore lacked and a "national interest" that individual leaders of alliance members could use to drum up political support for continued bombing and even the planning of ground deployments.

The Challenge of Human Smuggling

EU cooperation to reduce the number of bogus asylum claims by harmonization of the application process had been paired with increasing cooperation to reduce illegal migration through cooperation on visa policy and the erection of a common external border of more efficient controls. Such cooperation to combat illegal migration has been undermined by migrants' increasing use of smugglers to help them enter the EU clandestinely. Human smuggling thereby challenges the effectiveness of EU border control.

Although it is difficult to ascertain how many people have been smuggled into the EU, there have been many cases of traffickers ferrying migrants from North Africa to Spain and from Albania to Italy, Chinese flown into the EU via Moscow, and Russian and eastern European women trafficked throughout western Europe to work as prostitutes (IOM 1996, 1998; GSN 1997). Recently, increasing numbers of cases have been noted in Germany (MNS 1998d), the United Kingdom, and France (IOM 1996) as well as transit countries like Poland (PAP 1998) and Hungary (MTI 1998). The profit potential of exploiting vulnerable indentured labor was highlighted by a case in which Italian labor inspectors found 242 immigrants, mostly Chinese, working twelve-hour days in Tuscan leather workshops and earning about $11 per day (Reuters 1998). It is estimated that tens of thousands of women from Russia and eastern Europe have been smuggled into the EU under false pretenses of finding work as hostesses or dancers only to have their passports taken upon arrival, be forced into prostitution to work off their smuggler's fee, and ultimately find themselves in debt-bondage situations (IOM 1995; GSN 1997).

The largest flows have been those of Kurds and Kosovo Albanians fleeing conflicts within their countries. Between July 1997 and January 1998, some three thousand people, mostly Kurds from northern Iraq and south-western Turkey, paid smugglers $2,000 to $8,000 for passage to Italy by boat (IOM 1998). In 1997–98, Kosovo Albanians faced increasing attacks by Serbian police and paramilitary groups at home and a low probability of finding a safe haven within the EU, where there was no offer of tempo-rary protection. Thousands turned to smugglers to get them into the EU, particularly to Germany (MNS 1998d,g) that together with Switzerland al-ready hosted most of the EU's population of Kosovo Albanians. Of the twelve thousand persons apprehended while being smuggled into Germany in 1998, the largest group (between four and five thousand) were Kosovo Albanians (Dalka 1999).

Although human smuggling prompted JHA action as early as 1993, when the JHA Council agreed to a set of recommendations for member states to combat trafficking (JHA 1993), JHA ministers refocused their at-tention on human smuggling, particularly on the transportation of Turkish and Iraqi Kurds to Italian shores by Turkish and Italian criminal organiza-tions and the trafficking in women and children by Russian Mafiyas. In No-vember 1996, JHA ministers adopted a joint action initiated by the Com-mission to establish an information exchange between officials responsible for combating trade in human beings and the sexual exploitation of chil-dren (JHA 1996). The objectives of this joint action were partially realized in an October 1997 Conference of Ministers on the Prevention of Illegal Migration. The EU and other ministers involved in the so-called Berlin Pro-cess dealing with illegal migration as well as representatives from relevant international organizations adopted recommendations in areas including "harmonization of legislation to combat trafficking in aliens" and "linkage in trafficking in aliens and other forms of organized crime" (MNS 1997, 3–6). On January 26, 1998, EU foreign ministers adopted a forty-six-point plan directed at reducing the numbers of Kurds arriving illegally in the EU (MNS 1998a, 4–6). JHA ministers took up the action plan at their January 29–30 informal summit meeting in Birmingham, where Germany pressed for implementation of the plan and expressed fears that Kurds ar-riving in Italy would easily move on to Germany (ER 1998).

The January Action Plan aims to reduce the entrance of Turkish and Iraqi Kurds, described as "illegal refugees" as well as "illegal immigrants." The Council stated that these migrants "almost always make use of traf-fickers, of whom the majority appear to be part of organized crime net-works, with contacts in the EU" (qtd. in MNS 1998a, 4). Only three of the forty-six points were devoted to "ensuring that humanitarian aid makes an effective difference, while most points were focused on more restrictive measures—six on "effective application of asylum procedures"; six on "preventing abuse of asylum procedures; and twenty on "combating illegal immigration," most of which were devoted to enhanced border control and effective removal (MNS 1998a, 4–6).

Tougher border controls as well as visa and asylum policies make illegal migration more difficult and drive up its costs; however, these policies inadvertently prompt more migrants to use smugglers and entice more entrants into the increasingly profitable smuggling business. When refugees fleeing for their lives confront tougher asylum policies and increasing international cooperation to restrict access, they increasingly turn to smugglers, as the example of Kosovo Albanians amply demonstrated.

Nevertheless, the smuggling of Kosovo Albanians was transformed by the NATO military action. The refugee crisis fueled by NATO's action quickly melted resistance among EU member states to extend temporary protection status to Kosovo Albanians. With the extension of temporary protection and refugee status, Kosovo Albanians could enter the EU through regular asylum channels and therefore, should not have needed the smugglers. However, because the airlift evacuation focused on Macedonia and the Albanian government steadfastly kept its borders open and argued against removal of refugees from its territory, the option to be evacuated to the EU (or other countries) was not necessarily given to the bulk of the Kosovars in Albania. Moreover, receiving governments chose the refugees they would accept and bureaucratic red tape contributed to a situation in which some evacuation flights departed with a fifth of the seats empty (McGory 1999).

Many Kosovo refugees in Albania decided to leave without having to endure the application for evacuation to the EU from the camps. They made their way to Vlore (the primary embarkation point for the speed boats that cross the Adriatic to Italy) or accepted offers from Albanian smugglers who plied their services in Albanian cities and even the refugee camps. Since Italy declared its willingness to provide temporary protection, the Kosovars and their smugglers did not have to worry about deportations. Once in Italy, many Kosovars made their way, with or without the assistance of smugglers, to join relatives further north in Germany and Switzerland. Even if they were stopped at or near the Italian border, they were not returned to Yugoslavia as had previously often been the case. For example, in the beginning of April, France granted residency permits to twenty-seven Kosovars who clandestinely crossed the Italian-French border, and President Chirac declared that France would grant asylum to Kosovars who were driven out by ethnic cleansing (Reuters 1999).

With Serbian withdrawal from Kosovo, it would appear that Kosovo Albanians would no longer need the services of the smugglers. Despite the heartfelt desire to return that the refugees repeatedly expressed, the widespread destruction of homes and uncertain security future of Kosovo may lead a significant portion of the refugees to think twice about returning. Moreover, the EU quickly announced a reconstruction fund for Kosovo to the tune of $500 million per year for three years; however, much of the money for rebuilding Kosovar homes will most likely come from where it has in the recent past—Kosovo Albanians working abroad. According to a 1998 IMF estimate, Albanian migrant workers—many of whom are in the EU illegally—sent home remittances to the tune of $1 million per day (MN 1998). Given that Britain and other EU member states refused to provide funds to rebuild Serbia as long a Milosevic is in power, it is anticipated that "hundreds of thousands" of Serbs will go abroad in search of work (*Economist* 1999). Displaced Kosovo Serbs will most likely join displaced Kosovo Albanians among the destitute and desperate to whom the smugglers' market their services. If EU member states do not provide rapid and sufficient financial assistance to Kosovo and Serbia, there will be pressure for Kosovo Albanian and Serb families to institute their own foreign aid programs by sending one or more family members abroad. EU member states may choose to tolerate such illegal migration for the sake of lowering the need for official foreign aid (as the United States did for Central Americans in the aftermath of Hurricane Mitch). If not, one can be sure that smugglers will be waiting for the migrants.

EU member state cooperation on migration already exceeds that of other regional organizations of comparable advanced industrialized states. Member states may, for the most part, remain sovereign over migration from outside of the EU; however, they are not as sovereign as non-EU member states, due largely to the constraints of EU membership and the demands of continuing integration in general. Moreover, the Amsterdam treaty has initiated a course of action from intergovernmental cooperation toward the integration of member state migration policies on a European-wide basis. This deepening of European integration of migration policy and cooperation in Justice and Home Affairs is matched by its widening to embrace applicant states from central and eastern Europe. The Bosnian and Kosovo refugee crises as well as the increase in human smuggling have challenged EU cooperation on asylum policy and illegal migration. In the face of these challenges, the effectiveness of the EU's increasingly restrictive migration policies and border controls remain unclear. Nevertheless, if the recent EU activity to combat human smuggling is any indication, the policy discourse linking EU integration of migration policy to public concerns with personal security facilitates the formation of a political dynamic that may make major future transfers of sovereignty increasingly possible. The deepening and widening of integration in migration policy making and cooperation in Justice and Home Affairs are manifestations of a transformation of sovereignty in the emerging European polity that is far from over.

Conclusion

*T*his book demonstrates the influence of international migration and citizenship on the course of world politics: from the expansion of Europe over the rest of the world; to the rise of the United States and Russia as great powers; to changing nationality laws and the emergence of EU citizenship; to increasing EU cooperation on erecting a common external border; to, most recently, NATO intervention in Kosovo. At the same time, the book is also about the conceptualization of world politics and politics in general.

We tend to think of politics as taking place within and between the territories delineated by maps, and we draw our thickest lines around the 185 states that recognize each other as players in the game of international politics. Since most people are born, grow old, and die in the same state, we tend to take for granted that people line up with their designated states. If one stops to consider that the number of migrants worldwide equals the current population of Japan, the nice neat packages of nation-states, which encompass both people and territory, begin to fray around the edges. If one goes further when thinking about world politics and focuses on international migration and the political practices of people, it becomes more difficult to take the nation-state for granted and territoriality does not seem as solid a theoretical foundation as it once did. If one takes a step back and puts the nation-state in the perspective gained by considering migration throughout all of human history, one begins to wonder why the nation-state seemed to loom so large in the first place. The nation-state is not an eternal verity upon which to base general theories, but rather the central political institution of a quite limited period of time. Although world politics may currently be organized around the nation-state, it has not been so for all that long and it may not be the case in the future.

This book has depicted neorealism as a major culprit because it views existing territorial nation-states as the units of international relations analysis regardless of unwarranted assumptions of the continuity of people with place. Based on spatial and geographical referents, these assumptions lead to convenient, but overly simplistic and misconceived, understandings of identity and territoriality. While assumptions of territoriality made sense in the context of the historical development of the nation-state, when congruence between people and place as well as nation and state can no longer be taken for granted, territoriality impairs understanding. Once political identity can no longer be taken as a given in a territorial assumption, it becomes clear that the dynamics of individual political identity formation are critical to the delineation of the units of the international system. This process of identity formation hinges on the politics of citizenship, and citizenship laws are historically conditioned by the demographic context in which they developed. Since citizenship is shaped by international migration while the politics of citizenship is played out domestically, the process of identity formation is at the juncture of domestic and international politics. In this way, the politics of migration and citizenship is not only constitutive of the units of the international system, it also influences the interaction between them.

Although criticism has been primarily directed at neorealism and the state-centric conceptualization of world politics upon which it rests, the picture presented is also not that bright for various neoliberal arguments. For example, some argue that the spread of liberal democracy and free market economics has vanquished alternative ideologies (Fukuyama 1992) and others argue that democracies do not fight one another (Russett 1993). Theories that postulate changes in international politics due to democratization are also suspect because they generally assume the continuity of the demos and the democratic state it rules.

Peace among democratic states is conditioned by a demographic context that is generally overlooked. The expansion of what Dahl termed "restricted and full suffrage polyarchies" from three (the United States, Canada, and France) in 1880 to fifteen by the end of World War I (Dahl 1989, 234–39) occurred in the context of rapid population growth and unprecedented emigration. The first wave of democratization, in which most of world's long-established democracies were instituted, took place in a very unique demographic context that is unlikely to be repeated in the future due to the closing of New World frontiers and the global confluence of disease pools. While it may have been possible to assume the continuity of demos and democracy for these early democratic states due to the particular demographic context of the time, it may not be possible to do so for many contemporary and future democratizing states. In that the discontinuity of nation and state and demos and democracy is a potential source of international conflict, the experience of the long-established democracies may not be typical for future democracies.

Given falling fertility rates and increasing migration, the discontinuities between demos and democracy among established democratic states have been growing as well. Thus, migration clouds the neoliberal vision in several ways. Increasing migration and the exclusion of resident aliens calls into question the degree to which many established democracies are in fact democratic. Moreover, increasing migration prompts polarization of domestic politics within these established democracies and may put their political stability at risk. Either way, the problem of maintaining those democracies that already exist is at issue in the neoliberal presumption of a base of established democracies to which current democratization adds.

Moreover, in the context of the demographic expansion characteristic of the first wave of democratization, democratization is less likely to lead to conflicts among democratizing states than is democratization in the context of demographic contraction. For example, democratization of Serbia was susceptible to the manipulation of Serbian insecurities over relative population decline in comparison to Kosovo Albanians as demagoguery triumphed over democracy and ethnic conflict over multicultural accommodation.

This brings up perhaps the most problematic aspect of neo-Wilsonian liberalism—democratic self-determination. Again, the established democracies of western Europe gradually developed ethnically homogenous populations through expulsions in the sixteenth and seventeenth centuries and internal population growth in the eighteenth and early nineteenth centuries, long before democratizing in the later half of the nineteenth century and beginning of the twentieth centuries. This was not the case for many central and east European states. Democratic self-determination floundered on this demographic fact in the interwar period. It is also not the case for many of today's democratizing states. Democratization must increasingly take place in polyethnic societies, partly because the expulsions that helped form west European nation-states before their democratization are no longer tolerable. In polyethnic societies, democratization defined in terms of majority rule opens the possibility of secession and counter-secession based on democratic principles. In a conversation over Bosnian independence,

Richard Holbrooke (1999, 31) reports that one Yugoslav said, "Why should I be a minority in *your* state when you can be a minority in *mine*?" Since such acts of secession often lead to military as well as political conflict, democratization has the potential to increase rather than decrease war making, if not by internationally recognized states, then by ethnic groups in pursuit of statehood within which to constitute their democracy. Although long-established democracies may not go to war, democratizing states are another matter (Mansfield and Snyder 1995). This is particularly the case in the context of polyethnicity rendered by past migration.

Finally, just as Wilson assumed that democracy and federation were compatible, proponents of democracy as a solution to international conflict often see federation or confederation as the institutional structure for realizing further democratization (Barber 1995; Held 1995). Again, the problems of migration and citizenship have been overlooked in these conceptualizations, leaving these proponents susceptible to prescription based on inappropriate assumptions. In that the combination of migration and citizenship based on ancestral lineage leads to a conflict between democratic inclusiveness and federation in the EU, more ambitious proposals for utilizing confederalism or federalism as a framework for democratization on a global scale are ill-conceived. The projection of the United States to the global level, in which Wilson and his fellow advocates of democracy indulged, presupposed states in which citizenship was based on birthplace. Contemporary proposals stumble on the same point.

All too often, it seems as if international relations theory has become dominated by abstract debates over anonymous international actors and disembodied institutions. We easily forget that people make political institutions happen. Political institutions can die with the people who started them unless rules and conventions help successive generations reproduce the practices of their forebears. Rules and conventions, however, are not enough to maintain political institutions. Members of the group whose practices constitute the institution must reproduce themselves biologically and/or incorporate newcomers to the group if the political institutions in question are to survive. In a sense, indeed, demography is destiny. To understand the future as well as the past of the present political institutions, one must consider the demographic context of the development, maintenance, and demise of these political institutions. This brings us to the future of democracy and the nation-state in Europe as seen from the perspective of recent demographic trends.

Before proceeding, a note of caution: As the use of demographic statistics comparing the fertility rates of Serbs and Albanians should make painfully clear, demographic statistics and projections can become fuel for demagogues. Academic discussion of the political implications of demographic projections must by its very nature be very speculative. It is also fraught with potential misuse. Prudence may prescribe avoidance of such speculation altogether. Careful consideration of the policy implications of declining fertility may, however, prove more effective in warding off less reasoned analysis than would prudent silence.

According to Eurostat, the EU's 1996 population of 373 million inhabitants comprises 7 percent of total world population. Eurostat predicts that by the year 2050 the current fifteen member states of the EU will contain no more than 4 percent of the world's population (Eurostat 1997). Declining fertility rates mean a "births deficit" is leading to a situation in which deaths outnumber births. Some countries, such as Germany, have already experienced natural declines in native population. It is expected that Italy, Austria, and Denmark will soon follow, as will the rest of the EU member states in general. Even if the EU's total fertility rate increases from the 1997 level of 1.44 (Eurostat 1998) to the projected baseline levels of 1.55 in 2000 and 1.65 in 2020, the number of deaths will still exceed births sometime about the year 2010 (Eurostat 1997). Germany's population has only been maintained by net immigration, and that may soon be the case for the EU as a whole. From 1990 to 1994, net immigration added over five million people to the EU's population, and Eurostat predicts that net immigration in the medium to long term will vary between four hundred thousand and eight hundred thousand per year (Eurostat 1997).

As mentioned at the outset of this book, some European policymakers have described such flows in terms of a "migration crisis." European policymakers have mustered the political will to cooperate with one another in order to build an increasingly restrictionist regime governing migration to the EU. Building a "fortress Europe" at the EU's external borders, however, will not amount to a solution to the migration crisis that policymakers may perceive. Such restrictive policies do nothing to stop the underlying demographic trends toward depopulation of the EU that, in turn, increase the demand for immigration. If EU policymakers were actually able to stem the flows and stop the net migration that Eurostat predicts, the EU's population would only shrink faster.

Not only would there be fewer Europeans, but the population as a whole would be much older. As Peter Peterson (1999) puts it, at current fertility rates European states will soon have as many retirees as a percentage of their population as Florida does, where 18.5 percent of the population is sixty-five and older. Italy will become another Florida in 2003, Germany in 2006, the United Kingdom and France in 2016 (29). Without any reform of current pension systems, the ratio of working taxpayers to retirees eventually will drop in France and Germany to the current Italian ratio of 1.3 : 1, which has led to pension funding crises that have contributed to the demise of several governments (36–37).

Of course, there is the option of adopting pro-natalist policies. Sweden's generous parental leave subsidies and other social benefits have contributed to giving it the EU's highest fertility rate (2.04) during the period 1990–94 (Eurostat 1996d). It is questionable, however, as to whether an aging population of taxpayers can be convinced of the necessity of such major expenditures. More draconian pro-natalist polices, which infringe on the reproductive rights of women (such as had been taken to the extreme in Ceausescu's Romania), are unimaginable in Europe today.

Unless fertility rates increase dramatically over the next few decades, EU member states will most likely experience continued migration. Given that net migration to the EU has recently contributed to up to 70 percent of the EU's total population growth (Eurostat 1997), it is hard to imagine a future EU without significant net migration inflows in the hundreds of thousands per year. For those who believe that there is a European "migration crisis," an impermeable common EU border cannot be the "solution"— unless, of course, one views an EU with a shrinking, aging, and financially insecure population as a solution.

Barring self-defeating migration control policies and drastic changes in European reproductive practices, net migration to Europe will make European societies increasingly polyethnic. European policymakers should accept these demographic realities and begin to consider policies that foster greater political incorporation of their present resident alien population and prepare for those to come. Although I offer no specific policy recommendations in this regard, I do draw some conclusions about some of the policy options that have been taken and proposed.

European states with jus sanguinis citizenship laws inherited from the previous demographic context of large-scale emigration cannot maintain these laws in the context of increasing immigration without compromising their democracy. Growing populations of children who were not born into citizenship and cannot easily get it shrink the boundary of the demos in relation to the inhabitants of the state it rules. Although democracies can possibly tolerate this discrepancy at the margins and still be considered democratic, at a certain point they can no longer legitimately do so. Those European states that have accepted the reality of a future of immigration have liberalized their citizenship and naturalization policies, and even those that had long resisted similar changes are doing so as well. West European states have slowly, but surely, extended entitlements to citizenship to second-generation migrants (Hansen 1998). Together with Germany's latest reforms to introduce jus soli to third-generation, and in some cases second-generation, migrants, this liberalizing trend will help stem the growing number of "foreigners" being born in the EU who remain excluded from the demos. Given that increasing immigration has driven the recent trend of continental European states adopting jus soli, it bears out the argument made in chapter 4 that the demographic context of migration shapes states' citizenship laws.

Increasing immigration has also led some EU member states to extend political rights on the local level to non-nationals, and intra-EU migration has led to establishment of an EU citizenship that extends partial political rights to nationals of one EU state who live in another. EU citizenship has thereby reconfigured the European demos as a whole. If EU member states' liberalization of their citizenship laws for nationals of EU member states were to take place while they increased barriers to membership for immigrants from non-EU states, such change in policy would indicate citizenship law harmonization toward a form of EU jus sanguinis analogous to the German model of unification. The trend among EU member states to adopt jus soli that is applicable to all immigrants demonstrates movement in a contrary direction, toward the model of the American federation. Nevertheless, since full political rights on all levels are not extended to nationals of one EU member state living in another, and since EU citizenship only complements, rather than replaces, member state nationality, EU citizenship remains constitutive of a polity unlike traditional federations. Like the consociational democratic systems of several of its member states, the European polity seems headed in the near future toward political contestation on several dimensions organized along both territorial and non-territorial lines.

While immigration into several EU member states has come to rival that of the classic immigration countries of the United States, Canada, and Australia, the naturalization rates of European states have not, despite liberalization of naturalization rules. To remedy these low naturalization rates, some European states have eliminated renunciation requirements and policymakers and NGOs have advocated that other states permit dual nationality as well. Although there are reasons to believe that the option of dual nationality will increase naturalization, it may not have as great an impact as anticipated. The Netherlands experienced a record-breaking upsurge in naturalization after it dropped its renunciation requirement in

1991; however, the average naturalization rates of west European states that permitted dual nationality were not that much higher than those that required renunciation.[1] Still, over time, the trend among European states toward permitting dual nationality will gradually increase democratic inclusiveness through increasing naturalization.

Although the domestic politics of migration in several European states has led to policy changes embracing dual nationality to increase democratic inclusiveness, the declining demographic boundary regime has international consequences. Increasing cases of dual nationality are indicative of the trend toward overlapping authorities and multiple identities in an ever more complex European polity. They also have important policy implications for taxation, voting, and military service, which I plan to explore at length in the future but will only briefly mention at this time. Second nationalities enable economic elites to avoid taxes and conceal international travel. As nationalities of convenience are combined with offshore banking and the anonymous electronic money transfers of e-cash, even the most sophisticated states may confront obstacles to effective tax collection. Dual nationality also raises the prospect of individuals voting in two states. When combined with spreading democratization, the easing of prohibitions on dual nationality means that the potential of double voting could grow significantly. Perhaps most importantly, more dual nationals increase the potential for multiple military obligations. If international cooperation to minimize dual nationality is coming to an end, new forms of international cooperation on taxation, voting, and military service will become necessary to preempt the problems that prompted the development of international norms against dual nationality in the first place.

Dual nationality is closely linked with emigrant participation in home country politics. While home country participation of Croatians and Albanians (discussed in chapter 8) shows how emigrants can be a force for nationalism and separatism, in other cases emigrants have been forces for home country liberalization and democratization (Shain 1999). International migration along with advances in transportation and communications technology together with democratization foster a "globalization of the domestic politics" of many states that is similar to the globalization of national economies (for elaboration, see Koslowski 1994, 132–60). As emigrants increasingly become politically involved, the domestic politics of one state actually takes place in several states and becomes a dimension of politics neither within individual states nor between several states. In that this political practice is not captured by the imagery of domestic hierarchy/international anarchy, the globalization of domestic politics challenges traditional conceptualizations of world politics. A group of researchers and I have begun to analyze increasing emigrant political participation, the globalization of politics this activity represents, and impact of diasporas on international politics in general.[2] The rise of the KLA from a marginal rag-tag guerilla group to a negotiating party at the Rambouillet talks caught many foreign policymakers and analysts off guard. Hopefully, more research on emigrant participation in home country politics and the political and military impact of migrant worker remittances will improve future policy analysis as well.

The Bosnian and Kosovo refugee crises demonstrate that the EU cannot isolate itself from the political instability immediately beyond its frontiers. EU member states have either accepted hundreds of thousands of refugees at considerable economic and political cost or have participated in military intervention in efforts to stop such mass flight. Migration is not simply a function of relative economic growth rates but one of relative security as well. Many policymakers in EU member states may think restrictionist policies that increase the costs of migration beyond the gain of income-producing work in the EU will significantly reduce migration to the EU. As the European Commission (1994a, 13–19) pointed out, the desired results may not be possible without addressing migration's root causes—human rights abuses, civil war, economic disparities, population growth, and environmental degradation. The effectiveness of the EU's response to increasing human smuggling will provide a test of EU border control; however, that will have to be taken up in a future study.

Notes

INTRODUCTION

1. Due to the inherent methodological and administrative difficulties in gathering migration statistics from all of the world's states, these estimates are rather imprecise. Nevertheless, since these figures do not include illegal migrants, whose numbers are even more difficult to ascertain, they are unlikely to overstate the actual numbers of all migrants—legal and illegal.

2. For example, the *Economist* predicted that the number of immigrants "may continue in the low millions in each year of the 1990s" (*Economist* 1991, 11–12).

3. See Waever et al. 1993, especially chap. 8.

CHAPTER ONE

1. This phrase appears in official statements of the German interior ministry, including the "German National Report" for the 1994 U.N. Population and Development Conference in Cairo. See Münz and Ulrich 1995.

2. These are 1994 figures for children born with foreign citizenship as percentage of total births and legitimate children born to mixed German/foreign marriages as percentage of children born with German citizenship. See Frey and Mammey 1996, table A-6.

3. Contrast Morgenthau 1978 and Aron 1966 with Waltz 1979.

4. See, e.g., Thucydides 1972, 35–36; Schmitter Heisler and Heisler 1989.

5. For an overview, see Keohane and Nye 1972; Mansbach, Ferguson, and Lampert 1976; Risse-Kappen 1995.

6. Weiner 1989, 75, cited in Hollifield 1992, 21n. 5.

7. See Oye 1986 and especially Axelrod and Keohane 1986. See also Katzenstein's (1996b) commentary on the convergence of neorealism and neoliberalism.

8. My working definition of polity is adopted from Ferguson and Mansbach: "A polity (or political authority) has a distinct identity; a capacity to mobilize persons, that is, for value satisfaction; and a degree of institutionalization and hierarchy (leaders and constituents)" (Ferguson and Mansbach 1996, 34).

9. Similarly, the composition of the polity changes through the death of its members and the acceptance into the polity of children born to members. Assimilation of these children into the polity is also assumed.

10. The following discussion draws freely from Koslowski and Kratochwil 1994.

11. The constructivist approach employed in this paper parts company with the state-centric approach taken by Alexander Wendt (1994).

12. Those not born to constituent members of the association may gain formal state membership through naturalization.

CHAPTER TWO

1. On the concept of "spill over," see Haas 1958, 283–317; Nye 1971, 200. On the implicit federal goal of neofunctionalism, see Groom 1978.

2. "It is the distinguishing mark of the sovereign that he cannot in any way be subject to the commands of another, for it is he who makes law for the subject, abrogates laws already made and amends obsolete law" (Bodin 1967, 28).

3. For analytical purposes it is useful to differentiate between migration within the EU of member state nationals and migration to the EU of non-EU nationals, and to attribute different patterns of regime formation to each. This division, however, is problematic because there are many gray areas in between—such as the intra-EU migration of permanent resident aliens from non-EU countries and cooperation on border controls that simultaneously deals with both borders between EU member states and their common external border.

CHAPTER THREE

1. See Buzan, Jones, and Little 1993, 86–88.

2. The first paragraph of McNeill's *A World History* sets out the theme of the work: "The first great landmark of human history was the development of food production, which permitted an enormous multiplication of human numbers, and laid the basis for the emergence of civilizations. How, when, and where hunting and gathering gave way to farming and pastoralism is uncertain. One of the earliest and most important instances of this transition took place in the Middle East, perhaps between 8500 and 7000 B.C. Thence through migrations and borrowings, few of which can be reconstructed by modern scholars, grain cultivation spread into Europe and India, China, and parts of Africa. . . ." (McNeill 1967, 1).

3. See McNeill 1982, vii–viii. For a more extended discussion of the relationship between macroparasitism and microparasitism, see McNeill 1992, 69–131. Ironically, Steven Walt appeals to McNeill's *The Pursuit of Power* (1982) to argue against those who "have suggested broadening the concept of 'security' to include topics such as poverty, AIDS, environmental hazards, drug abuse, and the like. . . . However much we may regret it, organized violence has been a central part of human existence for millennia and is likely to remain so for the foreseeable future. Not surprisingly, therefore, preparations for war have preoccupied organized polities throughout history" (see Walt 1991, 213). Unfortunately, by relying on just *The Pursuit of Power* rather than consulting its "twin," *Plagues and Peoples,* Walt has used McNeill's work to argue against incorporating biological and environmental factors in understanding political change, precisely the accomplishment that McNeill is perhaps most known for. Moreover, Walt missed the point of McNeill's larger argument on the importance of cultural borrowing in *The Rise of the West,* to which *The Pursuit of Power* was "a belated footnote" (McNeill 1982, ix).

4. One need only consider the devastating outbreak of cholera that accompanied the 1994 mass migration of Rwandans fleeing ethnic conflict to gain an appreciation of the relationship between military movements and disease.

5. Although the size of the Amerindian populations before European conquest is the subject of extensive historical debate, the native die-off was very large. Tzvetan Todorov provides estimates in the upper range: "It will be recalled that in 1500 the world population is approximately 400 million, of whom 80 million inhabit the Americas. By the middle of the sixteenth century, out of these 80 million, there remain ten. Or limiting ourselves to Mexico: on the eve of conquest, its population is about 25 million; in 1600, it is one million" (Todorov 1982, 141).

6. See McNeill 1986, 34–56. Interestingly, the period in which nationalism among European political elites began to develop, particularly with the English revolution of 1640, coincided with a period of population growth between 1450 and 1650. See Fernand Braudel 1979, 33.

7. On the political consequences of urban dispersion, see Johnson 1991, 10–12.

8. Aristotle first made this connection. "He who would inquire into the essence and attributes of various kinds of governments must first of all determine 'What is a state?' . . . Some say that the state has done a certain act; others, no not the state, but the oligarchy or the tyrant. And the legislator or statesman is concerned entirely with the state; a constitution or government being an arrangement of the inhabitants of a states. But a state is composite, like any other whole made up of its parts;—these are the citizens, who compose it. It is evident, therefore, that we must begin by asking, Who is the citizen, and what is the meaning of the term?" (Aristotle 1941, 1176).

9. Eventually they elected the executive and upper house as well.

10. Brubaker's dissertation was published in a shorter version; see Brubaker 1992.

11. Figures are for 1993; see OECD 1995, 26, chart I.7.

12. See, e.g., Dahl 1989, 239, table 17.1.

CHAPTER FOUR

1. The restrictive citizenship law of 451 B.C. was repealed in 429 B.C. and then reinstated in 403 B.C. (Boegehold 1994).

2. Technically speaking, the principles of jus soli and jus sanguinis are associated with the ascription of nationality, or the international aspect of state membership. With respect to the problem of resident aliens for democracy, however, legitimization of the democratic state hinges on the acquisition of state membership in terms of the full political rights of citizenship. In modern representative democracies, that means the rights to vote and stand for election at all levels of the polity—local, regional, and national. Given my focus on democratic inclusiveness, I am primarily concerned here with the internal aspect of state membership, or citizenship, and the incumbent acquisition of full political rights. Hence, instead of exclusively referring to nationality with respect to jus sanguinis or jus soli, I often refer to citizenship, in terms of full political rights, in order to stress this internal aspect of formal state membership. In instances where the international aspect of state membership is of primary concern, I refer to nationality in order to make the distinction.

3. Jus soli was retained as certain subjects of the British empire came to be considered British citizens and others citizens of newly independent states, but the British nationality act of 1981 constricted that principle with jus sanguinis provisions. Now, a child born of aliens in the United Kingdom becomes a citizen only if at least one parent is a legal permanent resident

alien with no time limit on his or her stay. Children of illegal aliens, students, and those with limited visas are not automatically considered citizens. Previously, birth in a British colony entitled one to citizenship in the United Kingdom and its colonies, whereas now it only yields British Dependent Territories citizenship, with British citizenship reserved for those born in the United Kingdom itself. See Dummett and Nicol 1990, 231–59.

4. The French Constitution of 1791 unequivocally granted citizenship to the children of French fathers born in France, thereby adopting a combination of the jus sanguinis and jus soli principles. For those born of French parents outside of France and those of foreign fathers inside of France, a similar combination was used in naturalization that tended toward the jus soli principle. Later, with the development of the French Civil Code, the jus sanguinis principle came to inform law more extensively, tilting the balance in the opposite direction. For an extensive discussion of the initial delineation of French citizenship and combination of the principles of jus sanguinis and jus soli in that delineation, see Brubaker 1990, 100–115, 176–209; Grawert 1973, 165–70.

5. See AJIL 1929, 29. Of continental European countries, citizenship ascription in France, Belgium, Portugal, Spain, the Netherlands, Malta, and Bulgaria follow jus soli in certain cases in addition to jus sanguinis. See Council of Europe 1995; OECD 1995, 160, table III.2.

6. See "Nationality Law of July 22, 1913" in Flournoy and Hudson 1929, 306–13.

7. In the Americas, only Panama and Haiti base citizenship on jus sanguinis (Brubaker 1990, 169).

8. One could also apply to retain German citizenship after naturalization elsewhere, children of German emigrants born abroad who became citizens of jus soli countries at birth did not lose German citizenship, and military requirements were made easier to fulfill. See Brubaker 1992, 115.

9. "Unless otherwise provided by law, a German within the meaning of this Basic Law is a person who possesses German citizenship or who has been admitted to the territory of the German Reich within the frontiers of 31 December 1937 as a refugee or expellee of German stock (*Volkszugehörigkeit*) or as the spouse or descendent of such person." See the Basic Law printed in Hucko 1987, 255.

10. The residence rights of migrant workers from one EU member state working in another (e.g., Italians working in Germany or Spaniards in France) are based on the host country's EU treaty obligations rather than on individual labor contracts.

11. See treaties concluded by the Council of Europe, including the 1950 European Convention on Human Rights, the 1963 Fourth Protocol to the European Convention on Human Rights, the 1955 European Convention on Establishment, and the 1961 European Social Charter in Plender 1988b, 151–206.

CHAPTER FIVE

1. My argument at times seems critical of citizenship based on ancestral lineage, but my intent is to describe and analyze this principle of citizenship with respect to democracy rather than prescribe adoption of jus soli. Jus soli is not a cure-all. For instance, ascription of citizenship at birth based on jus soli raises other problems for the definition of the demos, particularly with respect to the children of illegal aliens and expatriates. See Schuck and Smith 1985. Similarly, I am not making an argument for or against European federalism or European citizenship as embodied in the Maastricht Treaty. I merely wish to examine some of the political consequences of migration for both.

2. This described the situation until November 1, 1993, when EU citizenship went into effect. See chapter 6.

3. See, e.g., Wheare 1964; Riker 1964; Duchacek 1986; King 1982; Elazar 1987.

4. See *The 1849 Constitution of the German Reich,* Part IV, Section I, reprinted in Hucko 1987.

5. Traditional federalist examinations of European integration focus on political frameworks, but they do not explore the stresses intra-European migration places on federal institutional arrangements. See Hay 1966; Friedrich 1968a, 1968b, 1969. Neither do more recent works on European federalism. See Forsyth 1981; Pinder 1991; Burgess 1989; Wistrich 1991.

6. Andrew Evans comes closest to the problem at hand by arguing that European integration challenges established citizenship laws of the member states, but he does not take the argument in the other direction. That is, he does not explore the consequences of member state citizenship laws for federalism. See Evans 1991, 190–215.

7. This assumes that B3 is not a descendent of citizens of A.

8. This alternative presupposes that both A and B permit dual nationality.

9. The inclusiveness of democracy in B may also be challenged. B3 may still participate in B and the composite community AB through his or her membership in B, but only if B3 can vote by absentee ballot, vote in B's consulate in A, or return to B for each election. Given these circumstances, the consistency and quality of B3's participation in community B may suffer after prolonged absence. If so, the other members of community B have reason to question B3's continuing membership. In fact, many countries do not allow citizens living abroad to vote in local and national elections.

CHAPTER SIX

1. See Lenaerts 1992. In the discussion following Dr. Lenaerts's presentation of this argument, he agreed that many of the cases critical to the constitutionalization of the treaty involved intra-EU migration.

2. France decentralized its administrative system at the beginning of the 1980s and thereby increased the powers of local government (Safran 1991, 211–18). Decentralizing administration differs from federalism (noncentralization) because local powers are not guaranteed and can be taken back by the central government just as easily as they were originally given (Elazar 1987, 34–38). In this way, the agenda of political choices is ultimately determined by the national government within which resident aliens have no say.

3. I owe this analogy to Jack Nagel.

CHAPTER SEVEN

1. Justice Felix Frankfurter commented that "no man should be permitted deliberately to place himself in a position where his services may be claimed by more than one government and his allegiance be due to more than one" (Frankfurter 1958). The German Constitutional Court echoed this argument (*Bundesverfassungsgericht* 1974, 254–55).

2. The U.N. International Law Commission drafted a Convention Relating to the Status of Stateless Persons in 1954 and a Convention on the Reduction of Statelessness in 1961. Signatory states took on a duty to extend nationality to those who would otherwise be stateless: "All persons are entitled to possess one nationality, but one nationality only" (ILC 1954).

3. A group of Harvard Law School researchers drew up the draft for the Hague Nationality Convention, and James Brown Scott—a leader of the effort to codify rules that would reduce cases of dual nationality—was also a U.S. delegate to the first Hague Peace Conferences, Secretary of the Carnegie Endowment for International Peace, and President of the American Society of International Law. (See Brown Scott 1930.)

4. "This convention does not prejudice the application of . . . the 1963 Convention on the Reduction of Cases of Multiple Nationality and Military Obligations in Cases of Multiple Nationality and its Protocols . . . in the relationship between the States Parties bound by these instruments" (Council of Europe 1997c).

5. The 1997 European Convention on Nationality was opened for signature on November 6, 1997, at which time it was signed by Austria, Denmark, Finland, Greece, Hungary, Iceland, Italy, the Netherlands, Norway, Portugal, Romania, Russia, Slovakia, Sweden, and the former Yugoslav Republic of Macedonia. It has subsequently been signed by Bulgaria and Moldova. As of June 15, 1999, only Austria and Moldova have ratified the Convention. See Council of Europe, European Treaties, Chart of Signatures and Ratifications, <http://www.coe.fr/tablconv/166t.htm>.

6. In 1995, the Lower Chamber of the Dutch Parliament passed a proposal to formalize the 1991 policy change and completely eliminate the prohibition on dual nationality in Dutch nationality law; however, the Upper Chamber blocked the change. Since then, the proposal lost critical support from the Christian Democrats in the Lower Chamber and the policy permitting dual nationality was reversed (ANP 1996). Beginning October 1, 1997, dual nationality would be permitted in only a very limited number of cases (Muus 1998).

7. See the Turkish Embassy web page, consular information for Turkish citizens, <http://turkey.org/services_fr.html>.

8. For details on Dominica's Economic Citizenship Programme, see <http://caribcats.com/citizenship.htm>.

CHAPTER EIGHT

1. For a perspective that stresses member state use of intergovernmental institutions, see Moravcsik 1991.

2. "An epistemic community is a network of professionals with recognized expertise and competence in a particular domain and an authoritative claim to policy-relevant knowledge within that domain or issue area" (Haas 1992b, 3).

3. For example, the March 1991 OECD International Conference on Migration.

4. See den Boer and Walker 1993, 9.

5. For a good account of unilateral, bilateral, and multilateral actions regarding asylum policy, see Ucarer 1997.

6. Quoted in International Intelligence Report 1994.

7. On the use of international norms by politicians to justify their actions, see Cortell and Davis 1996.

8. Nationals of certain Spanish-speaking Latin American states have only a one- or two-year residence requirement for naturalization instead of the usual ten. See Council of Europe 1995, 126.

9. The residency requirement of nationals of Portuguese-speaking states is six instead of ten years; however, "individuals who . . . are reputed to be of Portuguese descent or are members of Portuguese communities abroad, and foreigners who have carried out important work for the Portuguese State or who will be requested to do so in the future" may be dispensed from fulfilling residency and language requirements or demonstrating a "genuine link to the community." See Council of Europe 1995, 107. On accelerating naturalization through property purchases, see O'Nes 1990, 107–10.

10. When the Mexican government suggested labor migration be included in negotiations, the United States quickly rejected the idea knowing full well that any inclusion of labor migration into the agreement would make ratification impossible. See Weintraub 1992, 507.

11. Author's interview with Vesna Pusic on September 9, 1996. Pusic is a member of the Faculty of Philosophy, University of Zagreb; co-founder and director of the Erasmus Guild, a nongovernmental, nonpartisan think tank; and publisher of the journal *Erasmus*.

CONCLUSION

1. Refer to table 2. Compare average naturalization rates during 1991–96 for Belgium, France, Italy, the Netherlands, Switzerland, and the United Kingdom, which permitted dual nationality, with Austria, Denmark, Finland, Germany, Luxembourg, Spain, and Sweden, which did not. As a group the overall average naturalization of those countries that permitted dual nationality was 2.77, while the group average of those that did not was 2.33.

2. A workshop on *International Migration and the Globalization of Domestic Politics* was held at the Center on Global Change and Governance, Rutgers University, Newark, on May 14–15, 1999.

References

Adelman, Howard. 1997. "Why Refugee Warriors Are Threats." Presented at the International Studies Association Convention, Toronto, March.

Agence Europe. 1992. "France: Senate Approves Constitutional Revision Needed for Ratification of the Maastricht Treaty." *Agence Europe,* June 18.

——. 1995. "IGC Reflection Group—Majority in Favor of a Clause on Non-Discrimination." *Agence Europe,* September 27.

Agence France Presse. 1991. "Maastricht Prepares Europe as 'Greatest World Power,' France Says." *Agence France Presse,* December 11.

Aggarwal, Vinod. 1983. "The Unraveling of the Multi-Fiber Arrangement, 1981: An Examination of Regime Change." *International Organization* 37(4): 617–46.

AJIL (American Journal of International Law). 1929. Vol. 23, 2d supplement.

Alonso, William. 1987. "Identity and Population." In *Population in an Interacting World,* edited by William Alonso. Cambridge, Mass.: Harvard University Press.

Althusius, Johannes. 1964. *Politica Methodice Digesta, Atque Exemplis Sacris et Profanis Illustrata,* 3d ed., translated by Frederick S. Carney. In *The Politics of Johannes Althusius,* edited by Frederick S. Carney. Boston: Beacon Press.

Amsterdam Treaty. 1997. Conference of the Representatives of the Governments of the Member States, *Treaty of Amsterdam Amending, The Treaty on European Union, The Treaties Establishing the European Communities and Certain Related Acts Europa.*

Anderson, Malcolm, Monica den Boer, and Gary Miller. 1994. "European Citizenship and Cooperation in Justice and Home Affairs." In *Maastricht and Beyond,* edited by Andrew Duff, John Pinder, and Roy Price. London: Routledge.

ANP (Algemeen Nederlands Persbureau). 1995. "Some in EU Share Criticism of its Refugee Policy." *ANP English News Bulletin, Algemeen Nederlands Persbureau,* November 27.

——. 1996. "Schmitz Drops Idea of Dual Nationality." *ANP English News Bulletin,* November 7.

Appadurai, Arjun. 1996. *Modernity at Large: Cultural Dimensions of Globalization.* Minneapolis: University of Minnesota Press.

Arblaster, Anthony. 1987. *Democracy.* Minneapolis: University of Minnesota Press.

Archdeacon, Thomas J. 1983. *Becoming American: An Ethnic History.* New York: Free Press.

Ardittis, Solon. 1994. "East-West Migration: An Overview of Trends and Issues." In *The Politics of East-West Migration,* edited by Solon Ardittis. New York: St. Martin's Press.

Arendt, Hannah. 1951. *Origins of Totalitarianism.* New York: Harcourt, Brace.

Aristotle, 1941. *Politics.* In *The Basic Works of Aristotle,* edited by Richard McKeon. New York: Random House.

Armstrong, John A. 1982. *Nations before Nationalism.* Chapel Hill: University of North Carolina Press.

Aron, Raymond. 1966. *Peace and War: A Theory of International Relations.* New York: Praeger.

———. 1974. "Is Multinational Citizenship Possible?" *Social Research* 41: 638–56.

Art, Robert J., and Kenneth Waltz. 1971. "Technology, Strategy, and the Uses of Force." In *The Use of Force,* edited by Art and Waltz. Boston: Little, Brown.

Ausländerbeauftragte. 1997. *Facts and Figures on the Situation of Foreigners in the Federal Republic of Germany.* Bonn: Federal Government's Commissioner for Foreigners' Affairs.

Axelrod, Robert, and Robert Keohane. 1986. "Achieving Cooperation under Anarchy: Strategies and Institutions." In *Cooperation Under Anarchy,* edited by Kenneth Oye. Princeton: Princeton University Press.

Bade, Klaus J. 1980. "German Emigration to the United States and Continental Immigration to Germany in the Late Nineteenth and Early Twentieth Centuries." *Central European History* 13(4): 347–77.

Baker, David, Andrew Gamble, and Steve Ludlam. 1994. "The Parliamentary Siege of Maastricht 1993: Conservative Divisions and British Ratification." *Parliamentary Affairs* 47(1): 37–60.

Baldwin-Edwards, Martin. 1997. "The Emerging European Immigration Regime: Some Reflections on Implications for Southern Europe." *Journal of Common Market Studies* 35(4): 497–519.

Bancroft, George. 1849. Letter to Lord Palmerson, January 26. Reprinted in Sen. Ex. Docs. 38, 36th Congress, 1st Sess. 160 (1860).

Bar-Yaacov, Nissim. 1961. *Dual Nationality.* London: Praeger.

Barber, Benjamin R. 1984. *Strong Democracy: Participatory Politics for a New Age.* Berkeley: University of California Press.

Barber, Benjamin R. 1995. *Jihad vs. McWorld.* New York: Random House.

Barker, Anthony. 1998. "EU's Van den Broek Says Poland Must Tighten Border." *Reuters,* February 12.

Bauman, Zygmunt. 1997. *Postmodernity and Its Discontents.* New York: New York University Press.

Belgium. 1990. "Belgian Memorandum, 19 March 1990." In *Intergovernmental Conference on Political Union: Institutional Reforms, New Policies and International Identity of the European Community,* edited by Finn Laursen and Sophie Vanhoonacker. Dordrecht, Netherlands: Martinus Nijhoff Publishers (1992).

Bendix, Reinhard. 1964. *Nation-Building and Citizenship*. Berkeley: University of California Press.

Bernard, Cheryl. 1978. "Migrant Workers and European Democracy." *Political Science Quarterly* 93(2): 277–99.

Betz, Hans-Georg. 1994. *Radical Right-Wing Populism in Western Europe*. New York: St. Martin's Press.

Binyon, Michael. 1995. "Kohl 'heir' backs EU army." *The Times* (London), November 2.

Bishop, Cortland F. [1893] 1968. *History of Elections in the American Colonies*. New York: Burt Franklin.

Blejwas, Stanislaus A. 1995. "Polonia and Politics." In *Polish Americans and Their History,* edited by John J. Bukowczyk. Pittsburgh: University of Pittsburgh Press.

Bluntschli, J. K. 1895. *The Theory of the State*. Oxford: Clarendon Press.

Bobbio, Noberto. 1987. *The Future of Democracy*. Minneapolis: University of Minnesota Press.

Bodin, Jean. 1967. *Six Books of the Commonwealth*. Trans. Jean Tooley. Oxford: Oxford University Press.

Boegehold, Alan L. 1994. "Perikles' Citizenship Law of 451/0 B.C." In *Athenian Identity and Civic Ideology,* edited by Alan L. Boegehold and Adele C. Scafuro. Baltimore: Johns Hopkins University Press.

Boehning, Wolf R. 1972. *The Migration of Workers in the United Kingdom and the European Community*. London: Oxford University Press.

Bonjour, E., H. S. Offler, and G. R. Potter. 1952. *A Short History of Switzerland*. Oxford: Clarendon Press.

Bozeman, Adda. 1960. *Politics and Culture in International History*. Princeton: Princeton University Press.

Braudel, Fernand. 1972a. *The Mediterranean and the Mediterranean World in the Age of Philip II*. Vol. 1. New York: Harper and Row.

——. 1972b. *The Mediterranean and the Mediterranean World in the Age of Philip II*. Vol. 2. New York: Harper and Row.

——. 1979. *The Structures of Everyday Life: The Limits of the Possible*. New York: Harper and Row.

——. 1981. *The Structures of Everyday Life,* Vol. 1 of *Civilization and Capitalism: 15th–18th Century*. London: Collins.

——. 1990a. *The Identity of France*. Vol. 1. London: Collins.

——. 1990b. *The Identity of France*. Vol. 2. London: Collins.

Brown Scott, James. 1930. "Nationality: *Jus Soli* or *Jus Sanguinis*." *American Journal of International Law* 24: 58–64.

——. 1931. *Observations on Nationality*. New York: Oxford University Press.

Brubaker, Rogers. 1992. *Citizenship and Nationhood in France and Germany*. Cambridge, Mass.: Harvard University Press.

Brubaker, William Rogers. 1989. "Citizenship and Naturalization: Policies and Politics." In *Immigration and the Politics of Citizenship in Europe and North America,* edited by William Rogers Brubaker. New York: University Press of America.

——. 1990. *Citizenship and Nationhood in France and Germany*. Ph.D. dissertation, Columbia University.

Buchan, David. 1992. "The French Referendum: Wrong End of the Maastricht Stick—

Campaigners Are Misinterpreting the Treaty for Their Own Ends." *Financial Times,* September 3.

Buchanan, James M. 1990. "Europe's Constitutional Opportunity." In *Europe's Constitutional Future,* edited by James M. Buchanan, Karl Otto Pohl, Victoria Curzon Price, and Frank Vibert. London: Institute of Economic Affairs.

Bull, Hedley. 1977. *The Anarchical Society: A Study of Order in World Politics.* New York: Columbia University Press.

Bull, Hedley, and Adam Watson, eds. 1984. *The Expansion of International Society.* Oxford: Oxford University Press.

Bundesverfassungsgericht. 1974. Judgment of May 21, 37 BVerGE 217.

Burgess, Michael, ed. 1986. *Federalism and Federation in Western Europe.* London: Croom Helm.

——. 1989. *Federalism and European Union: Political Ideas, Influences and Strategies in the European Community, 1972–1987.* London: Routledge.

Burley, Ann Marie, and Walter Mattli. 1993. "Europe before the Court: A Political Theory of Legal Integration." *International Organization* 47(1): 41–76.

Burton, John W. 1972. *World Society.* Cambridge: Cambridge University Press.

Buzan, Barry, Charles Jones, and Richard Little. 1993. *The Logic of Anarchy: Neorealism to Structural Realism.* New York: Columbia University Press.

Capelletti, Mauro, Monica Seccombe, and Joseph Weiler. 1986. *Integration through Law: Europe and the American Experience.* Berlin: Walter de Gruyter.

Caporaso, James A. 1993. "International Relations Theory and Multilateralism: The Search for Foundations." In *Multilateralism Matters,* edited by John Gerard Ruggie. New York: Columbia University Press.

Carens, Joseph H. 1989. "Membership and Morality: Admission to Citizenship in Liberal Democratic States." In *Immigration and the Politics of Citizenship in Europe and North America,* edited by William Rogers Brubaker. New York: University Press of America.

——. 1992. "Migration and Morality: A Liberal Egalitarian Perspective." In *Free Movement: Ethical Issues in the Transnational Migration of People and of Money,* edited by Brian Barry and Robert E. Goodin. University Park: Pennsylvania State University Press.

Castles, S., and G. Kosak. 1973. *Migrant Workers and Class Structure in Western Europe.* Oxford: Oxford University Press.

Castles, S., H. Booth, and T. Wallace. 1984. *Here For Good.* London: Pluto Press.

Castles, Stephen, and Mark J. Miller. 1998. *The Age of Migration: International Population Movements in the Modern World.* 2d ed. New York: Guilford Press.

CDU/CSU/FDP. 1994. *Koalitionsvertrag.* Bonn, November 21.

Chayes, Abram, and Antonia Handler Chayes. 1995. *The New Sovereignty: Compliance with International Regulatory Agreements.* Cambridge, Mass.: Harvard University Press.

Claude, Inis L. 1964. *Swords into Plowshares: The Problems and Progress of International Organization.* 3d ed., revised. New York: Random House.

——. 1966. "Collective Legitimization as a Political Function of the UN." *International Organization* 20: 267–79.

Cobban, Alfred. 1970. *Nation State and Self-Determination.* New York: Thomas Y. Crowell Co.

Cohen, Robin. 1997. *Global Diasporas: An Introduction.* London: UCL Press.

Connolly, William. 1991. *Identity Difference: Democratic Negotiations of Political Paradox.* Ithaca: Cornell University Press.

Cornelius, Wayne A., Philip L. Martin, and James F. Hollifield. 1994. *Controlling Immigration: A Global Perspective.* Stanford: Stanford University Press.

Cortell, Andrew P., and James W. Davis, Jr. 1996. "How Do International Institutions Matter? The Domestic Impact of International Rules and Norms." *International Studies Quarterly* 40: 451–78.

Council of Europe. 1963. "Convention on the Reduction of Cases of Multiple Nationality." *European Treaty Series,* no. 43 (Strasbourg: Council of Europe).

——. 1993a. "Second Protocol Amending the Convention on the Reduction of Cases of Multiple Nationality and Military Obligations in Cases of Multiple Nationality." *European Treaty Series,* no. 149 (Strasbourg: Council of Europe).

——. 1993b. "Existing Fora for Inter-governmental Co-Operation on Asylum, Refugee and Migration Problems in the European Region." October 15, doc. no. CDMG (93) 20 rev. (Strasbourg: Council of Europe).

——. 1995. *European Bulletin on Nationality.* January 1, doc. no. DIR/JUR (95) (Strasbourg: Council of Europe).

——. 1996. "A Review of the Implementation of Community Relations Policies," by the Migration Policy Group, presented to the 6th Conference of European Ministers Responsible for Migration Affairs, doc. no. MMG-6 (96) 1E (Brussels: Migration Policy Group).

——. 1997a. *European Bulletin on Nationality.* March, doc. no. DIR/JIR (97) 4 (Strasbourg: Council of Europe).

——. 1997b. "European Convention on Nationality and Explanatory Report (Provisional)." May 14, doc. no. DIR/JIR (97) 6 (Strasbourg: Council of Europe).

——. 1997c. "European Convention on Nationality." *European Treaty Series* no. 166 (Strasbourg: Council of Europe).

Cowhey, Peter F. 1990. "The International Telecommunications Regime: The Political Roots of Regimes for High Technology." *International Organization* 44: 169–99.

Crawford, Beverly. 1996. "Explaining Defection from International Cooperation: Germany's Unilateral Recognition of Croatia." *World Politics* 48(4): 482–521.

Crawford, Neta C. 1994. "Cooperation Among Iroquois Nations." *International Organization* 48(3): 345–85.

Criddle, Byron. 1993. "The French Referendum on the Maastricht Treaty, September 1992." *Parliamentary Affairs* 46(2): 228–38.

Crosby, Alfred. 1972. *The Columbian Exchange, Biological and Cultural Consequences of 1492.* Westport, Conn.: Greenwood Press.

——. 1986. *Ecological Imperialism: The Biological Expansion of Europe 900–1900.* Cambridge: Cambridge University Press.

Dahl, Robert A. 1989. *Democracy and Its Critics.* New Haven, Conn.: Yale University Press.

——. 1994. "A Democratic Dilemma: System Effectiveness vs Citizen Participation." *Political Science Quarterly* 109(1): 23–34.

Dalka, Karin. 1999. "Smuggling of Human Beings Experiencing Upswing." *Frankfurter Rundschau,* March 12.

D'Amato, Gianni. 1997. "Gelebte Nation un Einwanderung Zur Trans-Nationalisierung von Nationalstaaten durch Immigrantenpolitik am Beispiel der Schwiez." In *Transnationale Staatsbürgerschaft,* edited by Heinz Kleger. Frankfurt and New York: Campus Verlag, 1997.

Davies, Norman. 1982. *God's Playground: A History of Poland.* New York: Columbia University Press.

den Boer, Monica, and Neil Walker. 1993. "European Policing after 1992." *Journal of Common Market Studies* 31(1): 3–28.

Denmark. 1990. "Memorandum from the Danish Government (4 October 1990)." In *Intergovernmental Conference on Political Union: Institutional Reforms, New Policies and International Identity of the European Community,* edited by Finn Laursen and Sophie Vanhoonacker. Dordrecht, Netherlands: Martinus Nijhoff Publishers (1992).

de Rham, Gerard. 1990. "Naturalization: The Politics of Citizenship Acquisition." In *Political Rights of Migrant Workers in Western Europe,* edited by Zig Layton-Henry. London: Sage.

Dessler, David. 1989. "What's at Stake in the Agent-Structure Debate." *International Organization* 43 (summer): 441–73.

Deutsch, Karl W., Sidney A. Burrell, Robert A. Kann, Maurice Lee, Jr., Martin Licterman, Raymond E. Lindgren, Francis L. Loewenheim, and Richard W. Van Wagenen. 1957. *Political Community in the North Atlantic Area.* Princeton: Princeton University Press.

Diamond, Jared. 1997. *Guns, Germs, and Steel: The Fates of Human Societies.* New York: Norton.

Dillon, Sam. 1996. "Mexico Is Near to Granting Expatriates Voting Rights." *New York Times,* June 16.

d'Oliveria, Hans Ulrich Jessurun. 1995. "Union Citizenship: Pie in the Sky?" In Allan Rosas and Esko Antola, *A Citizens' Europe: In Search of a New Order.* London: Sage.

Dowty, Alan, and Gil Loescher. 1996. "Refugee Flows as Grounds for International Action." *International Security* 21(1): 43–71.

Doyle, Michael W. 1986. *Empires.* Ithaca: Cornell University Press.

Drozdiak, William. 1998. "Exiles' Donations Fund Kosovo Rebels." *The Washington Post,* July 27.

Duchacek, Ivo D. 1986. *The Territorial Dimension of Politics: Within, Among, and Across Nations.* Boulder, Colo.: Westview Press.

Dummett, Ann, and Andrew Nicol. 1990. *Subjects, Citizens and Others: Nationality and Immigration Law.* London: Weidenfeld and Nicholson.

ECJ. 1963. Reports of the European Court of Justice, Case 41/74.

———. 1989. Reports of the European Court of Justice, Case 186/87.

Economist (London). 1991. "Poor Men at the Gate." March 11.

———. 1999. "Rebuilding the Balkans." June 19.

Elazar, Daniel J. 1987. *Exploring Federalism.* Tuscaloosa: University of Alabama Press.

ER (*European Report*). 1998. "Justice and Home Affairs: EU Struggles to Define CEEC Strategy." No. 2288, February 4.

Eurobarometer. 1994. No. 41 (July).

———. 1995a. No. 42 (spring).

———. 1995b. No. 43 (autumn).

———. 1996a. No. 44 (April).

——. 1996b. No. 45 (December).

——. 1997. No. 47 (October).

——. 1998. No. 48 (September).

——. 1999. No. 50 (March).

European Commission. 1961. Regulation no. 15/61 of the Council of 16 August 1961.

——. 1964. Regulation no. 38/64 of the Council of 15 March 1964 on the freedom of movement for workers within the Community, *Official Journal of the European Communities* 965/64.

——. 1968. Regulation no. 1612/68 of the Council of 15 October 1968 on freedom of movement for workers within the Community, *Official Journal of the European Communities* L257/2.

——. 1975. "Towards European Citizenship: Implementation of Point 10 of the Final Communique Issued at the European Summit Held in Paris on 9 and 10 December 1974." *Bulletin of the European Communities* Supplement 7/75.

——. 1985. "A People's Europe: Reports from the Ad Hoc Committee." *Bulletin of the European Communities* Supplement 7/85.

——. 1986. "Voting Rights in Local Elections for Community Nationals: A Report from the Commission to the European Parliament." *Bulletin of the European Communities* Supplement 7/86.

——. 1988. "A People's Europe: Proposal for a Council Directive on Voting Rights for Community Nationals in Local Elections in Their Member State of Residence." *Bulletin of the European Communities* Supplement 2/88.

——. 1993. "Council Directive 93/109 of 6 December 1993." *Official Journal of the European Communities* L329/34.

——. 1994a. "Communication from the Commission to the Council and the European Parliament on Immigration and Asylum Policies." Com (94) 23 final, Brussels, February 23.

——. 1994b. "Council Directive 94/80 of 19 December 1994." *Official Journal of the European Communities* L368.

——. 1995a. "Decision of the Representatives of the Governments of the Member States Meeting within the Council of 19 December 1995 Protection for Citizens of the European Union by Diplomatic and Consular Representations." *Official Journal of the European Communities* L314/73.

——. 1995b. *Commission Report for the Reflection Group.* Luxembourg: Office for Official Publications of the European Communities.

——. 1997a. Second report of the European Commission on Citizenship of the Union. <http://europa.eu.int/comm/internal_market/en/update/report/citen.htm>.

——. 1997b. "The Effects on the Union's Polices of Enlargement to the Applicant Countries of Central and Eastern Europe." *Agenda 2000.*

——. 1997c. "Commission Opinion on the Czech Republic's Application for Membership of the European Union." *Agenda 2000.*

——. 1997d. "Commission Opinion on Estonia's Application for Membership of the European Union." *Agenda 2000.*

——. 1997e. "Commission Opinion on Hungary's Application for Membership of the European Union." *Agenda 2000.*

——. 1997f. "Commission Opinion on Poland's Application for Membership of the European Union." *Agenda 2000.*

——. 1997g. "Commission Opinion on Slovenia's Application for Membership of the European Union." *Agenda 2000.*

European Council. 1992. "Conclusions of the Presidency, European Council in Edinburgh 11–12 December 1992."

European Insight. 1995. "EU Makes Protection of Refugees Less Secure." *European Insight, European Information Service,* December 1.

Eurostat. 1993a. *Rapid Reports: Population and Social Conditions,* no. 6.

——. 1993b. *Eurostat CD-ROM* database, ed. 1.

——. 1994. *Demographic Statistics 1994.* Luxembourg: Office for Official Publications of the European Communities.

——. 1995a. "Results of Monthly Surveys of European Opinion (July, September, October 1995)." *Europinion,* no. 6, October.

——. 1995b. *Migration Statistics 1995. Population and Social Conditions Series.* Luxembourg: Office for Official Publications of the European Communities.

——. 1996a. "Asylum-Seekers in Europe 1985–1995." *Statistics in Focus: Population and Social Conditions,* no. 1.

——. 1996b. "Non-nationals Make Up Less Than 5% of the Population of the European Union on 1/1/1993." *Statistics in Focus: Population and Social Conditions,* no. 2.

——. 1996c. "Results of Monthly Surveys of European Opinion (May, June, July 1996)." *Europinion,* no. 9, September.

——. 1996d. "Decline in Migration Stopped in 1995; Principle Demographic Trends in the EU in 1995." *Statistics in Focus: Population and Social Conditions,* no. 6.

——. 1997. "Beyond the Predictable: Demographic Changes in the EU up to 2050." *Statistics in Focus: Population and Social Conditions,* no. 7.

——. 1998. "First Results of the Demographic Data Collection for 1997 in Europe." *Statistics in Focus: Population and Social Conditions,* no. 9.

Evans, Andrew C. 1984. "European Citizenship: A Novel Concept in EEC Law." *American Journal of Comparative Law* 32: 679–715.

——. 1991. "Nationality Law and European Integration." *European Law Review* 16: 190–215.

FAZ (Frankfurter Allgemeine Zeitung). 1999. "Im Bundestag soll es einem Gruppenantrag geben." *Frankfurter Allgemeine Zeitung,* March 13.

Feldblum, Miriam. 1998. "Reconfiguring Citizenship in Western Europe." In *Challenge to the Nation-State: Immigration in Western Europe and the United States,* edited by Christian Joppke. Oxford: Oxford University Press.

Ferguson, Yale H., and Richard W. Mansbach. 1996. *Polities: Authorities, Identities and Change.* Columbia: University of South Carolina Press.

Fichtner, Paula S. 1976. "Dynastic Marriage in Sixteenth Century Hapsburg Diplomacy and Statecraft: An Interdisciplinary Approach." *American Historical Review* 81(2): 243–65.

Fischer, David Hacket. 1989. *Albion's Seed: Four British Folkways in America.* New York: Oxford University Press.

Fischer, Markus. 1992. "Feudal Europe, 800–1300: Communal Discourse and Conflictual Practices." *International Organization* 46 (spring): 426–66.

——. 1993. "On Context, Facts and Norms: A Response to Hall and Kratochwil." *International Organization* 47 (summer): 492–500.

Flournoy, Richard W., Jr., and Manley O. Hudson, eds. 1929. *A Collection of Nation-*

ality Laws of Various Countries as Contained in Constitutions, Statutes and Treaties. New York: Oxford University Press.

Forsyth, Murray. 1981. *Unions of States: The Theory and Practice of Confederation.* New York: Leicester University Press.

Franck, Thomas M. 1996. "Clan and Superclan: Loyalty, Identity and Community in Law and Practice." *American Journal of International Law* 90 (July): 359–83.

Frankfurter, Felix. 1958. Majority opinion, *Perez v. Brownell* 356 U.S. at 50.

Frazer, Mathew. 1993. "No Birthright: French Law Turns Children into Citizens of No Country." *The Gazette* (Montreal), May 16.

Freeman, Gary P. 1985. "Migration and the Political Economy of the Welfare State." In *From Foreign Workers To Settlers? Transnational Migration and the Emergence of New Minorities,* edited by Martin O. Heisler and Barbara Schmitter Heisler. *The Annals of the American Academy of Political and Social Science,* no. 485. Beverly Hills: Sage.

——. 1994. "Can Liberal States Control Unwanted Migration?" In *Strategies for Immigration Control,* edited by Mark J. Miller. *The Annals of the American Academy of Political and Social Science* 534 (May): 17–30.

——. 1998. "The Decline of Sovereignty? Politics and Immigration Restriction in Liberal States." In *Challenge to the Nation-State: Immigration in Western Europe and the United States,* edited by Christian Joppke. Oxford: Oxford University Press.

Frey, Martin, and Ulrich Mammey. 1996. *Impact of Migration in the Receiving Countries: Germany.* Geneva: International Organization for Migration.

Friedrich, Carl J. 1968a. *Constitutional Government and Democracy: Theory and Practice in Europe and America.* 4th ed. Waltham, Mass.: Blaisdell Publishing.

——. 1968b. *Trends in Federalism in Theory and Practice.* New York: Praeger.

——. 1969. *Europe: An Emergent Nation.* New York: Harper and Row.

Frowein, Jochen Abraham, Stephen Schulhofer, and Martin Shapiro. 1986. "The Protection of Fundamental Human Rights as a Vehicle of Integration." In *Integration through Law: Europe and the American Experience,* edited by Mauro Capelletti, Monica Seccombe, and Joseph Weiler. Berlin: Walter de Gruyter.

FT (*The Financial Times*). 1997. "Enlargement May Test EU's Treaty: The Achievements of the Amsterdam Summit Cannot Mask the Divisions That Remain." June 19.

Fukuyama, Francis. 1992. *The End of History and the Last Man.* New York: Free Press.

Funk, Albrecht. 1995. "Immigration Policy of the EU: Common Challenges, Common Responses, Common Policies." Paper presented for the Fourth Biennial International Conference of the European Community Studies Association, May 11–14.

Garth, Bryant. 1986. "Migrant Workers and the Rights of Mobility." In *Integration through Law: Europe and the American Experience,* edited by Mauro Capelletti, Monica Seccombe, and Joseph Weiler. Berlin: Walter de Gruyter.

Gaunt, Jeremy. 1996. "Flexible Europe is Problem for EU Negotiators." *The Reuter European Community Report,* May 31.

Gilpin, Robert. 1981. *War and Change in World Politics.* Cambridge: Cambridge University Press.

Glenny, Misha. 1992. *The Fall of Yugoslavia.* London: Penguin.

Glick Schiller, Nina, Linda Basch, and Cristina Blanc-Szanton. 1992. *Toward a Transnational Perspective on Migration: Race, Class, Ethnicity and Nationalism Reconsidered. Annals of the New York Academy of Sciences,* vol. 465, July 6.

Goldstein, Eugene, and Victoria Piazza. 1996. "Naturalization, Dual Citizenship and the Retention of Foreign Citizenship: A Survey." *Interpreter Releases* 73(16): 517–21.

Gooch, G. P. 1947. *Frederick: The Ruler, the Writer, the Man.* New York: Alfred Knopf.

Gorham, Eric B. 1992. *National Service, Citizenship, and Political Education.* Albany: State University of New York Press.

Gottlieb, Gidon. 1993. *Nation against State: A New Approach to Ethnic Conflicts and the Decline of Sovereignty.* New York: Council on Foreign Relations Press.

Grawert, Rolf. 1973. *Staat und Staatsangehörigkeit, Verfassungsgeschichte Untersuchungen zur Entstehung der Staatsangehörigkeit, Schriften zur Verfassungsgeschichte, Band 17.* Berlin: Duncker and Humbolt.

Greenfeld, Liah. 1992. *Nationalism: Five Roads to Modernity.* Cambridge, Mass.: Harvard University Press.

Grieco, Joseph M. 1988. "Anarchy and the Limits of Cooperation: A Realist Critique of the Newest Liberal Institutionalism." *International Organization* 42 (August): 485–507.

Groom, A. J. R. 1978. "Neofunctionalism: A Case of Mistaken Identity." *Political Science* 30(1): 15–28.

GSN (Global Survival Network). 1997. *Crime and Servitude: An Exposé of the Traffic in Women for Prostitution from the Newly Independent States.* Washington, D.C.

Guetzkow, Harold. 1955. *Multiple Loyalties: Theoretical Approach to a Problem in International Organization.* Princeton, N.J.: Center for Research on World Political Institutions.

Haas, Ernst B. 1958. *Uniting of Europe: Political, Economic, and Social Forces, 1950–1957.* London: Stevens and Sons.

——. 1968. *Beyond the Nation-State.* Stanford: Stanford University Press.

Haas, Peter M., ed. 1992a. *Knowledge, Power, and International Policy Coordination.* A special issue of *International Organization* 46(1).

——. 1992b. "Epistemic Communities and International Policy Coordination." Introduction to *Knowledge, Power and International Policy Coordination,* a special issue of *International Organization* 46(1): 1–36.

Habermas, Jürgen. 1992. "Citizenship and National Identity: Some Reflections on the Future of Europe." *Praxis International* 12(1): 1–19.

Hailbronner, Kay. 1989. "Citizenship and Nationhood in Germany." In *Immigration and the Politics of Citizenship in Europe and North America,* edited by William Rogers Brubaker. New York: University Press of America.

——. 1992. *Einbürgerung von Wanderarbeitnehmern und doppelte Staatsangehörigkeit.* Baden-Baden: Nomos.

Hall, Rodney Bruce, and Friedrich Kratochwil. 1993. "Medieval Tales: Neorealist 'Science' and the Abuse of History." *International Organization* 47 (summer): 479–91.

Hammar, Tomas. 1985. "Dual Citizenship and Political Integration." *International Migration Review* 19(3): 438–50.

——. 1990a. *Democracy and the Nation-State: Aliens, Denizens and Citizens in a World of International Migration.* Aldershot: Avebury.

——. 1990b. "Civil Rights." In *Political Rights of Migrant Workers in Western Europe,* edited by Zig Layton-Henry. London: Sage.

Handlin, Lilian. 1984. *George Bancroft: The Intellectual as Democrat.* New York: Harper and Row.

Hansen, Randall. 1998. "A European Citizenship or a Europe of Citizens? Third Country Nationals in the EU." *Journal of Ethnic and Migration Studies* 24(4): 751–68.

Harvard Law School. 1929. "Nationality, Responsibility of States, and Territorial Waters. Drafts of Conventions Prepared in Anticipation of the First Conference on Codification of International Law, The Hague, 1930." *American Journal of International Law* 23 (Supplement) (April).

Hay, P. H. 1966. *Federalism and Supranational Organizations: Patterns for New Legal Structures.* Urbana, Ill.: University of Illinois Press.

Hayes, Carlton J. H. 1931. *The Historical Evolution of Nationalism.* New York: R. Smith.

Heater, Derek. 1990. *Citizenship: The Civic Ideal in World History, Politics and Education.* London: Longman.

Hedges, Chris. 1999. "Kosovo's Next Masters?" *Foreign Affairs* 78(3): 24–42.

Heisler, Martin O., and Barbara Schmitter Heisler, eds. 1985. *From Foreign Workers to Settlers? Transnational Migration and the Emergence of New Minorities. The Annals of the American Academy of Political and Social Science,* no. 485. Beverly Hills: Sage.

Held, David. 1987. *Models of Democracy.* Stanford: Stanford University Press.

——. 1995. *Democracy and the Global Order.* Stanford: Stanford University Press.

Hendrickson, David C. 1992. "Migration in Law and Ethics: A Realist Perspective." In *Free Movement in the Transnational Migration of People and of Money,* edited by Brian Barry and Robert E. Goodin. University Park: Pennsylvania State University Press.

Herald, The. 1993. "Euro-Rebels Crushed in Lords Vote." Glasgow, June 23.

Herz, John. 1959. *International Politics in the Atomic Age.* New York: Columbia University Press.

Hinsley, F. H. 1963. *Power and the Pursuit of Peace: Theory and Practice in the History of Relations Between States.* Cambridge: Cambridge University Press.

——. 1973. *Nationalism and the International System.* London: Hodder and Stoughton.

Hoffmann, Stanley. 1966. "Obstinate or Obsolete? The Fate of the Nation-State and the Case of Western Europe." *Daedalus* 95: 862–915.

——. 1993. "Thoughts on the French Nation Today." *Daedalus* 122(3): 63–79.

Hoffmann-Novotny, Hans Joachim. 1997. "World Society and the Future of International Migration: A Theoretical Perspective." In *Immigration into Western Societies: Problems and Policies,* edited by Emek Ucarer and Donald J. Puchala. London: Pinter Press.

Holbrooke, Richard. 1999. *To End a War.* New York: Modern Library.

Hollifield, James F. 1992a. *Immigrants, Markets, and States: The Political Economy of Postwar Europe.* Cambridge, Mass.: Harvard University Press.

——. 1992b. "Migration and International Relations: Cooperation and Control in the European Community." *International Migration Review* 26(2).

Holmes, George, ed. 1992. *The Oxford History of Medieval Europe.* Oxford: Oxford University Press.

Hovy, Bela, and Hania Zlotnik. 1994. "Europe Without Internal Frontiers and International Migration." *Population Bulletin of the United Nations,* no. 36: 19–42.

Hucko, Elmar M. 1987. *The Democratic Tradition: Four German Constitutions.* New York: Berg.

Huntington, Samuel P. 1991. *The Third Wave: Democratization in the Late Twentieth Century.* Norman: University of Oklahoma Press.

Iggers, George G. 1968. *The German Conception of History: The National Tradition of Historical Thought from Herder to the Present.* Middletown, Conn.: Wesleyan University Press.

ILC (International Law Commission). 1954. *International Law Commission Yearbook 1954* II, Section 42, 48.

International Intelligence Report. 1994. "Kohl Views 1993 Achievements, 1994 Tasks." January 3.

IOM (International Organization for Migration). 1995. *Trafficking and Prostitution: The Growing Exploitation of Migrant Women From Central and Eastern Europe.* Geneva: International Organization for Migration.

——. 1996. "Organized Crime Moves into Migrant Trafficking." *Trafficking in Migrants, Quarterly Bulletin,* no. 11 (June).

——. 1998. International Organization for Migration, *Trafficking in Migrants, Quarterly Bulletin,* no. 17 (January).

Isaac, Julius. 1947. *Economics of Migration.* London: Kegan Paul, Trench, Trubner.

Jackson, J. A. 1963. *The Irish in Britain.* London: Routledge and Kegan Paul.

Jackson, Robert H. 1990. *Quasi-States: Sovereignty, International Relations and the Third World.* Cambridge: Cambridge University Press.

Jacobson, David. 1996. *Rights across Borders: Immigration and the Decline of Citizenship.* Baltimore: John Hopkins University Press.

Jacobson, Harold K. 1984. *Networks of Interdependence.* 2d ed. New York: Alfred A. Knopf.

Jedruch, Jacek. 1982. *Constitutions, Elections and Legislatures of Poland, 1493–1977.* Washington, D.C.: University Press of America.

Jensen, Merrill. 1962. *The New Nation: A History of the United States during the Confederation 1781–1789.* New York: Knopf.

JHA (Justice and Home Affairs). 1993. Council of the European Union, "Recommendation on Trafficking in Human Beings." Council Press Release 10550/93 of 29 and 30 November.

——. 1996. Justice and Home Affairs, Joint Action 96/700/JHA.

——. 1999. Special Council Meeting—Justice and Home Affairs, Press Release, Brussels (07-04-99)—Nr. 6973/99 (Presse 93).

Johnson, Esther, and David O'Keefe. 1994. "From Discrimination to Obstacles to Free Movement: Recent Developments Concerning the Free Movement of Workers 1989–1994." *Common Market Law Review* 31: 1313–46.

Johnson, Nevil. 1991. "Territory and Power: Some Historical Determinants of the Constitutional Structure of the Federal Republic of Germany." In *German Federalism Today,* edited by Charlie Jeffery and Peter Savigear. New York: St. Martin's Press.

Jones, E. L. 1987. *The European Miracle: Environments, Economies and Geopolitics in the History of Europe and Asia.* 2d ed. Cambridge: Cambridge University Press.

Joppke, Christian. 1998. "Asylum and State Sovereignty: A Comparison of the United States, German, and Britain." In *Challenge to the Nation-State: Immigration in Western Europe and the United States,* edited by Christian Joppke. Oxford University Press.

Kant, Immanuel. 1970. "Perpetual Peace." In *Kant's Political Writings,* edited by Hans Reiss. Cambridge: Cambridge University Press.

Katzenstein, Peter J. 1996a. *The Culture of National Security: Norms and Identity in World Politics.* New York: Columbia University Press.

———. 1996b. "Conclusion: National Security in a Changing World." In *The Culture of National Security: Norms and Identity in World Politics,* edited by Peter J. Katzenstein. New York: Columbia University Press.

Keane, John. 1988. *Democracy and Civil Society.* London: Verso.

Kearney, Michael. 1995. "The Local and the Global: The Anthropology of Globalization and Transnationalism." *Annual Review of Anthropology* 24.

Keely Charles B. 1996. "How Nation-States Create and Respond to Refugee Flows." *International Migration Review* 30(4): 1046–66.

Kennedy, Paul. 1987. *Rise and Fall of the Great Powers.* New York: Random House.

Keohane, Robert O. 1984. *After Hegemony: Cooperation and Discord in the World Political Economy.* Princeton, N.J.: Princeton University Press.

———. 1988. "International Institutions: Two Approaches." *International Studies Quarterly* 32: 379–96.

———. 1977. *Power and Interdependence.* Boston: Little Brown.

Keohane, Robert O., and Helen V. Milner. 1996. *Internationalization and Domestic Politics.* Cambridge: Cambridge University Press.

Keohane, Robert O., and Joseph S. Nye, Jr., eds. 1972. *Transnational Relations and World Politics.* Cambridge, Mass.: Harvard University Press.

Kessler, Alan. 1997. "Managing Migration: Domestic or International Policy Choices." Paper presented at the International Studies Association Meeting, March 18–22.

Kindleberger, Charles P. 1967. *Europe's Postwar Growth: The Role of Labor Supply.* Cambridge, Mass.: Harvard University Press.

King, Preston. 1982. *Federalism and Federation.* London: Croom Helm.

Kohl, Helmut, and Jacques Chirac. 1995. "Délaration du chancelier Helmut Kohl et du président Jacques Chirac au président du Conseil europeen." December 6.

Koslowski, Rey. 1994. "International Migration, European Political Institutions and International Relations Theory." Ph.D. dissertation, University of Pennsylvania.

———. 1998. "EU Migration Regimes: Established and Emergent." In *Challenge to the Nation-State: Immigration in Western Europe and the United States,* edited by Christian Joppke. Oxford: Oxford University Press.

Koslowski, Rey, and Friedrich Kratochwil. 1994. "Understanding Change in International Politics: The Soviet Empire's Demise and the International System." *International Organization* 48(2): 215–47.

Koslowski, Rey, and Antje Wiener. 1998. "Practicing Democracy Transnationally." Paper presented at the Third Pan-European International Relations Conference and Joint Meeting with the International Studies Association (ISA), Vienna, September 16–20.

Krasner, Stephen D., ed. 1983. *International Regimes.* Ithaca: Cornell University Press.

Kratochwil, Friedrich. 1982. "On the Notion of Interest." *International Organization* 36(1): 1–30.

———. 1986. "Of Systems, Boundaries and Territoriality." *World Politics* 34(1): 753–75.

———. 1989. *Rules, Norms and Decisions: On the Conditions of Practical and Legal Rea-*

soning in International Relations and Domestic Affairs. Cambridge: Cambridge University Press.

———. 1995. "Sovereignty as *Dominium:* Is There a Right of Humanitarian Intervention?" In *Beyond Westphalia? State Sovereignty and International Intervention,* edited by Gene M. Lyons and Michael Mastanduno. Baltimore: Johns Hopkins University Press.

Kratochwil, Friedrich, and John Gerard Ruggie. 1986. "International Organization: A State of the Art on an Art of the State." *International Organization* 40: 753–75.

Lahav, Gallya. 1998. "Immigration and the State: The Devolution and Privatization of Immigration Control in the EU." *Journal of Ethnic and Migration Studies* 24(1): 675–94.

Lapid, Yosef. 1994. "Theorizing the 'National' in International Relations Theory: Reflections on Nationalism and Neorealism." In *International Organization: A Reader,* edited by Friedrich Kratochwil and Edward Mansfield. New York: HarperCollins.

Laxer, James. 1992. "As Mitterrand Found, a Referendum's Fraught with Peril." *Toronto Star,* September 22.

League of Nations. 1930a. "Hague Convention on Certain Questions Relating to the Conflict of Nationality Laws." April 12, 179 League of Nations Treaty Series 89.

———. 1930b. "Military Obligations in Certain Cases of Double Nationality." 178 League of Nations Treaty Series 227.

———. 1930c. "Special Protocol Concerning Statelessness." U.K Treaty Series 112.

———. 1930d. "Certain Case of Statelessness." 179 League of Nations Treaty Series 116.

Lee, Loyd E. 1980. *The Politics of Harmony.* Newark: University of Delaware Press.

Lenaerts, Koen. 1992. "Federalism and Rights in the European Community." Presented at the Federalism and Rights convention, Center for the Study of Federalism, Temple University, Philadelphia, November 16.

Lijphart, Arend. 1984. *Democracies.* New Haven, Conn.: Yale University Press.

———. 1985. "Non-Majoritarian Democracy: A Comparison of Federal and Consociational Theories." *Publius* 15 (spring): 3–15.

Little, Richard. 1993. "Rethinking System Continuity." In *The Logic of Anarchy: Neorealism to Structural Realism,* edited by Barry Buzan, Charles Jones, and Richard Little. New York: Columbia University Press.

Loescher, Gil. 1993. *Beyond Charity: International Cooperation and the Global Refugee Crisis.* Oxford: Oxford University Press.

———. 1994. "The International Refugee Regime: Stretched to the Limit?" *Journal of International Affairs* 47(2): 351–77.

Magiera, Sigfried. 1988. "Kommunalwahlrecht in den EG-Mitgliedstaaten." *Europea-Archiv* 16: 475–80.

———. 1991. "A Citizens Europe: Personal, Political, and Cultural Rights." In *The State of the European Community,* edited by Leon Hurwitz and Christian Lequesne. Boulder, Colo.: Lynne Reiner.

Mancini, G. Federico. 1991. "The Making of a Constitution for Europe." In *The New European Community: Decision Making and Institutional Change,* edited by Robert O. Keohane and Stanley Hoffmann. Boulder, Colo.: Westview Press.

Mansbach, Richard W., Yale Ferguson, and Donald E. Lampert. 1976. *The Web of*

World Politics: Nonstate Actors in the Global System. Englewood Cliffs, N.J.: Prentice-Hall.

Mansbridge, Jane. 1983. *Beyond Adversary Democracy.* Chicago: University of Chicago Press.

Mansfield, Edward D., and Jack Snyder. 1995. "Democratization and the Danger of War." *International Security* 20: 5–35.

Marshall, T. H. 1964. "Citizenship and Social Class." In *Class, Citizenship and Social Development: Essays by T. H. Marshall.* Chicago: University of Chicago Press.

Maxson, Charles Hartshorn. 1930. *Citizenship.* New York: Oxford University Press.

Mazzini, Giuseppe. 1864. *Life and Writings.* London: Smith, Elder.

McGory, Daniel. 1999. "Scandal of the Empty Seats on Mercy Flights." *The Times* (London), May 26.

McNeill, William H. 1967. *A World History.* New York: Oxford University Press.

———. 1977. *Plagues and Peoples.* Garden City, N.Y.: Anchor Books.

———. 1978. "Human Migration: A Historical Overview." In *Human Migration: Patterns and Policies,* edited by William H. McNeill and Ruth S. Adams. Bloomington: Indiana University Press.

———. 1982. *The Pursuit of Power.* Chicago: University of Chicago Press.

———. 1986. *Polyethnicity and National Unity in World History.* Toronto: University of Toronto Press.

———. 1987. "Migration in Premodern Times." In *Population in an Interacting World,* edited by William Alonso. Cambridge, Mass.: Harvard University Press.

———. 1992. *The Global Condition: Conquerors Catastrophes and Community.* Princeton, N.J.: Princeton University Press.

Mearsheimer, John J. 1990. "Back to the Future: Instability in Europe After the Cold War." *International Security* 15 (summer): 5–56.

———. 1994. "The False Promise of International Institutions." *International Security* 19(3): 5–49.

Meehan, Elizabeth. 1993. *Citizenship and the European Community.* London: Sage Publications.

Miller, Kerby. 1985. *Emigrants and Exiles: Ireland and the Irish Exodus to North America.* New York: Oxford University Press.

Miller, Mark J. 1978. "The Problem of Foreign Worker Participation and Representation in France, Switzerland and the Republic of Germany." Ph.D. dissertation, University of Wisconsin.

———. 1979. "Reluctant Partnership: Foreign Workers in Franco-Algerian Relations 1962–1979." *Journal of International Affairs* 33(2): 219–37.

———. 1981. *Foreign Workers in Western Europe: An Emergent Political Force.* New York: Praeger.

———. 1989. "Dual Citizenship: A European Norm?" *International Migration Review* 23(4): 945–50.

———. 1997. "International Migration and Security: Towards Transatlantic Convergence?" In *Immigration into Western Societies: Implication and Policy Choices,* edited by Emek M. Ucarer and Donald Puchala. London: Pinter.

Mirovitskaya, Natalia S., Margaret Clark, and Ronald G. Purver. 1993. "North Pacific Fur Seals: Regime Formation as a Means of Resolving Conflict." In *Polar Politics:*

Creating International Environmental Regimes, edited by Oran R. Young and Gail Osherenko. Ithaca: Cornell University Press.

Mitchell, Christopher. 1989. "International Migration, International Relations and Foreign Policy." *International Migration Review* 23(3): 681–708.

Mitrany, David. 1946. *A Working Peace System.* London: Oxford University Press.

MN (Migration News). 1998. Vol. 5, no. 3 (March).

MNS (Migration News Sheet). 1995a. "The 15 Adopt Principles of Sharing the Costs of Temporary Reception of Displaced Persons." No. 148/95-07 (July): 5.

——. 1995b. "Most Member States Unwilling to Take in Ex-Yugoslav Refugees." No. 151/95–10 (October): 4–5.

——. 1997. "Conference of Ministers on the Prevention of Illegal Migration." No. 177/97–12 (December): 3–6.

——. 1998a. "Influx of Kurds Prompts Adoption of a 46–Point Action Plan." No. 179/98–02 (February): 4–6.

——. 1998b. "Special Meeting to Combat Illegal Migration." No. 185/98–08 (August): 5–6.

——. 1998c. "EU Enlargement Must Include Waiting Period of 12 to 15 Years for Free Movement." No. 186/98–09 (September): 2.

——. 1998d. "More Human Smuggling Across the Eastern Border." No. 186/98–09 (September): 5.

——. 1998e. "Germany Cannot Receive Kosovo Albanians." No. 186/98–09 (September): 12.

——. 1998f. "No Temporary Protection for Kosovo Albanians." No. 186/98–09 (September): 10.

——. 1998g. "Large Smuggling Ring Broken Up." No. 186/98–09 (September): 6.

——. 1998h. "EU 'Remains Gravely Concerned' at the Plight of Kosovo Refugees but Stubbornly Refuses to Offer Temporary Protection." No. 188/98–11 (November): 6.

——. 1998i. "Most Bosnian Refugees Have Left Germany." No. 189/98–12 (December): 11.

——. 1999a. "Another 10,000 Kosovars to be Evacuated to Germany, but the Reception the Second Half Depends on Whether Other EU States Honour Pledges." No. 195/99–06 (June): 14.

——. 1999b. "Former Chancellor Kohl Criticises Certain EU States for Not Receiving Kosovar Refugees." No. 195/99–06 (June): 9.

——. 1999c. "UK 'Responded within Hours' to Appeal to Evacuate Kosovar Refugees." No. 195/99–06 (June): 19.

Moch, Leslie Page. 1992. *Moving Europeans: Migration in Western Europe since 1650.* Bloomington: Indiana University Press.

Mockler, Anthony. 1970. *Mercenaries.* London: McDonald.

Mohawk, John C. 1992. "Indians and Democracy: No One Ever Told Us." In *Exiled in the Land of the Free: Democracy, Indian Nations and the U.S. Constitution,* edited by Oren Lyons, John Mohawk, Vine Deloria, Jr., Lawrence Hauptman, Howard Berman, Donald Grinde, Jr., Curtis Berkey, and Robert Venables. Santa Fe, N.M.: Clear Light Publishers.

Molle, W., and A. Van Mourik. 1988. "International Movements of Labour under Conditions of Economic Integration: The Case of Western Europe." *Journal of Common Market Studies* 26(3): 317–42.

Moltmann, Guenter. 1980. "American-German Return Migration in the Nineteenth and Early Twentieth Centuries." *Central European History* 13(4): 378–92.

Moravcsik, Andrew. 1991. "Negotiating the Single European Act: National Interests and Conventional Statecraft in the European Community." *International Organization* 45(1): 651–88.

Morgenthau, Hans. 1978. *Politics among Nations.* 5th ed. New York: Knopf.

MTI (Magyar Távirati Iroda). 1998. "Conference on Border Control." MTI Hungarian News Agency, April 22.

Münz, Rainer, and Ralf Ulrich. 1995. *Too Many Foreigners? Demographic Developments Changing Patterns of Migration and the Absorption of Immigrants; The Case of Germany, 1945–1994.* Washington, D.C.: Center for German and European Studies, Georgetown University.

Murphy, Brian. 1998. "Kosovo Rebels Support Abroad." *Associated Press,* 19 June.

Muus, Philip J. 1998. *Migration, Immigrants and Policy in the Netherlands: Recent Trends and Developments.* Report for the Continuous Reporting System of Migration (SOPEMI) of the Organization for Economic Co-Operation and Development.

Nathan, Richard. 1991. "Implications for Federalism of European Integration." In *Political Power and Social Change: The United States Faces a United Europe,* edited by Norman J. Ornstein and Mark Perlman. Washington, D.C.: AEI Press.

Neue Zürcher Zeitung. 1993. "Over 500,000 Swiss Citizens Live Abroad Permanently." 11 August.

Neuman, Gerald L. 1993. "Buffer Zones against Refugees: Dublin, Schengen, and the German Asylum Amendment." *Virginia Journal of International Law* 33(3): 503–26.

———. 1998. "Nationality Law in the United States and Germany." In *Paths to Inclusion: The Integration of Migrants in the United States and Germany,* edited by Peter H. Schuck and Rainer Münz. New York: Berghahn Books.

Niessen, Jan. 1994. "The Role of Non-Governmental Organizations in Standard Setting and Promoting Ratification." In *The Use of International Conventions to Protect the Rights of Migrants and Ethnic Minorities,* edited by Julie Cator and Jan Niessen. Strasbourg: Churches Commission for Migrants in Europe.

Nye, Joseph S., Jr. 1971. "Comparing Common Markets: A revised Neofunctional Model." In *Regional Integration: Theory and Research,* edited by Leon N. Lindberg and Stuart A. Scheingold. Cambridge, Mass.: Harvard University Press.

OECD (Organization for Economic Cooperation and Development). 1992. *SOPEMI: Continuous Reporting System on Migration.* Paris: OECD.

———. 1995. *SOPEMI: Trends in International Migration, Annual Report 1994.* Paris: OECD.

———. 1998. *SOPEMI: Trends in International Migration, Annual Report 1998.* Paris: OECD.

Ogata, Sadako. 1992. "Refugees: A Humanitarian Strategy." Statement by Mrs. Sadako Ogata, United Nations High Commissioner for Refugees at the Royal Institute for International Relations, Brussels, November 25, <http://www.unhcr.ch>.

O'Leary, Siofra. 1995. "The Relationship between Community Citizenship and the Protection of Fundamental Rights in Community Law." *Common Market Law Review* 32: 519–54.

O'Nes, D. *The Guide to Legally Obtaining a Foreign Passport.* New York: Shapolsky Publishers, Inc., 1990.

Onuf, Nicholas. 1989. *World of Our Making.* Columbia: University of South Carolina Press.

Onuf, Peter S. 1983. *The Origins of the Federal Republic: Jurisdictional Controversies in the United States.* Philadelphia: University of Pennsylvania Press.

Oppenheim, Lassa. 1995. *International Law.* 8th ed., edited by Hirsch Lauterpacht. London: Longman.

Orzack, Louis. 1991. "The General Systems Directive and the Liberal Professions." In *The State of the European Community: Policies, Institutions, and Debates in the Transition Years,* edited by Leon Hurwitz and Christian Lequesne. Boulder, Colo.: Lynne Rienner Publishers.

Oye, Kenneth, ed. 1986. *Cooperation under Anarchy.* Princeton, N.J.: Princeton University Press.

Özdemir, Cem. 1996. Presentation by Cem Oezdemir at "Immigration, Incorporation and Citizenship in Advanced Industrial Democracies," the German American Academic Council, Summer Institute, New School for Social Research, July 17–27.

PAP (Polska Agendja Prasowa). 1998. "Interior Minister Reports Crime Rise in 1997." PAP Polish Press Agency, February 18.

Papdemetriou, Demetios G. 1996. *Coming Together or Pulling Apart? The European Union's Struggle with Immigration and Asylum.* Washington, D.C.: Carnegie Endowment for International Peace.

Pennsylvania. 1776. *1776 Pennsylvania Constitution, the Declaration of the Rights of the Inhabitants of the Commonwealth, or State of Pennsylvania.* In *Constitutions of Pennsylvania, Constitution of the United States,* prepared by John H. Fertig and Frank M. Hunter. Harrisburg, Pa.: W. S. Ray, state printer, 1916.

Peterson, Peter G. 1999. *Gray Dawn.* New York: Times Books.

Pfaff, William. 1992. "Unity Agreement Causing Wave of Anxiety in Europe." *Chicago Tribune,* May 17.

Pinder, John. 1991. *European Community: The Building of a Union.* Oxford: Oxford University Press.

Plender, Richard. 1988a. *International Migration Law.* Dordrecht, Netherlands: Martinus Nijhoff Publishers.

———. 1988b. *Basic Documents on International Migration Law.* Dordrecht, Netherlands: Martinus Nijhoff Publishers.

Poggi, Gianfranco. 1978. *The Development of the Modern State.* Stanford: Stanford University Press.

Portes, Alejandro. 1995. "Transnational Communities: Their Emergence and Significance in the Contemporary World System." Keynote address to the 19th Annual Conference on the Political Economy of the World System, University of Miami, April 21.

Posen, Barry R. 1996. "Military Responses to Refugee Disasters." *International Security* 21(1): 72–111.

Pounds, Norman John Greville. 1990. *An Historical Geography of Europe.* Cambridge: Cambridge University Press.

Putnam, Robert D. 1988. "Diplomacy and Domestic Politics: The Logic of Two Level Games." *International Organization* 42 (summer): 427–61.

Rath, Jan. 1990. "Voting Rights." In *The Political Rights of Migrant Workers in Western Europe,* edited by Zig Layton-Henry. London: Sage Publications.

Reif, Karlheinz. 1993. "Cultural Convergence and Cultural Diversity as Factors in European Identity." In *European Identity and the Search for Legitimacy,* edited by Soledad Garcia. London: Pinter.

Renner, Karl. 1918. *Das Selbstbesimmungsrecht der Nationen in besonderer Anwendung auf Öesterreich.* Vienna: F. Deuticke.

Reuters. 1992a. "French Senate Waters Down Maastricht." June 16.

———. 1992b. "Thatcher Sees Advantages in European Currency Crises." *The Reuter Library Report,* September 19.

———. 1993. "France Moves Toward Tightening Nationality Law." *The Reuter Library Report,* April 29.

———. 1998. "Chinese Exploited in Italian Leather Workshops." May 28.

———. 1999. "France Takes in Border-Crossing Kosovo Refugees." April 7.

Rheinische Post (Düsseldorf). 1999. "Koch: Unterschriftenaktion fortsetzen." March 19.

Rice, Eugene F., Jr. 1970. *The Foundations of Early Modern Europe 1460–1559.* New York: W. W. Norton.

Riesenberg, Peter. 1992. *Citizenship in the Western Tradition: Plato to Rousseau.* Chapel Hill: University of North Carolina Press.

Riker, William. 1964. *Federalism: Origins, Operation, Significance.* Boston, Little, Brown.

———. 1982. *Liberalism Against Populism.* San Francisco: W. H. Freeman.

Risse-Kappen, Thomas. 1995. *Bringing Transnational Relations Back In: Non-State Actors, Domestic Structures and International Institutions.* Cambridge: Cambridge University Press.

Rousseau, Jean-Jacques. 1991. "Abstract and Judgement of Saint-Pierre's Project for Perpetual Peace." In *Rousseau on International Relations,* edited by Stanley Hoffmann and David P. Fidler. Oxford: Clarendon Press.

Roy, W. T. 1983. "A Note on the Role of Maoris in New Zealand Politics." *Plural Societies* 3/4: 69–76.

Ruggie, John Gerard. 1983. "Continuity and Transformation in the World Polity: Toward a Neorealist Synthesis." *World Politics* 35 (January): 261–85.

———. 1993. "Territoriality and Beyond." *International Organization* 47(1): 139–74.

Russett, Bruce. 1993. *Grasping the Democratic Peace.* Princeton, N.J.: Princeton University Press.

Sabine, George H. 1961. *A History of Political Theory.* 3d ed. New York: Holt, Rinehardt, and Winston.

Sack, Robert David. 1986. *Human Territoriality: Its Theory and History.* Cambridge: Cambridge University Press.

Safran, William. 1991. *The French Polity.* 3d ed. London: Longman.

Saint-Simon, Henri Comte de. [1814] 1952. "The Reorganization of the European Community." In *Henri Comte de Saint-Simon (1760–1825) Selected Writings,* edited by F. M. H. Markham. Oxford: Blackwell.

Salt, John. 1989. "A Comparative Overview of International Trends and Types, 1950–1980." *International Migration Review* 23(2): 431–56.

———. 1992. Migration Processes among the Highly Skilled in Europe." *International Migration Review* 26(2): 484–505.

———. 1993. "The Future of International Migration." *International Migration Review* 26(4): 1077–111.

Santel, Bernhard. 1995. "Loss of Control: The Build-up of a European Migration and Asylum Regime." In *Migration and European Integration,* edited by Robert Miles and Dietrich Thraenhardt, 75–91. London: Pinter Press.

Sartori, Giovanni. 1987. *The Theory of Democracy Revisited.* Chatham, N.J.: Chatham House.

Sassen, Saskia. 1996. *Losing Control? Sovereignty in an Age of Globalization.* New York: Columbia University Press.

Savill, Anika. 1992. "Hurd Urges EC to Focus on Migration." *The Independent* (Dublin), September 16.

Schmitter Heisler, Barbara, and Martin O. Heisler. 1989. "Comparative Perspectives on Security and Migration: The Intersection of Two Expanding Universes." Presented at the Annual Meeting of the American Sociological Association, San Francisco, August 9–13.

Schuck, Peter H. 1989. "Membership in the Liberal Polity: The Devaluation of American Citizenship." In *Immigration and the Politics of Citizenship in Europe and North America,* edited by Rogers Brubaker. Lanham, Md.: University Press of America.

Schuck, Peter H., and Rogers M. Smith 1985. *Citizenship without Consent.* New Haven, Conn.: Yale University Press.

Schwartz, Sally. 1987. *A Mixed Multitude: The Struggle for Toleration in Colonial Pennsylvania.* New York: New York University Press.

Scoville, W. C. 1951. "Minority Migrations and the Diffusion of Technology." *Journal of Economic History* 11(4): 347–60.

Shain, Yossi. 1999. *Marketing the American Creed Abroad: Diasporas in the U.S. and their Homelands.* Cambridge: Cambridge University Press.

Sheehan, James J. 1989. *German History, 1770–1866.* Oxford: Oxford University Press.

Sherwin-White, A. N. 1939. *The Roman Citizenship.* Oxford: Clarendon.

Simmel, Georg. 1950. *Sociology of Georg Simmel.* Translated and edited by Kurt H. Wolff. New York: Free Press.

Solberg, Winton U., ed. 1958. *The Federal Convention and the Formation of the Union of the American States.* Indianapolis, Ind.: Bobbs-Merrill.

Sommer, Theo. 1993. "Fremde zu Bürgern Machen." *Die Zeit,* June 11.

Soysal, Yasemin Nuhoglu. 1994. *Limits of Citizenship: Migrants and Postnational Membership in Europe.* Chicago: University of Chicago Press.

Spain. 1991. "Spanish Delegation, Intergovernmental Conference on Political Union, European Citizenship (21 February 1991)." In *The Intergovernmental Conference on Political Union: Institutional Reforms, New Policies and International Identity of the European Community,* edited by Finn Laursen and Sophie Vanhoonacker. Dordrecht, Netherlands: Martinus Nijhoff Publishers (1992).

Spiro, Peter J. 1997. "Dual nationality and the Meaning of Citizenship." *Emory Law Journal* 46: 1412–85.

Stanton Russell, Sharon. 1992. "Migrant Remittances and Development." *International Migration* 30: 267–87.

Stanton Russell, Sharon, and Michael S. Teitelbaum. 1992. *International Migration and International Trade.* Washington, D.C.: World Bank.

Starchild, Adam. 1993. *Second Passports and Dual Nationality.* Baltimore: Agora.

Stein, Eric. 1981. "Lawyers, Judges, and the Making of a Transnational Constitution." *American Journal of International Law* 75: 1–27.

Stourzh, Gerald. 1991. "Problems of Conflict Resolution in a Multiethnic State: Lessons from the Austrian Historical Experience, 1848–1918." In *State and Nation in Multi-ethnic Societies: The Breakup of Multinational States,* edited by Uri Raánan, Maria Mesner, Keith Armes, and Kate Martin. Manchester, UK: Manchester University Press.

Straubaar, Thomas. 1988. "International Labour Migration within a Common Market: Some Aspects of EC Experience." *Journal of Common Market Studies* 27: 45–62.

Suganami, Hidemi. 1989. *The Domestic Analogy and World Order Proposals.* Cambridge: Cambridge University Press.

Swardson, Anne. 1993. "The Croats of Canada Prove Their Hearts in the Homeland." *Washington Post,* March 8.

Taylor, Paul. 1990. "Consociationalism and Federalism as Approaches to International Integration." In *Frameworks for International Cooperation,* edited by A. J. R. Groom and Paul Taylor. New York: St. Martin's Press.

Teitelbaum, Michael S., and Myron Weiner, eds. 1995. *Threatened Peoples, Threatened Borders: World Migration and U.S. Policy.* New York: W. W. Norton.

Thatcher, Margaret. 1993. Speech of June 7. *The Parliamentary Debates,* House of Lords, vol. 546.

Thomas, Brinley. 1961. *International Migration and International Development.* Paris: UNESCO.

Thraenhardt, Dietrich. 1997. "The Political Uses of Xenophobia in England, France and Germany." In *Immigration into Western Societies: Problems and Policies,* edited by Emek Ucarer and Donald J. Puchala. London: Pinter Press.

Thucydides. 1972. *History of the Peloponnesian War.* Translated by Rex Warner. London: Penguin.

Tocqueville, Alexis de. [1840] 1969. Translated by George Lawrence. *Democracy in America.* Garden City, N.Y.: Doubleday & Co.

Todorov, Tzvetan. 1982. *The Conquest of America.* New York: Harper & Row.

Tönnies, Ferdinand. 1887. *Gemeinshaft und Gesellschaft.* Leipzig: Fues Verlag.

Treaty on European Union (TEU). 1992. Luxembourg: Office for the Official Publications of the European Communities.

Tucker, Robert W., Charles B. Keely, and Linda Wrigley. 1990. *Immigration and U.S. Foreign Policy.* Boulder, Colo.: Westview Press.

TWIG (This Week In Germany). 1995. April 21.

Ucarer, Emek M. 1997. "Europe's Search for Policy: Asylum Policy Harmonization and European Integration." In *Immigration into Western Societies: Problems and Policies,* edited by Emek M. Ucarer and Donald J. Puchala. London: Pinter Press.

U.N. (United Nations). 1995. "U.N. Department for Economic and Social Information and Policy Analysis, Population Division. *Trends in Total Migrant Stock,* Revision 3. Doc. no. POP/1B/DB/95/1/REV.3.

UNHCR (United Nations High Commissioner for Refugees). 1993. *The State of the World's Refugees, 1993.* London: Penguin. <http://www.unhcr.ch/refworld/pub/state/sowrtoc.htm>.

———. 1995. *The State of the World's Refugees, 1995.* <http://www.unhcr.ch/refworld/pub/state/95/contents.htm>.

———. 1999a. "Asylum Applications Lodged by Citizens of the Federal Republic of Yugoslavia during 1998 and 1999." *Kosovo Crisis Update,* table 3. <http://www.unhcr.ch/world/euro/fryugo.htm>.

———. 1999b. "UNHCR Urges Non-European Countries to Take Kosovo Refugees as the

Refugee Crisis in the FRY of Macedonia Worsens." Press Release, United Nations High Commissioner for Refugees, Geneva, April 30.

——. 1999c. "UNHCR/IOM Humanitarian Evacuation Program of Kosovar Refugees from the FYR of Macedonia 5 April through 15 June 1999." *Kosovo Crisis Update,* table 2. <http://www.unhcr.ch/news/media/kosovo.htm>.

Vagts, Alfred. 1959. *A History of Militarism, Civilian and Military.* New York: Free Press.

van den Berghe, Guido. 1982. *Political Rights for European Citizens.* Aldershot, UK: Gower.

Vranken, Jan. 1990. "Industrial Rights." In *Political Rights of Migrant Workers in Western Europe,* edited by Zig Layton-Henry. London: Sage.

Waever, Ole. 1995. "Identity, Integration and Security: Solving the Sovereignty Puzzle in E.U. Studies." *Journal of International Affairs* 48(2): 389–431.

Waever, Ole, et al. 1993. *Identity, Migration and the New Security Agenda in Europe.* New York: St. Martin's Press.

Walker, Mack. 1971. *German Home Towns: Community, State and General Estate, 1648–1871.* Ithaca: Cornell University Press.

Wallace, William. 1983. "Less than a Federation, More than a Regime: The Community as a Political System." In *Policy-Making in the European Community,* edited by Helen Wallace, William Wallace, and Carole Webb. Chichester, UK: John Wiley and Sons.

Walt, Stephen M. 1991. "The Renaissance of Security Studies." *International Studies Quarterly* 35(2): 211–39.

Waltz, Kenneth N. 1959. *Man, the State and War.* New York: Columbia University Press.

——. 1979. *Theory of International Politics.* New York: Random House.

——. 1990. "Realist Thought and Neorealist Theory." *Journal of International Affairs* 44(1): 21–37.

Walzer, Michael. 1971. "The Obligation to Die for the State." In *Obligations: Essays on Disobedience, War, and Citizenship,* edited by Michael Walzer. Cambridge, Mass.: Harvard University Press.

——. 1983. *Spheres of Justice.* New York: Basic Books.

Weber, Eugen. 1976. *Peasants into Frenchmen: The Modernization of Rural France 1870–1914.* Stanford: Stanford University Press.

Weber, Max. 1946. "Politics as a Vocation." In *From Max Weber: Essays in Sociology,* edited by H. H. Gerth and C. Wright Mills. New York: Oxford University Press.

Weiler, J. H. H. 1991. "The Transformation of Europe." *The Yale Law Journal* 100(8): 2403–83.

——. 1997. "The Reformation of European Constitutionalism." *Journal of Common Market Studies* 35(1): 97–131.

Weiner, Myron. 1989. "The Political Aspects of International Migration." Paper presented at the meeting of the International Studies Association, March 30.

——, ed. 1993. *International Migration and Security.* Boulder, Colo.: Westview Press.

——. 1995. *The Global Migration Crisis: Challenge to States and to Human Rights.* New York: HarperCollins College Publishers.

——. 1996. "Bad Neighborhoods: An Inquiry into the Causes of Refugee Flows." *International Security* 21(1): 5–42.

Weintraub, Sidney. 1992. "North American Free Trade and the European Situation Compared." *International Migration Review* 26(2): 506–24.

Weis, Paul. 1979. *Nationality and Statelessness in International Law*. Alpen aan den Rijn, Netherlands: Sijthoff & Noordhoff.

Wendt, Alexander. 1987. "The Agent-Structure Problem in International Relations Theory." *International Organization* 41 (summer): 291–425.

———. 1992. "Anarchy is What States Make of It: The Social Construction of Power Politics." *International Organization* 46 (spring): 391–425.

———. 1994. "Collective Identity Formation and the International State." *American Political Science Review* 88 (June): 384–96.

Werner, Heinz. 1993. "Migration Movements in the Perspective of the European Single Market." In *The Changing Course of International Migration*, edited by the OECD. Paris: OECD.

Wheare, Kenneth C. 1964. *Federal Government*. New York: Oxford University Press.

Whelen, Frederick. 1983. "Democratic Theory and the Boundary Problem." In *Liberal Democracy, Nomos XXV*, edited by J. Roland Pennock and John W. Chapman. New York: New York University Press.

Widgren, Jonas. 1990. "International Migration and Regional Stability." *International Affairs* 66(4): 749–66.

Wistrich, Ernest. 1991. *After 1992: The United States of Europe*. London: Routledge.

Zimmerman, Warren. 1996. *Origins of a Catastrophe*. New York: Times Books.

Zolberg, Aristide R. 1985. "The Formation of New States as a Refugee-Generating Process." In Elizabeth G. Ferris, *Refugees and World Politics*. New York: Praeger.

———. 1992. "Labour Migration and International Economic Regimes: Bretton Woods and After." In *International Migration Systems: A Global Approach*, edited by Mary M. Kritz, Lin Lean Lim, Hania Zlotnik. Oxford: Clarendon Press.

Zolberg, Aristide R., Astri Suhrke, and Sergio Aguayo. 1989. *Escape from Violence*. New York: Oxford University Presss.

Index